Global Power Shift

Ample empirical evidence points to recent power shifts in multiple areas of international relations taking place between industrialized countries and emerging powers, as well as between states and non-state actors. However, there is a dearth of theoretical interpretation and synthesis of these findings, and a growing need for coherent approaches to understand and measure the transformation. The central issues to be addressed include theoretical questions and empirical puzzles: How can studies of global power shift and the rise of 'emerging powers' benefit from existing theories, and which alternative aspects and theoretical approaches might be suitable? How can the meanings, perceptions, dynamics, and consequences of global power shift be determined and assessed? This edited series will include highly innovative research on these topics. It aims to bring together scholars from all major world regions as well as different disciplines, including political science, economics and human geography. The overall aim is to discuss and possibly blend their different approaches and provide new frameworks for understanding global affairs and the governance of global power shifts.

All titles in this series are peer-reviewed.

This book series is indexed in Scopus.

Lev Topor

Cyber Sovereignty

International Security, Mass Communication, and the Future of the Internet

Springer

Lev Topor
ISGAP-Woolf Institute
Cambridge, UK

ISSN 2198-7343 ISSN 2198-7351 (electronic)
Global Power Shift
ISBN 978-3-031-58198-4 ISBN 978-3-031-58199-1 (eBook)
https://doi.org/10.1007/978-3-031-58199-1

This Springer imprint is published by the registered company Springer Nature Switzerland AG
The registered company address is: Gewerbestrasse 11, 6330 Cham, Switzerland

Paper in this product is recyclable.

To Funny Cat Videos online. May this content never be blocked.

Preface

Within the span of a generation, the world has experienced a seismic shift caused not by tectonic plates but by cables connecting computers and running lines of code and project information to us all. The internet, once a hopeful utopia of boundless connection, has transformed into a turbulent digital archipelago. Countries (nation-states), no longer confined by physical borders, are staking a claim to their own sovereign cyberspaces by erecting firewalls and digital borders or disconnecting themselves from the global grid altogether through sheer tenacity. This book plots a daring course through this fragmented landscape, charting the treacherous shoals of national regulation, restricted access and the ever-present threat of complete disconnection.

The beginning of the twenty-first century has witnessed an unprecedented surge in the importance of cyberspace as a crucial arena for economic, political and social interaction. The internet, once heralded as a harbinger of global unity, now finds itself at a crossroads. The utopian vision of a borderless network, a free-flowing exchange of ideas and information, is increasingly under siege. From North Korea's Kwangmyong internet to the Great Firewall of China to Iran's Shabake-ye Melli-ye Ettelā'āt (National Information Network) to Russia's RuNet project and even the European Union's regulatory struggle for individual privacy, countries are crafting their own bespoke versions of the online world, often at the expense of open access and free speech. This book meticulously dissects these diverse cyber domains, revealing the unique challenges and motivations that drive each nation's digital agenda. One thing is clear: they are not afraid to compete with the Western dominance over the web.

This shift towards "cyber sovereignty" is not merely a technical phenomenon; it represents a fundamental reassessment of power and control in the twenty-first century. Information, once the lifeblood of democratic societies, is now wielded as a tool of both empowerment and repression. Information is now mis/disinformation. Governments, concerned about national security, social stability, and the erosion of cultural identities, are increasingly turning to digital gatekeeping to safeguard their interests. However, this comes at a steep price. As the book eloquently argues, the fragmentation of the internet into siloed cyber spaces risks severing the very communication arteries that facilitate global dialogue, economic exchange and scientific collaboration.

The consequences of this fragmentation are far-reaching and multifaceted. The book outlines the impact on matters like human rights and free speech, global trade and scientific progress. The silencing of dissident voices within national firewalls, the chilling effects of self-censorship, and the potential for a "digital balkanization" are just some of the possibilities that loom on the horizon. The fight for a global internet, one that respects national sovereignty while upholding fundamental human rights, remains a complex and ongoing struggle. This book serves as a crucial roadmap for navigating this contested terrain, offering nuanced analyses of potential solutions and frameworks for international cooperation in the case of Secure Cyber Domains and cyber blocs.

But beyond the policy prescriptions and technical frameworks, this book also delves into the deeper philosophical questions that underpin the very notion of cyber sovereignty. It grapples with the tension between individual autonomy and national security, the delicate balance between free speech and societal cohesion, and the challenges of reconciling cultural diversity with a globalized digital realm. These are not merely technical problems to be solved but profound ethical dilemmas that demand careful consideration and ongoing dialogue. This book is a clarion call for a future where the internet can connect but respect. It is a call for a digital world that respects national sovereignty while fostering global connection, a world where the free flow of information empowers individuals and strengthens societies, and where the vast potential of the internet is harnessed for the betterment of all, not the abuse of all. As we embark on this digital odyssey, this book serves as a vital compass, guiding us through the uncharted binary waters of cyber sovereignty and towards a future where the internet remains a beacon of connection, not a weapon of division.

Cambridge, UK Lev Topor

Acknowledgements I would like to express my sincere gratitude to the following individuals and organizations who have contributed to the completion of this book: Prof. Arie Kacowicz, who advised on an early draft paper on the topic of cyber blocs presented at the Israeli Association for International Studies, Prof. Eldar Haber, with whom I have published a paper on the topic of sovereign cyber domains (which we referred to as "internet bubbles"), Dr. Alexander Tabachnik, who contributed his great insight on the Russian cyber domain, and the Center for Cyber Law and Policy at the University of Haifa, Israel.

Contents

Abbreviations

AI	Artificial Intelligence
APNIC	Asia Pacific Network Information Centre
APT	Advanced Persistent Threat
AR	Augmented Reality
ARPANET	Advanced Research Projects Agency Network
BIS	Bureau of Industry and Security
BRI	Belt and Road Initiative
CCDCOE	Cooperative Cyber Defence Centre of Excellence
CCP	Chinese Communist Party
CCPA	California Consumer Privacy Act
ccTLDs	Country Code Top-Level Domains
CDA	Communications Decency Act
CDN	Content Delivery Network
CERT-EU	Computer Emergency Response Team for the EU
CIS	Commonwealth of Independent States (former Soviet countries)
CISA	Cybersecurity and Infrastructure Security Agency
CISA	Cybersecurity Information Sharing Act
CNNIC	China Internet Network Information Center
CSIS	Center for Strategic and International Studies
CSO	Civil Society Organization
CST	Communications, Space and Information Technology Commission
DARPA	Defense Advanced Research Projects Agency
DIME	Diplomatic, Information, Military and Economic
DMA	Digital Markets Act
DNS	Domain Name System
DoS	Denial of Service
DPI	Deep Packet Inspection
DSA	Digital Services Act
ECJ	European Court of Justice
EIF	European Internet Forum
ENISA	European Union Agency for Cybersecurity

FCC	Federal Communications Commission
GCHQ	Government Communications Headquarters
GCI	Global Cybersecurity Index
GCSC	Global Commission on the Stability of Cyberspace
GDPR	General Data Protection Regulation
GEC	Global Engagement Center
GFW	Great Firewall
GGE	Group of Governmental Experts
GSP	Golden Shield Project
IAB	Internet Architecture Board
IANA	Internet Assigned Numbers Authority
ICANN	Internet Corporation for Assigned Names and Numbers
ICS	Industrial Control Systems
ICT	Information and Communication Technology
IDF	Israel Defense Force
IETF	Internet Engineering Task Force
IGF	Internet Governance Forum
IIX	Israeli Internet Exchange
INCD	Israel National Cyber Directorate
IoT	Internet of Things
IP	Internet Protocol
IRTF	Internet Research Task Force
ISO	International Organization for Standardization
ISOC	Internet Society
ISP	Internet Service Provider
IT	Information Technology
ITU	International Telecommunication Union
IUCC	Israeli inter-University Computation Center
IXP	Internet Exchange Point
MAD	Mutual Assured Destruction
NATO	North Atlantic Treaty Organization
NCA	National Cybersecurity Authority
NCC	National Center for Cyberspace
NCP	Network Control Protocol
NCSC	National Cyber Security Centre
NHS	National Health Service
NIC	Network Information Center
NIN	National Information Network
NIS	Network and Information Systems
NIST	National Institute of Standards and Technology
NSC	National Security Council
NTIA	National Telecommunications and Information Administration
OEWG	Open-Ended Working Group
OFCOM	Office of Communications

OGAS	National Automated System for Computation and Information Processing (from Russian: ОГАС—Общегосударственная автоматизированная система учёта и обработки информации)
ONI	Open Net Initiative
OSA	Online Safety Act
OSI	Open System Interconnection
OT	Operational Technologies
PRC	People's Republic of China
PTI	Public Technical Identifiers
R2P	Responsibility to Protect
RIR	Regional Internet Registry
SATNET	Atlantic Ocean Packet Satellite Communications Network
SCC	Supreme Council of Cyberspace
SCD	Secure Cyber Domain
SMA	Secure Messaging Application
SORM	System of Operational-Investigatory Measures
TCP	Transmission Control Protocol
TLD	Top-Level Domain
UNGA	United Nations General Assembly
UPS	Uninterruptible Power Supply
US-CERT	United States Computer Emergency Readiness Team
VCD	Vulnerable Cyber Domain
VK	VKontakte
VR	Virtual Reality
W3C	World Wide Web Consortium
WEF	World Economic Forum

List of Figures

List of Tables

Chapter 1
Introduction

The internet, or cyberspace, refers to a virtual world of computers and "smart" devices that facilitate online communication and the transmission of information through interconnected digital environments. With the global population soon to reach 8 billion people (as of 2023), only approximately 2.6 billion of us are still offline. Approximately, 67%, or 5.4 billion people, are now using the internet. Regionally, 91% of Europeans are connected, 89% of the population of the Commonwealth of Independent States (CIS, former Soviet countries) is connected, 66% of the people in the Asia–Pacific region are connected, 69% of the population of Arab countries is connected, 87% of Americans (South, Central and North) are connected and 37% of Africans are connected. Most communication occurs via submarine fiber-optic cables and terrestrial cables (approximately 95%; some utilizes satellites). It seems like the whole world is being uploaded; since the internet has indeed become a form of mass communication—people are connected, organizations are connected and countries are connected—it has become a major proxy for international security.[1]

The cyber domain has emerged as the perfect platform for international influence and power struggles on the world stage. Now, not only global powers but also terror organizations, rogue lone-wolf terrorists and criminals execute their attacks in the cyber domain as well as in the real kinetic domain.[2] Just as Alfred T. Mahan observed in the late nineteenth century that "whoever rules the waves rules the world,"[3] it has become clear that whoever rules the cyber domain rules mass communications and, consequently, the world (or at least, a significant part of global affairs). In fact, the cyber domain can be considered a perfect platform for international influence not only because it enables global powers to virtually—but in a very real sense—invade and intervene in their adversaries with a few (very skilled) mouse clicks but also because, in the current state of affairs, there are no binding international laws and no clear

[1] See International Telecommunication Union (2023).

[2] See, generally, Lin and Zegart (2019).

[3] Mahan (2011).

L. Topor, *Cyber Sovereignty*, Global Power Shift,
https://doi.org/10.1007/978-3-031-58199-1_1

norms regarding cyberspace—every country can do what it considers appropriate. Successful attempts to agree upon such laws seem distant (i.e., the Tallinn Manual, the United Nations' GGE and OEWG),[4] although some legislative efforts such as the European General Data Protection Regulation (GDPR), Digital Services Act (DSA) and Digital Markets Act (DMA), as well as specific national legislations, do seem more likely to succeed.[5] Nevertheless, such regulations mainly concern blocs like Europe or sovereign nations such as Russia, China and a few others, not the entire world. Even in Europe, each nation has its own norms and regulations.

Meanwhile, under the present legislative conditions, cyberattacks and influence campaigns are perfectly legal. That is, the spread of malicious software, mis/disinformation campaigns, and leaks are not illegal. Cyberattacks that directly cause damage, human injuries or death may be retaliated against, but one has to forensically prove their source—an objective that is very difficult to achieve, as elaborated throughout this book. Since many cyber criminals utilize digital and real proxies, attribution is very difficult.[6] It is true that under the Charter of the United Nations, Chapter VII, Article 51, a country can take physical (kinetic) action against an armed attack, even an armed cyberattack; however, in its current structure, as Martin C. Libicki noted, cyberspace is tailor-made for strategic ambiguity.[7] Furthermore, the Twitter Revolution,[8] the Arab Spring,[9] and interventions in electoral and democratic processes by foreign actors, such as the United States presidential elections or cases like Brexit, have proven that even manipulated information in cyberspace can cause tremendous damage, often more than a kinetic attack.

Thus, what can nations do to protect themselves in this Wild West, in this lawless virtual domain? Since international relations and politics, in general, are reactionary, it is probable that countries will strive to control their cyberspaces and protect themselves.[10] As examples throughout this book make clear, countries like Russia and China are already taking action.

The main argument presented in this book, based on observation and formulated from a strategic point of view, is that because nations worldwide are currently striving to restrict their cyber domains in order to better control their domestic affairs and

---

[4] See Schmitt (2017); UN GGE—Group of Governmental Experts, UNGA Res. 73/266; UN OEWG—Open-ended Working Group, UN GA Res. 73/27.

[5] Digwatch (n.d.) and Shuker and Topor (2021).

[6] Harknett and Nye Jr. (2017).

[7] Libicki (2011). See United Nations (1945).

[8] The term "Twitter Revolution" has been used to refer to various revolutions and protests that utilized the social networking site Twitter as a communication tool. It has been associated with events such as the 2009 Moldova civil unrest, the 2009–2010 Iranian election protests, the political movements in Egypt during January and February 2011 and more.

[9] The Arab Spring refers to a series of anti-government protests, uprisings and armed rebellions that spread across the Arab world in the early 2010s. Social media, including Twitter, played a significant role in the Arab Spring by facilitating communication and interaction among activists, allowing them to organize demonstrations, disseminate information and raise global awareness of the events.

[10] See, generally, Lin and Zegart (2019).

better protect themselves from foreign cyberattacks and unwanted influences, we may, in the near future, see a different type of internet—a more restricted one. This, I call a Secure Cyber Domain (SCD). Simply put, an SCD is a border intended to preserve national sovereignty, specifically by controlling domestic mass communications and keeping out unwanted content of any kind. SCD is a flexible term that can be used to describe a country with a protected cyber domain, a standalone cyber domain or one shared with others (which I refer to as a cyber bloc), as long as it is secure and not (or less) susceptible to foreign influence and manipulation. In contrast, a Vulnerable Cyber Domain (VCD) is a domain that prioritizes freedom of information, whether true, false or harmful, over national resilience and public order.

Countries can manage to disconnect from globalization in this age of information just as they managed to halt certain aspects of globalization through lockdowns and border closures when the COVID-19 pandemic struck. In the case of the pandemic, nations eventually opened their borders to those tested for the virus and/or vaccinated against it. Closing cyber borders may be a bit more complex, but it is a very manageable task, as I demonstrate in subsequent chapters. Following on from this observation and argument, I also ask: How will the global internet be structured in future? Will processes of de-proliferation of connectivity undermine processes of globalization? How will such changes in mass communication affect human cooperation? How will this "digital balkanization" continue to develop?[11]

In a paper co-authored with Eldar Haber, these efforts to restrict the internet were referred to as "internet bubbles," meaning that a nation may create its own sovereign internet bubble—an enclosed national intranet.[12] Since writing that paper, I have developed this concept further as the international spread of mis/disinformation and cyberattacks has proliferated. Such sovereign cyberspaces, SCDs, might not only be constructed within nations but also within blocs and partnerships. Nations are taking advantage of the lack of regulations and legal frameworks to create such spheres. Nowadays, this is particularly true for Russia and China, which perceive the internet, a largely American project, as a domain that enables their global adversary—the United States—to maintain its power and global influence. In a world that is framed as tri-polar (or multipolar), Russian and Chinese concerns are not far-fetched; the United States has developed much of the global internet and controls its infrastructure either directly or via business proxies, high-tech companies, social media and secure messaging applications (SMAs).[13] Even the European Union, with the GDPR, DSA and DMA in place, has expressed concerns over American and corporate influence.[14]

It is important to note that the observations and arguments in this book focus on strategy, sovereignty and international relations and not on international human rights or debates on freedom of speech or freedom of information and truth—although the latter is touched upon. Furthermore, even though I personally lean toward the liberal

[11] Economist (2010).

[12] Haber and Topor (2023).

[13] Elkin-Koren and Haber (2016).

[14] For instance, the European Commission has challenged Meta (Facebook) over what in Europe are perceived as abusive practices. See European Commission (2022a) and Machangama (2022).

West, national sovereignty is of vast importance to the majority of nations in the world, even if they are less liberal and less democratic, and even if, personally, as a human but also as a researcher of politics and international affairs, I do not agree with them. In this book, I attempt to decouple from normative perspectives and focus on national strategy. Therefore, I explore how a country should act if it wants to either preserve or increase its sovereignty, considering the fact that countries—nations—generally seek to have greater sovereignty. The concept of sovereignty will be presented and explained in detail in Chap. 3, which deals with sovereignty, power and international security. The term sovereignty is, as the English historian Francis Harry Hinsley notes, complex but flexible:

> Men do not wield or submit to sovereignty. They wield or submit to authority or power. Authority and power are facts as old and ubiquitous as society itself; but they have not everywhere and at all times enjoyed the support or suffered the restraints which sovereignty, a theory or assumption about political power, seeks to construct for them. Although we talk of it loosely as something concrete which may be lost or acquired, eroded or increased, sovereignty is not a fact. It is a concept which men in certain circumstances have applied – a quality they have attributed or a claim they have counterposed – to the political power which they or other men were exercising.[15]

The situation is changing even as these lines are being written. Russia continues to develop its cyber sovereignty through its so-called RuNet project and is developing strict regulations against unwanted influences, including the Yarovaya law and the "sovereign internet" law. Russia also requires that a specific application be installed on new smartphones and other smart devices.[16] China continues its regulation and restriction of foreign platforms using its "Great Firewall"; Google, Apple, Meta (Facebook) and other American-based tech giants are not welcome in the People's Republic of China.[17] China also plans to rival the private American Starlink venture in space and launch its own constellation of satellites.[18] Furthermore, China is pursuing independence from the American-backed internet infrastructure as it works to rival, and presumably replace, American-backed undersea fiber-optic cables.[19] North Korea controls its own communication systems with the Kwangmyong intranet, which is entirely separate from the global grid.[20] Furthermore, even within the United States, private business entities are attempting to create restricted and sovereign business zones (i.e., "Innovation Zones" in Nevada), chipping away at American sovereignty.[21]

What motives have led countries to restrict their internet? The internet as we know it today is a largely American project. It was developed by American and Western defense and research entities and projects like the Advanced Research Projects

---

[15] Hinsley (1986: 1).

[16] Topor and Tabachnik (2021) and Wang (2020).

[17] Chandel et al. (2019).

[18] Cadell (2023).

[19] Brock (2023).

[20] Warf (2015).

[21] Metz (2021).

Agency Network (ARPANET), and it is currently also controlled by American-led international organizations such as the Internet Corporation for Assigned Names and Numbers (ICANN) and the Internet Assigned Numbers Authority (IANA), as well as many others, as described in Chap. 2. The internet is also predominantly owned by American and Western technology companies like Microsoft, Amazon, Meta, Apple, IBM, Lumen Technologies and many others. These companies own and operate various internet infrastructures, including the internet's backbone of undersea cables, satellites, internet exchange points (IXPs), data centers, cloud infrastructure and platforms, services, social media and more.

As long ago as 2013, Edward Snowden leaked that the West not only controls global communications but also spies on the entire globe (with programs like PRISM). For instance, the British Government Communications Headquarters (GCHQ) alongside other organizations had gained (and probably still has) access to the network of cables that carry the world's phone calls and internet traffic. As Snowden noted, the United Kingdom has had the greatest success in surveillance and eavesdropping of all members of the Five Eyes alliance (an intelligence alliance of English-speaking countries, including the United States, the United Kingdom, Canada, New Zealand and Australia).[22] However, global communication involves not just wires but also services. For instance, before, during and even after the Arab Spring of 2010–2012, protesters used social media platforms like Twitter to organize a series of uprisings in the Arab world and other countries, sharing information to organize themselves in real-time. Protests like the Occupy Wall Street and Black Lives Matter movements in the United States were also organized largely via such social media platforms, as were Brexit-related protests in the United Kingdom, the Yellow Vests Protests in France and many others.[23]

This situation of bias and lack of control has led sovereign countries, including many global powers, to restrict their cyber domains and resist Western dominance. In fact, many countries worldwide restrict rather than free the internet. The West itself suffers from foreign *sharp power*—the utilization of asymmetry between open and closed countries. And although the internet might be very open and free in the West, it is certainly not private.

In direct contradiction to common Western understanding, in many countries, the internet is anything but open and free. According to the organization Freedom House, the internet can be described as "Not Free" in Azerbaijan, Bahrain, Belarus, China, Cuba, Egypt, Ethiopia, Iran, Kazakhstan, Myanmar, Pakistan, Russia, Rwanda, Saudi Arabia, Sudan, Turkey, Thailand, the United Arab Emirates, Uzbekistan, Venezuela and Vietnam. Moreover, in addition to these twenty-one countries, thirty-two more countries are described by Freedom House as "Partly Free." As presented in Table 1.1, in an assessment of internet freedom in seventy countries, many countries already display cyber sovereignty, at least to some extent, since only seventeen countries are described as "Free."[24]

---

[22] MacAskill et al. (2013).

[23] Kumar (2022) and Hadero (2023).

[24] See Freedom House (n.d.). Scores are based in a scale of 0 (least free) to 100 (most free).

Table 1.1 Assessment of internet freedom in 70 countries (0—least free, 100—most free)

Country	Total score and status	Obstacles to access	Limits on content	Violations of user rights
Angola	61 partly free	11	29	21
Argentina	71 free	19	27	25
Armenia	74 free	20	28	26
Australia	76 free	23	28	25
Azerbaijan	38 not free	12	15	11
Bahrain	29 not free	16	6	7
Bangladesh	43 partly free	13	18	12
Belarus	28 not free	12	10	6
Brazil	65 partly free	20	24	21
Cambodia	43 partly free	13	18	12
Canada	87 free	23	32	32
China	10 not free	8	2	0
Colombia	64 partly free	19	24	21
Costa Rica	88 free	21	34	33
Cuba	20 not free	4	9	7
Ecuador	64 partly free	18	24	22
Egypt	27 not free	13	10	4
Estonia	93 free	25	31	37
Ethiopia	27 not free	5	13	9
France	76 free	23	29	24
Georgia	78 free	19	31	28
Germany	77 free	23	28	26
Ghana	64 partly free	14	27	23
Hungary	69 partly free	22	24	23
Iceland	95 free	25	34	36
India	51 partly free	13	21	17
Indonesia	49 partly free	14	17	18
Iran	16 not free	7	5	4
Iraq	42 partly free	12	16	14
Italy	75 free	21	29	25
Japan	77 free	22	29	26
Jordan	47 partly free	14	17	16
Kazakhstan	32 not free	10	11	11
Kenya	68 partly free	16	27	25
Kyrgyzstan	53 partly free	15	22	16
Lebanon	51 partly free	11	22	18

(continued)

Table 1.1 (continued)

Country	Total score and status	Obstacles to access	Limits on content	Violations of user rights
Libya	44 partly free	8	21	15
Malawi	57 partly free	11	25	21
Malaysia	59 partly free	18	22	19
Mexico	61 partly free	18	25	18
Morocco	51 partly free	15	21	15
Myanmar	12 not free	2	6	4
Nicaragua	45 partly free	11	17	17
Nigeria	57 partly free	16	24	17
Pakistan	26 not free	6	13	7
Philippines	65 partly free	17	26	22
Russia	23 not free	11	6	6
Rwanda	37 not free	13	11	13
Saudi Arabia	24 not free	12	8	4
Serbia	72 free	22	25	25
Singapore	54 partly free	19	17	18
South Africa	73 free	18	29	26
South Korea	67 partly free	22	24	21
Sri Lanka	48 partly free	9	22	17
Sudan	29 not free	5	13	11
Taiwan	79 free	24	30	25
Thailand	39 not free	16	14	9
The Gambia	56 partly free	12	24	20
Tunisia	61 partly free	16	26	19
Turkey	32 not free	14	10	8
Uganda	50 partly free	12	19	19
Ukraine	59 partly free	18	21	20
United Arab Emirates	28 not free	12	9	7
United Kingdom	79 free	24	30	25
United States	76 free	21	30	25
Uzbekistan	27 not free	9	11	7
Venezuela	30 not free	7	12	11
Vietnam	22 not free	12	6	4
Zambia	58 partly free	15	23	20
Zimbabwe	49 partly free	8	23	18

Source Freedom House

Furthermore, governments around the world not only control or manipulate content but can also block internet access altogether. Internet shutdowns have become a common tool used by governments around the world to suppress dissent, control information, maintain power and block unwanted foreign information and communication. According to Access Now, a non-profit organization that defends digital rights, the internet was shut down 182 times in 2021, 129 times in 2020, 213 times in 2019 and 196 times in 2018. It is mainly non-democratic countries that engage in internet shutdowns as a form of despotic power.[25]

Some of the longest shutdowns include a shutdown in Tigray, Ethiopia, still ongoing since November 4, 2019, a shutdown in Jammu and Kashmir from August 5, 2019, until February 5, 2021, and a shutdown in Rakhine, Myanmar, from June 22, 2019, until February 2021; one of the longest shutdowns in history was Pakistan's shutdown in tribal areas from June 12, 2016, until December 28, 2021. In 2021, India shut down the internet 106 times in various areas in response to protests. Facebook, WhatsApp, Twitter, Telegram, Instagram and Google Services are some of the main platforms that are blocked and censored. In addition, countries not only shut down internet connections but can also throttle the internet to make it less usable.[26] Of course, it should be noted that Access Now has legal entities in Western countries like the United States (a country which also operates the infamous TOR Dark Web). Thus, countries that oppose a Western orientation and prioritize their sovereignty and power over human rights are shutting down what they consider a Western form of internet.

Non-Western nations are not the only ones restricting the internet. Restrictions and regulations in Europe were mentioned above (GDPR, DSA, DMA), and even the United States with its free market regulates some aspects related to the global internet. For instance, the United States has banned the Chinese company Huawei and its networking equipment, including 5G hardware, after fears this equipment could be used as a surveillance tool by the Chinese government. Huawei, alongside sixty-eight foreign Huawei affiliates, was added to the United States Department of Commerce's Bureau of Industry and Security (BIS) Entity List in May 2019 (Chinese companies ZTE, Hikvision, Dahua and Hytera were also banned).[27] The United Kingdom has also banned Huawei's 5G equipment, demanding the removal and/or replacement of it by the end of 2027,[28] and Canada has banned Chinese Huawei and ZTE 5G equipment.[29] Furthermore, the United States has labeled the Chinese social media app TikTok as worrisome and banned it from government-owned or assigned devices; individual states have also banned the app, as well as some colleges and universities.[30]

---

[25] Access Now (2022).

[26] Ibid.

[27] BBC (2022).

[28] Department for Digital, Culture, Media & Sport and The Rt Hon Michelle Donelan MP (2022).

[29] Gillies (2022).

[30] Maheshwari and Holpuch (2023).

Google's Transparency Report gives more interesting details further exemplifying how governments advance their interests on the internet. It records government requests to remove content, and the number of items named for removal since 2011 (true to January 18, 2024) totals 4,487,919. The main reasons for such requests are national security, violence, adult content, impersonation, defamation and hate speech. Other reasons include privacy-related or copyright issues. The majority of requests were from executive governmental bodies and authorities of information and communication, not from police or military forces. For example, the United Kingdom has requested the removal of 41,973 items since 2011, the United States 263,047 items, Russia 2,162,096 items, China 18,697 items, Iran 8 items and Israel 16,567 items.[31] Removal requests thus come from democratic and less democratic and less liberal countries alike.

These are just a few examples. It is evident from these few paragraphs that countries ban, restrict or manipulate foreign content, software and hardware, as well as demand access to foreign devices and software used by their own citizens and demand the removal of content. Why do they do that? The long answer is presented throughout this book; however, here, I will highlight the short and simple answer: countries are sovereign and would like to control and maintain their sovereignty as much as possible. It is their nature to be sovereign and to ban foreign influence, whatever form it might take.

These struggles for sovereignty, which are building incrementally as we advance in the twenty-first century, will change people's use of the internet; responsiveness, ease of use, speed, availability of content and freedom of speech will take a backseat to cybersecurity, national security and censorship of unwanted information. That is, until and unless the international community develops and enacts laws regarding cyberspace—a process that is not likely to take place in the near future.[32] Currently, Russia and China are very advanced in their domestic regulations while using their sharp power to spread influence in less-regulated cyber domains like the United States and Europe. One can only imagine how the American presidential elections or the Brexit issue in the United Kingdom would have turned out if their cyber domains had been better regulated, monitored and protected. Regarding the British example, it is true that Brexit did not appear out of nowhere—foreign influence agents did not suddenly invent it and the many social rifts and problems associated with it. However, they did manage to enhance the social rifts between the left and the right and to increase negative attitudes toward foreign labor, immigration and international cooperation. This strategy of enhancing social problems, commonly used by global powers to influence each other and smaller nations, is evident in many European countries.[33]

Regarding the global use of the internet, I argue that countries worldwide will increase their regulation, monitoring and restriction of their cyber domains not only when it comes to social media and news platforms but throughout the whole structure

---

[31] See Google Transparency Report (n.d.).

[32] Fischerkeller (2021).

[33] Ruy (2020).

and layers of the cyber domain. The cyber domain can be generally segmented into four main layers: (1) the physical infrastructure layer, which consists of fiber-optic cables, satellites and nodes; (2) the logic layer, which can be regarded as the central nervous system of the internet; (3) the information layer, which consists of encoded text, video, audio and any other type of stored data and (4) the user layer, which consists of actual users—regular users but also malicious users. All these layers together shape the global internet. Interestingly, however, while the self-regulated, market-driven internet is very susceptible to cyberattacks in more democratic and liberal but less-regulated countries like the United States, nations like Russia, China, Iran and even North Korea are better protected against cyber influence campaigns, strategically speaking.[34]

In historical terms, this prediction is very similar to the emergence of the concept of sovereignty at the time of the Treaty of Westphalia, which, in the field of international relations, is considered a significant event in the development of modern sovereignty and the emergence of independent nations. During and following Westphalia, the power of Ferdinand III, Holy Roman Emperor, was stripped from him and returned to the imperial states.[35] In the present context, the global internet is comparable to Ferdinand III's actions as both have reduced the sovereignty of states/nations. Since nations generally act to preserve their sovereignty at all costs, they will most likely strip the internet, as we know it today, of its powers by creating their own restricted cyber domains, SCDs, whether spanning all layers or some, and whether as individual nations or within internet blocs.

The idea of cyber sovereignty is very reasonable, and this book is certainly not the first to present the concept. However, it is the first significant comparative study that seeks to understand the future of the internet and the possible consequences on global affairs, be that diplomacy or warfare. As early as 1997, before significant online "fake news" campaigns, before social media, and before every child, adolescent and grownup had a smartphone glued to their hands, the American legal scholar Timothy S. Wu wrote about cyber sovereignty. In his journal article, Wu asked two questions: Is it possible to regulate the internet? And will countries regulate the internet? As this book shows, the internet can indeed be regulated, and countries do regulate it. Wu arrived at these answers as well, and he quotes Wu Jichuan, the former Minister of Posts and Telecommunications and former Minister of the Ministry of Industry and Information Technology in China. The quote from 1995 reads:

> By linking with the Internet, we don't mean absolute freedom of information. I think there is a general understanding about this. If you go through customs, you have to show your passport. It's the same with management of information. There is no contradiction at all between the development of telecommunications infrastructure and the exercise of state sovereignty.[36]

However, creating a completely isolated national intranet like that of North Korea is not the only option. My main prediction is that due to the lawlessness and lack of

---

[34] Topor (2022: 20–38), Choucri and Clark (2012) and Benkler (2006: 23).

[35] Croxton (1999) and Osiander (2001).

[36] Wu (1996).

norms in cyberspace, and the need to protect themselves from malicious or unwanted influences, more nations, particularly those with VCDs, will start to restrict their cyber domains, creating SCDs. Russia, China, North Korea and others are already establishing SCDs—and due to the [ab]use of sharp power, more will follow. What exactly these SCDs will be like is beyond my ability to predict. The feasible probability is that different countries will decide on different measures, according to their overall strategic abilities and objectives, and according to political and even cultural notions. While Russia, China and others work to create SCDs, the United States and the European Union, for instance, are promoting a vision for cooperation. In a formal document titled "A Declaration for the Future of the Internet," they describe how they aim to gather a pact—a bloc—of more open and liberal countries that under the leadership of the United States and the European Union will together create a new common internet (or keep it as it is—relatively open):

> We call for a new Declaration for the Future of the Internet that includes all partners who actively support a future for the Internet that is an [*sic*] open, free, global, interoperable, reliable, and secure. We further affirm our commitment to protecting and respecting human rights online and across the digital ecosystem. Partners in this Declaration intend to work toward an environment that reinforces our democratic systems and promotes active participation of every citizen in democratic processes, secures and protects individuals' privacy, maintains secure and reliable connectivity, resists efforts to splinter the global Internet, and promotes a free and competitive global economy. Partners in this Declaration invite other partners who share this vision to join us in working together, with civil society and other stakeholders, to affirm guiding principles for our role in the future of the global Internet.[37]

Yet, from this study arise several main possibilities for how the future of the global internet will take shape. After the publication of this book, only time will tell what our internet will look like in five, ten or twenty years. Generally, and conceptually, there are four main options for the future of the internet, according to the evidence from this study. That is, if one acknowledges a more realistic point of view, including global shifts in power and a global struggle for dominance by various powers. The options are:

- ***Status Quo***: The global internet remains an American-led project, and American legislation, cyber capabilities, technology companies and social media platforms lead the global cyber domain as they have done in the past and, in many respects, do now. This outcome is supported by other Western countries like the United Kingdom.
- ***Internet Bubbles***: The global internet breaks down into internet bubbles, as coined by Haber and Topor.[38] Each country disconnects from the global internet grid and creates its own closed-circuit intranet. Any exchange of information (content) must pass through cyber-borders that scan for compliance (i.e., whether certain information is appropriate for the specific nation's citizens—generally called

[37] European Commission (2022b) and The White House (2022).

[38] Haber and Topor (2023).

censorship) and malware.[39] Such internet bubbles may be wholistic, meaning that all the layers of the internet are restricted, or partial.

- ***Internet Blocs***: The global internet breaks down into blocs defined by cultural and strategic similarities. Countries that are politically and economically aligned and cooperate, and that do not perceive one another as pure adversaries, will form a bloc that allows the open transfer of information, software and operations. This formation of internet blocs is very similar in nature to economic blocs, security alliances or border-free zones like the European Union or the North Atlantic Treaty Organization (NATO). Blocs could be based on geographical proximity (i.e., a bloc in each continent) or by cultural and strategic proximity (i.e., blocs of like-minded nations, even by Samuel Huntington's concept of the *Clash of Civilizations*). An example of an emerging cyber bloc is the United States and the European Union, with their *Declaration for the Future of the Internet*, as mentioned above. A more robust model is the European Union cyber bloc, which is described in Chap. 7.
- ***Emergence of Globally Applicable Law Regarding Cyberspace***: The development of and influence on the global internet is divided among more countries worldwide, especially among global powers, and countries establish respected norms about the usage of the internet. It is ruled by international law, once most countries adopt it. Though very similar to maritime law, this option is, due to the use of proxy warfare, somewhat unlikely—at least in the near future.

As shown in Table 1.2, the four options each have certain distinctive features, advantages and disadvantages. That is, without considering my own preference for a pro-liberal democratic world (that censors radical content like racism, antisemitism and hate in general).

Each option also reflects a different approach in the field of international affairs. Calculated predictions of these options will be consolidated in due course. However, each approaches the problem from a different angle. Some options, like the "internet bubbles" or "internet blocs," are more realistic, while approaches that emphasize cooperation, such as the emergence of internationally applicable law, are more liberal or constructivist. Interpretation can, of course, utilize a Marxist approach as well, as the internet is led by giant conglomerates and powerful governments, or it can apply the approach of the English School, when governments do find a middle ground. Whether the internet will become more Hobbesian, Grotian or Kantian is beyond my abilities to predict, as noted previously. Nevertheless, I further address this issue throughout the book as I refer to concepts or actions as more realistic or more cooperative.

What is the contribution of these predictions and suggestions? The expected contribution of this project is threefold. First, its predictions, which, as exemplified throughout the book, are taking shape in many countries as these lines are being written, are expected to contribute to theories in the field of international relations, specifically the debate between Realism, Liberalism and Constructivism, as well

[39] Malware—malicious computer software that is designed to cause disruption of any kind. Malware can take many forms, including viruses, worms, trojan horses, ransomware and spyware.

Table 1.2 Four options for the future of the internet

	Status quo	Internet bubbles	Cyber blocs	Emergence of globally applicable law regarding cyberspace
Feature	American/ Western-led project of mass communication	Restricted internets resembling intranets: secure cyber domains (SCDs)	A cyber domain developed and used by several countries forming a cyber bloc, whether by technical means, regulatory means or both	International laws and norms, dictating legal and illegal actions regarding cyberspace, including a sanction regime
Advantages	Advances American/ Western aims, global communication grid, openness	Complete cyber sovereignty for each individual country according to its desires	Protected cyberspace between several countries, more usable than internet bubbles but slightly less protected	A global regime of norms and laws, mutual development and accountability, enhanced usability
Disadvantages	Open countries like the United States are more susceptible to foreign influence; most countries have to rely on American-based development	Cyber domain is restricted to individual countries, less international development, restricted information and services (considered desirable by some countries)	Compromise between more powerful and less powerful countries: some may act as stakeholders regarding operations, foreign information	Every country is restricted in its use of cyber warfare strategies and tactics. Importantly, countries and their proxies are held accountable for cyber actions, although attribution remains an issue
Prominent example	The United States	North Korea	The European Union (GDPR, DSA, DMA), intelligence sharing by the five eyes	The Budapest convention on cybercrime

as further debates about the future of globalization. Second, this project makes an empirical contribution as it detects, reviews and compares cyber sovereignty processes that are already taking place—presenting very mature models of such "cyberspaces," SCDs, along with less developed ones. Third, this project contributes to the actual work of policymakers and practitioners by enabling them to better understand common issues and problems in the cyber domain. Moreover, it will guide human online activities, and public presentations of this project will, hopefully, lead to better and safer use of the internet.

1.1 An Answer to the "So What?" Question

Given the current state of the internet, countries are susceptible to cyberattacks carried out by proxies of other nations, and they are susceptible to foreign influence and mis/disinformation. Although, in forensic terms, it is difficult to attribute cyberattacks and influence to other countries or their proxies, some have made this attempt. One of the most well-known cases was when the United States accused Russia of attempting to influence its 2016 presidential elections.[40] Other well-known examples that are mentioned in later chapters of this book include the alleged Russian intervention and influence in the United Kingdom's referendum on European Union membership (Brexit), as well as its alleged intervention in Ukraine and intervention and influence in the Baltic countries that sought to join and/or collaborate with NATO and more. At first glance, interventions in the form of spreading mis/disinformation, unwanted information or even some hacking actions may seem insignificant. One might ask whether countries would really go to war or change the global order because of social media posts or news publications, or because one country hacked another's computer system. Will the lawlessness of cyberspace really change the global order as we know it? The answer is yes. But why?

As explained by Jeffery Hart in 1976, countries seek control in their efforts to increase three main measurements of power. They seek to control resources, other international actors and outcomes. However, particularly since the Peace of Westphalia in 1648, countries have borders and autonomy in decision-making and the use of force. A country thus controls its land, resources and people. So, how can a country increase the other measurements of power? Either by economic and diplomatic means, whether fair or unfair, or by military means and intervention.[41] As further explained in Chap. 3, Fredric S. Pearson suggested that countries have six reasons for intervening in others' affairs: a desire to acquire territory or other domains, a desire to protect social/identity groups, a desire to protect or promote economic interests, a desire to protect or promote diplomatic and/or military interests, a desire to protect or promote ideology and, lastly, a desire to maintain or adjust the regional

[40] Mueller III (2019) and Gayle (2016).

[41] Hart (1976).

balance of power.[42] Thus, as long as the cyber domain allows countries to either fulfill the abovementioned six objectives or sabotage others' efforts to do so, they will strive to contain or control cyberspace. This is the naturally feasible outcome.

1.2 Relation to Other Publications

As mentioned, the concepts of cyber sovereignty and internet governance are not new. Nor is the discussion about the dangers of cyberspace. Many practitioners and scholars have addressed these concepts in the fields of cyber security, law and international relations. My argument is built upon their findings and reasoning, extending them and further developing the concept. Using real and ongoing practices and processes in the cyber domain, I attempt to empirically and theoretically demonstrate that cyber sovereignty is not just a theoretical concept or a minor action that countries and even corporations take. Cyber sovereignty, or the de-proliferation of the internet as we know it, is one of the most significant global processes since Westphalia or since the peak of globalization, and while researchers like Milton L. Mueller argue against the fragmentation of the internet, they do so from a normative point of view that regards globalization and freedom of communications as supreme values. In this book, however, I do not focus on these values but on strategic and, importantly, realistic shifts in global power.[43]

Yochai Benkler, Robert Faris and Hal Roberts discussed the many vulnerabilities of cyberspace in their book *Network Propaganda*.[44] In *Bytes, Bombs, and Spies*, Herbert Lin and Amy Zegart showed that cyber warfare is a significantly growing trend among countries, terror organizations, cybercriminals and individuals. Lin and Zegard argued that offensive cyber operations have become an integral part of foreign policy and national strategy. This strategy is not only offensive in nature but defensive as well—countries also need the ability to protect themselves from cyberattacks.[45] In *Wars of Disruption and Resilience*, Chris Demchak presented a strategy of "security resilience" to address the many complexities, dangers and vulnerabilities of cyberspace.[46] Moreover, Bruce Schneier addressed the concept of cyber sovereignty in his 2015 book *Data and Goliath* and noted that countries like Russia, China and Saudi Arabia are already taking measures to strengthen their role in their own cyber domains.[47] Cyber sovereignty has also been discussed by Yi Shen in the Chinese Political Science Review Journal and by Eric T. Jensen in the Texas International Law Journal.[48]

---

[42] Pearson (1974).

[43] Mueller (2017, 2020).

[44] See, generally, Benkler et al. (2018).

[45] See Lin and Zegart (2019).

[46] Demchak (2011).

[47] See Schneier (2015).

[48] Shen (2016) and Jensen (2015).

Indeed, countries like China and Russia have already begun controlling their own cyber domains. Binxing Fang discussed the Chinese case thoroughly in his 2018 article *Cyberspace Sovereignty: Reflections on Building a Community of Common Future in Cyberspace.*[49] Russia has also initiated a cyber sovereignty project with its own internal internet, RuNet, and through legislative actions like the Yarovaya law and the "sovereign internet" law. Scott Jasper reviewed the Russian cyber offensive approach in his book *Russian Cyber Operations: Coding the Boundaries of Conflict*. Furthermore, together with my co-author, I have published two articles for the U.S. Marine Corps and the Russian International Affairs Council (RIAC) that present and discuss the Russian grand strategy for cyberspace.[50] Russia and China have already gained significant benefits from their implementation of regulations, and in recent years even the United States has begun working toward a more feasible solution with its publicly published cyber sovereignty workshop series.[51] In this regard, Sarah Kreps has addressed the issue of social media and international relations and showed how foreign governments employ social media for strategic purposes.[52]

The debate about cyber sovereignty, and even its implementation, is on the rise. This book aims to enhance and extend the theoretical and philosophical arguments of the mentioned scholars and practitioners, offering a "go-to" guide readers can consult to learn about the theoretical aspects of international relations and cyber sovereignty, as well as the practical implementations of this sovereignty, along with an actual overview of cyberspace structure, as presented in Chap. 2.

1.3 Research Design and Methodology

This study is an analysis of the international arena, specifically of the international struggle for dominance and the struggle for sovereignty. The approach taken here is a realistic approach—it stresses that countries are the main actors within the international system, and while organizations and individuals do have an impact, this impact is often limited and under the auspices of countries. This study was inspired by the observation that countries have been undermined using the internet—cyberspace—and that they are taking what might be called selfish actions in an attempt to control their sovereignty. Countries do cooperate when it is beneficial to them, but it is only logical to assume that they will put security and national stability before cooperation and human rights.

Methodologically, this is a comparative study. I examine and compare global and local trends concerning cyberspace, cyber warfare and international security. I use both qualitative and quantitative analysis to examine cyberspace, elaborating on the methodology of each individual chapter in its introduction. I review international

[49] See Fang (2018).

[50] Topor and Tabachnik (2021).

[51] Haber and Topor (2023).

[52] Kreps (2020).

norms and laws, regulations, trends in cyber warfare strategies and tactics, social media trends, measurements of internet usage, and review case studies. In Chap. 2, which follows this introduction, I present the structure of cyberspace and explain various associated issues, including its use, the way it operates and its vulnerabilities. In Chap. 3, I present the concepts of sovereignty and power and discuss the lack of international norms and laws regarding cyberspace. In Chap. 4, I present the trends of 500 cyberattacks and review a few cases in-depth, not only cases of "harder" cyberattacks but also cases of soft cyberattacks like mis/disinformation campaigns or "fake news." The results suggest that the main issue with the internet is information flow—be that mis/disinformation or unwanted information. Thus, in Chap. 5, I ask: are countries immune to mis/disinformation campaigns or are "fake news" posts on Facebook or Twitter or circulated stories on WhatsApp or Telegram a real threat to countries? To answer this question, I review the impact of mis/disinformation influence campaigns on national resilience and stability using recent cases from around the world.

The next question is how countries might cope with these cyberattacks. To propose several solutions, in Chap. 6, I present and elaborate on the concept of SCDs and give examples of mature models of such cyber domains, including those of North Korea, China, Russia, Iran and Saudi Arabia. In contrast, in Chap. 7, I present vulnerable and open cyber domains including those of the United States, the United Kingdom and Israel, as well as the European example, which is an attempt to create an international bloc, at least to some extent. Methodologically, in Chaps. 6 and 7, I analyze the cyber domains of the abovementioned countries using a structured review based on the structure of cyberspace: I analyze the physical layer of cyberspace, the logical layer, the information layer, and the user layer. Subsequently, I compare the cases with one another. Lastly, in Chap. 8, I present the conclusions of the study and elaborate on the emergence of cyber blocs within global affairs, be they geographical or economic and political cyber blocs.

1.3.1 Selection of Case Studies

The case studies that were selected for Chaps. 6 and 7, the cardinal chapters of this book, were chosen based on several considerations. First, for Chap. 6, based on information from the non-profit organizations Freedom House (see Table 1.1) and Access Now, I chose the most restricted cyber domains—those most secure in terms of strategic security. Another important consideration was power. Since history has taught us that powers set the global scene, I chose to focus on countries that are powerful enough, globally and regionally, to compete with the United States—the Western country that developed cyberspace in the first place. The selected powers compete with the United States to exert global influence and are even developing their own cyber initiatives to function as alternatives for Western cyber-related things. China, for instance, has developed WeChat as an alternative messaging application, Weibo as the "Chinese Twitter," Douyin (TikTok), Baidu as an alternative search engine, Alibaba as an e-commerce platform, Huawei as an alternative to Western smartphones and computers (hardware), and many other initiatives. The cases presented in Chap. 6 are those of North Korea, China, Russia, Saudi Arabia and Iran.

For Chap. 7, I chose the least Secure Cyber Domains among the countries that are considered global or regional powers. While these cyber domains are open and free, promoting free speech and the open flow of information, they are more susceptible to cyberattacks and the exertion of sharp power. Although these global and regional powers attempt to remain free and open, following the American example, these are also the least Secure Cyber Domains in terms of strategic security. The cases are those of the United States, the United Kingdom, Israel and the European Union, the latter of which serves as an example of an evolving cyber bloc.

References

Access Now. 2022. The return of digital authoritarianism—Internet shutdowns in 2021, April 2022. https://www.accessnow.org/wp-content/uploads/2022/05/2021-KIO-Report-May-24-2022.pdf.

BBC. 2022. US bans sale of Huawei, ZTE tech amid security fears. *BBC*, November 26. https://www.bbc.com/news/world-us-canada-63764450.

Benkler, Yochai. 2006. *The wealth of networks: How social production transforms markets and freedom*. New Haven, CT: Yale University Press.

Benkler, Yochai, Robert Faris, and Hal Roberts. 2018. *Network propaganda: Manipulation, disinformation, and radicalization in American politics*. Oxford University Press.

Brock, Joe. 2023. Exclusive: China plans $500 million subsea internet cable to rival US-backed project. *Reuters*, April 6. https://www.reuters.com/world/china/china-plans-500-mln-subsea-internet-cable-rival-us-backed-project-2023-04-06/.

Cadell, Cate. 2023. China's military aims to launch 13,000 satellites to rival Elon Musk's Starlink. *Washington Post*, April 6. https://www.washingtonpost.com/national-security/2023/04/06/elon-musk-china-starlink-pla/.

Chandel, Sonali, Jingji Zang, Yunnan Yu, Jingyao Sun, and Zhipeng Zhang. 2019. The golden shield project of China: A decade later—An in-depth study of the great firewall. In *2019 International Conference on Cyber-Enabled Distributed Computing and Knowledge Discovery (CyberC)*, 111–119. IEEE.

Choucri, Nazli, and David D. Clark. 2012. Integrating cyberspace and international relations: The co-evolution dilemma. In *Explorations in cyber international relations*. MIT.

Croxton, Derek. 1999. The peace of Westphalia of 1648 and the origins of sovereignty. *The International History Review* 21 (3): 569–591.

Demchak, Chris C. 2011. *Wars of disruption and resilience: Cybered conflict, power, and national security*. University of Georgia Press.

Department for Digital, Culture, Media & Sport and The Rt Hon Michelle Donelan MP. 2022. Huawei legal notices issued. *United Kingdom Government*, October 13.

Digwatch. n.d. EU's Digital Services Act (DSA) & Digital Markets Act (DMA). https://dig.watch/processes/eu-digital-service-act-dsa-digital-market-act-dma.

Economist. 2010. A virtual counter-revolution. *Economist*, September 2. https://www.economist.com/briefing/2010/09/02/a-virtual-counter-revolution.

Elkin-Koren, Niva, and Eldar Haber. 2016. Governance by proxy: Cyber challenges to civil liberties. *Brooklyn Law Review* 82: 105.

European Commission. 2022a. Antitrust: Commission sends statement of objections to Meta over abusive practices benefiting Facebook marketplace, December 19. https://ec.europa.eu/commission/presscorner/detail/en/ip_22_7728.

European Commission. 2022b. EU and international partners put forward a Declaration for the Future of the Internet, April 28. https://ec.europa.eu/commission/presscorner/detail/en/ip_22_2695.

Fang, Binxing. 2018. *Cyberspace sovereignty: Reflections on building a community of common future in cyberspace*. Springer.

Fischerkeller, Michael P. 2021. Current international law is not an adequate regime for cyberspace. *Lawfare Blog*, April 22. https://www.lawfareblog.com/current-international-law-not-adequate-regime-cyberspace.

Freedom House. n.d. Internet freedom scores. https://freedomhouse.org/countries/freedom-net/scores?sort=asc&order=Country. Accessed August 22, 2023.

Gayle, Damien. 2016. CIA concludes Russia interfered to help Trump win election, say reports. *Guardian*, December 10. https://www.theguardian.com/us-news/2016/dec/10/cia-concludes-russia-interfered-to-help-trump-win-election-report.

Gillies, Rob. 2022. Canada bans China's Huawei Technologies from 5G networks. *AP News*, May 20. https://apnews.com/article/politics-technology-justin-trudeau-canada-ec8046f8f85f3e70fb3800a0f749ced5.

Google Transparency Report. n.d. Government requests to remove content. https://transparencyreport.google.com/government-removals/government-requests/AE?hl=en. Accessed January 18, 2024.

Haber, Eldar, and Lev Topor. 2023. Sovereignty, cyberspace, and the emergence of internet bubbles. *Journal of Advanced Military Studies* 14 (1): 144–165.

Hadero, Haleyulaa. 2023. Why social media is being blamed for fueling the riots in France. *AP*, July 1. https://apnews.com/article/france-shooting-riots-social-media-tiktok-snapchat-c6328bdfbaf8be851c84416993e09cbf.

Harknett, Richard J., and Joseph S. Nye Jr. 2017. Is deterrence possible in cyberspace? *International Security* 42 (2): 196–199.

Hart, Jeffrey. 1976. Three approaches to the measurement of power in international relations. *International Organization* 30 (2): 289–305.

Hinsley, Francis H. 1986. *Sovereignty*, 2nd ed. Cambridge University Press.

International Telecommunication Union. 2023. *Fact and figures 2023*. https://www.itu.int/itu-d/reports/statistics/facts-figures-2023/.

Jensen, Eric Talbot. 2015. Cyber sovereignty: The way ahead. *Texas International Law Journal* 50: 275.

Kreps, Sarah. 2020. *Social media and international relations*. Cambridge University Press.

Kumar, Raksha. 2022. Not quite the Arab Spring: How protestors are using social media in innovative ways. *Reuters Institute*, December 6. https://reutersinstitute.politics.ox.ac.uk/news/not-quite-arab-spring-how-protestors-are-using-social-media-innovative-ways.

Libicki, Martin C. 2011. The strategic uses of ambiguity in cyberspace. *Military and Strategic Affairs* 3 (3): 3–10.

Lin, Herbert, and Amy Zegart (eds.). 2019. *Bytes, bombs, and spies: The strategic dimensions of offensive cyber operations*. Brookings Institution Press.

MacAskill, Ewen, Julian Borger, Nick Hopkins, Nick Davies, and James Ball. 2013. GCHQ taps fibre-optic cables for secret access to world's communications. *Guardian*, June 21. https://www.theguardian.com/uk/2013/jun/21/gchq-cables-secret-world-communications-nsa.

Machangama, Jacob. 2022. The real threat to social media is Europe. *Foreign Policy*, April 25. https://foreignpolicy.com/2022/04/25/the-real-threat-to-social-media-is-europe/.

Mahan, Alfred T. 2011. *The influence of sea power upon history, 1660–1783*. CreateSpace Independent Publishing Platform.

Maheshwari, Sapna, and Amanda Holpuch. 2023. Why countries are trying to ban TikTok. *New York Times*, August 16. https://www.nytimes.com/article/tiktok-ban.html.

Metz, Sam. 2021. Nevada tech company asks to withdraw 'Innovation Zones' plan. *AP News*, October 8. https://apnews.com/article/technology-nevada-blockchain-legislature-a84007f8d5894a8411e915f3eab2c5e5.

Mueller, Milton L. 2017. *Will the internet fragment? Sovereignty, globalization and cyberspace*. Wiley.

Mueller, Robert S. III. 2019. *Report on the investigation into Russian interference in the 2016 presidential election—Volume I of II*. Washington, DC: US Department of Justice.

Mueller, Milton L. 2020. Against sovereignty in cyberspace. *International Studies Review* 22 (4): 779–801.

Osiander, Andreas. 2001. Sovereignty, international relations, and the Westphalian myth. *International Organization* 55 (2): 251–287.

Pearson, Frederic S. 1974. Foreign military interventions and domestic disputes. *International Studies Quarterly* 18 (3): 259–290.

Ruy, Donatienne. 2020. Did Russia influence Brexit? *CSIS*, July 21. https://www.csis.org/blogs/brexit-bits-bobs-and-blogs/did-russia-influence-brexit.

Schmitt, Michael N. (ed.). 2017. *Tallinn manual 2.0 on the international law applicable to cyber warfare*, 2nd ed. Cambridge University Press.

Schneier, Bruce. 2015. *Data and goliath: The hidden battles to collect your data and control your world*. WW Norton & Company.

Shen, Yi. 2016. Cyber sovereignty and the governance of global cyberspace. *Chinese Political Science Review* 1: 81–93.

Shuker, Pnina, and Lev Topor. 2021. Russian influence campaigns against NATO in the Baltic region: Spread of chaos and divide et impera. In *The Russian Federation in global knowledge warfare*, 295–314. Cham: Springer.

The White House. 2022. A Declaration for the Future of the Internet, April 2022. United States of America. https://www.whitehouse.gov/wp-content/uploads/2022/04/Declaration-for-the-Future-for-the-Internet_Launch-Event-Signing-Version_FINAL.pdf.

Topor, Lev. 2022. *Phishing for Nazis: Conspiracies, anonymous communications and white supremacy networks on the Dark Web*. Routledge.

Topor, Lev, and Alexander Tabachnik. 2021. Russian cyber information warfare: International distribution and domestic control. *Journal of Advanced Military Studies* 12 (1): 112–127.

United Nations. 1945. *Charter of the United Nations, Chapter VII, Article 51*.

Wang, Anqi. 2020. Cyber sovereignty at its boldest: A Chinese perspective. *Ohio State Technology Law Journal* 16: 395.

Warf, Barney. 2015. The Hermit Kingdom in cyberspace: Unveiling the North Korean internet. *Information, Communication & Society* 18 (1): 109–120.

Wu, Timothy S. 1996. Cyberspace sovereignty—The Internet and the international system. *Harvard Journal of Law & Technology* 10: 647.

Chapter 2
Cyberspace: Structure, Functionality and Vulnerabilities

In this chapter, I explain what the internet is, its structure, how it operates, and the main vulnerabilities of each layer of cyberspace ("cyberspace" and "internet" are used interchangeably). This will serve as the basis of the analysis in the subsequent chapters as I will use the terms and concepts discussed in this chapter to demonstrate how nations control their own cyberspaces. The first part of this chapter offers a brief history of the internet, including its origins in the American ARPANET projects, a review of failed competing projects, such as the Soviet OGAS project, as well as the different stages of the ever-developing internet, such as the emergence of interconnected networks, its gradual civilian adoption for communications in the 1980s with emails and USENET groups, the dot-com boom of the 1990s and the consolidation and refinement of the internet—of cyberspace—in the early 2000s, which led to the emergence of social media and artificial intelligence (AI). I also present the concept of top-level domains (TLD) and explain that even the rights to domains like *.gov* or *.ru* are highly contested.

In the second part of this chapter, I present the structure of cyberspace from a semi-technical and socio-political perspective. The TCP/IP and OSI models of the internet are introduced and explained. Next, the four-layer model of cyberspace is presented, which describes cyberspace as having an infrastructure layer, a logical layer, an information (data) layer and a user layer. These three models are compared and elucidated. The worldwide internet cable connections are illustrated in Figs. 2.1 and 2.2. Figure 2.1 shows the global dissemination of submarine and land connections, and Fig. 2.2 provides an example of an isolated country, North Korea, which has no publicly visible connections—though some experts think it probable that, apart from satellite connections, it is connected to a few Chinese cables with very limited access.

The third part of this chapter deals with power and control. Two questions are asked: Who runs the internet? And who owns the internet? In this section, I provide an overview of the main entities that control, monitor and regulate cyberspace—entities

L. Topor, *Cyber Sovereignty*, Global Power Shift,
https://doi.org/10.1007/978-3-031-58199-1_2

Fig. 2.1 Global map of submarine fiber-optic cables and land (terrestrial) links. Gray indicates submarine fiber-optic cables and blue indicates land links. *Source* Infrastructure Connectivity Map, International Telecommunication Union

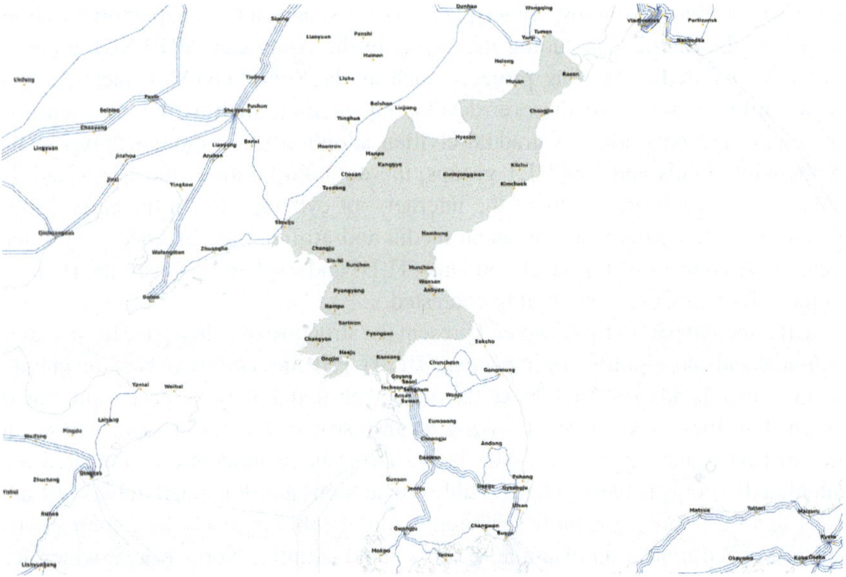

Fig. 2.2 Connections with North Korea. Gray indicates submarine fiber-optic cables and blue indicates land links. *Source* Infrastructure Connectivity Map, International Telecommunication Union

like sovereign countries but mainly entities like international regulatory organizations and companies, which together make up the internet ecosystem. These include entities like ICANN, the Internet Engineering Task Force (IETF) and Internet Architecture Board (IAB), the International Telecommunication Union (ITU) and many others. Companies also play a significant role and serve, at times, as proxies. Companies develop and provide infrastructure, platforms and clouds, services and social media. Prominent examples are Microsoft, Apple, Telegram, DanceByte (TikTok) and many more, such as Lumen Technologies, Cogent Communications, Rostelecom and China Telecom. Not all entities control every aspect of cyberspace. Some control naming and addressing, others control development and standards, some focus on services and some on policies and education; together they make up the internet ecosystem.

In the last part of this chapter, before the conclusion, I present and explain the main socio-political threats and vulnerabilities of cyberspace, which include not only the threat of cyberattacks by countries but also individual user privacy concerns about fair information usage, government surveillance, censorship and concerns over discerning fact and fiction online—the impact of mis/disinformation, algorithmic biases and platforms' manipulation of users. Other concerns include online harassment and bullying, as well as the digital divide—the unequal access to and use of cyberspace among different socioeconomic groups and regions. These socio-political threats are explained and discussed in depth in many of the cases throughout this book, especially in Chaps. 4 and 5; in this chapter, however, they are brought up to make a point: a lawless cyberspace can be a dangerous domain.

2.1 A Short History of the Internet

All of us, mainly but not exclusively in developed countries, use the internet to consume, create and share. But how did humans communicate before the internet? Generally, humans have had various options for consuming and sharing information, for communication. Skipping over the time of smoke signals, blowing a horn, and making public announcements in the village center, people had postal services and/or couriers, as well as print and radio communications. In general, these are methods of either mass communication or long-distance communication. The features of some communication methods are explained further in this chapter; in general, however, the development and increased affordability of personal computers and other devices and the internet—the network of networks—have allowed people from all over the world to communicate easily for the first time, with almost no delay between one end and the other and with less chance of a third party "peeking" at the personal messages between parties. Even before the internet, methods to ensure authenticity and confidentiality were used when sending letters by courier or post. For instance, letters would be closed with a personal wax seal for authentication of the sender's identity, and the receiver would know the letter had been read or tampered with if the wax seal was broken.[1] Today, of course, we have encryption and personal signatures and certificates to authenticate and keep messages private.

Wired and wireless communication methods, like radio or signals, have been used by the civil and military services of countries like Russia, China, England and other developed countries since the late nineteenth century. However, another unique feature of the internet is that the information can be stored, unlike a radio wave that is only available as it moves in space between the sender and the receiver. Once a message has been received, the wave is gone (unless the message has been recorded and stored on a third device). Another feature of the internet is that it is a decentralized and distributed network. That is, at least in its early design and theory. While it is true that the internet is not designed to have a center, it does have a center of gravity, the United States of America, as the historical development of the internet shows. Of course, in an attempt to exert more control, other global powers and countries try to compete with this status quo, as I explain throughout this book.[2]

The internet has grown into our primary platform for communication; while people, organizations and countries still use postal services, couriers, radio and other types of communication, the internet has become the most convenient and the fastest. Over five billion people worldwide use the internet, and most own computers and/or smartphones.[3] The internet stands as one of the most transformative inventions in human history, revolutionizing communication, commerce, education and virtually every aspect of modern life. Its origins can be traced back to the mid-twentieth century when it emerged from a combination of technological breakthroughs and visionary ideas. In the 1960s, during the Cold War era, the United States was investing heavily in scientific research and technology. The concept of packet switching, a method of transmitting electronic data over a network in small packets, was a critical breakthrough. In the early 1960s, Paul Baran proposed the idea of distributed communication networks, which laid the foundation for the development of the American Advanced Research Projects Agency Network (ARPANET). From the 1960s onwards, the internet was developed by American researchers and engineers and the American government. This fact is crucial to understanding the global struggle over cyberspace as further elaborated in this book.[4]

In August 1962, Joseph Carl Robnett Licklider of the Massachusetts Institute of Technology (MIT) wrote a series of memos describing a concept he called the "Galactic Network." This network would connect computers globally, allowing people to access data and programs from any location. Licklider, the first head of the computer research program at the Defense Advanced Research Projects Agency (DARPA),[5] convinced his successors, Ivan Sutherland, Bob Taylor and Lawrence G.

[1] Bedos-Rezak (2000).

[2] Topor (2022: 20–38), Leiner et al. (2009) and Ryan (2010).

[3] DataReportal (2023).

[4] Internet Society (1997).

[5] The Defense Advanced Research Projects Agency (DARPA) is a research and development agency of the United States Department of Defense, it was founded on February 7, 1958, by President Dwight D. Eisenhower.

Roberts, of the importance of this idea. Leonard Kleinrock of MIT published a paper on packet-switching theory in July 1961 that convinced Roberts that communication using packets instead of circuits was feasible. In 1965, Roberts and Thomas Merrill connected the TX-2 computer in Massachusetts to explore how to make computers communicate with each other. These were key steps toward computer networking, which eventually led to the internet we know today.[6]

During the early stages of computer networking, a group of researchers conducted an experiment in which time-shared computers were able to work together effectively. However, they found that the circuit-switched telephone system was not adequate for the job. This led to the realization that packet switching was necessary. In 1967, Roberts developed a plan for the ARPANET, and in 1969, the first message was successfully transmitted over the ARPANET between the University of California, Los Angeles, and the Stanford Research Institute.[7] The ARPANET was a decentralized network that aimed to ensure communication resilience in the event of a nuclear attack. The key innovation was the development of the Transmission Control Protocol (TCP) and the internet protocol (IP), collectively known as TCP/IP, which established a standardized method for data transmission and communication between different networks. By the end of 1969, four host computers had been connected to form the initial ARPANET, marking the beginning of the internet. The research on networking involved both work on the underlying network and how to utilize it. Many more computers were added to the ARPANET in the following years, and work proceeded on creating a functionally complete host-to-host protocol and other network software.[8]

In December 1970, the Network Working Group led by S. Crocker finalized the Network Control Protocol (NCP), the initial ARPANET host-to-host protocol. This allowed network users to start developing applications as the ARPANET sites implemented NCP between 1971 and 1972. In October 1972, Bob Kahn organized a highly successful demonstration of the ARPANET at the International Computer Communication Conference, marking the first public display of this innovative network technology. The first "hot" application, electronic mail, was introduced in the same year, with Ray Tomlinson at Bolt Beranek and Newman (BBN) creating the basic sending and reading software for email messages in March. In July, Roberts expanded the software's utility by writing the first email program that could list, selectively read, file, forward and respond to messages. For over a decade, email was the most significant application of the network, signaling the rise of "people-to-people" or "user-to-user" traffic that we see on the World Wide Web today. The 1970s thus witnessed significant advances in networking protocols, leading to the establishment of email as a means of electronic communication. Ray Tomlinson's introduction of the "@" symbol as a separator in email addresses was a crucial development during this period. Additionally, the term "internet" was coined to describe a network of

[6] Internet Society (1997).

[7] Kleinrock (2019).

[8] Internet Society (1997).

networks, highlighting the interconnected nature of the evolving technology.[9] A further decentralized platform emerged in the 1980s: User Network or USENET. USENET was a network of clients and servers. Unlike early emails that were sent from a single user to another, USENET users could read or post messages, called articles, or share files. USENET was organized into groups, and every discussion was threaded, as we still see in web forums or bulletin boards today. This made it a convenient way to spread information.[10]

The initial American ARPANET served as the foundation for the development of the internet. The internet was based on the concept of having several autonomous networks with varying designs. The ARPANET was the first packet switching network, but the internet soon included other packet satellite and ground-based packet radio networks. The internet's core technical concept is open-architecture networking. This means that network providers can choose any network technology and interconnect it with other networks through a meta-level "internetworking architecture." Before this development, circuit switching was the primary method for connecting networks. However, in 1961, MIT's Leonard Kleinrock showed that packet switching was more efficient. Additionally, the internet allows other options, such as special-purpose interconnection arrangements between networks. Rather than functioning as equals in providing end-to-end service, one network may serve as a component of another in an open-architecture network. Each network can be designed with its own unique interface to cater to specific user requirements and environments. The inclusion of various types of networks and their geographic scope is generally unrestricted, barring practical limitations. Other internet providers can also be included in the network. This design makes the internet, in theory, decentralized.[11]

Another significant moment was the development of the Atlantic Ocean Packet Satellite Communications Network (SATNET). This early satellite network formed an initial segment of the internet, allowing data to be transmitted through satellites and not cables. It was implemented by BBN Technologies under the direction of the Advanced Research Projects Agency (ARPA). The first heterogeneous computer network was implemented in 1973, connecting the ARPANET to University College London, and this evolved into SATNET. The first Transmission Control Program demonstration, linking SATNET, the ARPANET and the packet radio network (PRNET), took place on November 22, 1977, forming the first heterogeneous interconnected network in the world. This event was unique because it demonstrated the possibility of interconnecting different types of networks, each based on different transmission technologies and featuring different interfaces, packet sizes, labeling, conventions and transmission rates. The successful interconnection of these networks was a significant milestone in the development of the internet, as it demonstrated the viability of internetworking and the TCP protocol for connecting diverse network technologies.[12] The internet—literally a global network of networks—was born.

[9] Ibid.

[10] See Hauben and Hauben (1997) and Pfaffenberger (2003).

[11] Ibid.

[12] Rajaraman (2022a, b).

The 1980s brought further progress with the emergence of the World Wide Web, and in this decade many Western countries, and some non-Western countries, began using network technologies. In 1985, the National Science Foundation Network (NSFNET) was established to coordinate and develop projects about networking; it was funded by the American National Science Foundation and remained active until 1995, helping to further develop and deploy the American internet backbone of cables and hubs. In 1989, Tim Berners-Lee, a British computer scientist, proposed a system for sharing information through a "web" of linked documents. In 1990, he developed the first web browser and web server, allowing users to access and navigate interconnected web pages using hypertext links. The ability to easily share and access information marked a turning point in the internet's history as it made the creation, consumption and sharing of information open to all.[13] The 1990s witnessed the commercialization of the internet, leading to the explosive growth of online businesses and services. The introduction of graphical web browsers like Netscape Navigator made the internet more user-friendly and accessible to a wider audience. This period also witnessed the emergence of e-commerce giants like Amazon and eBay, signaling the potential for online retail. The late 1990s saw the dot-com boom, characterized by a speculative frenzy around internet-related companies. While this era led to the creation of numerous startups and innovations, it culminated in the dot-com bubble burst of the early 2000s, resulting in the collapse of many internet companies.[14]

The 2000s and early 2010s witnessed the consolidation and refinement of the internet's infrastructure and services. The development of broadband and high-speed internet connections enabled the proliferation of multimedia content, paving the way for streaming services, online gaming and social media platforms. The rise of social media, exemplified by platforms like Facebook, Twitter and Instagram, redefined how people connect and communicate online. These platforms facilitated the sharing of personal experiences, opinions and media, transforming the way information spread and influencing various aspects of culture and society. Unlike user-to-user interactions, social media allowed people to spread unrestricted—and in the United States, uncensored—information to the masses. In addition, the advent of smartphones in the late 2000s brought about a new era of internet usage. Mobile devices allowed individuals to access the internet on the go, leading to the development of mobile apps and responsive web design. This shift significantly impacted communication, entertainment and entire industries. Simultaneously, the concept of the Internet of Things (IoT) emerged, wherein everyday objects and devices were connected to the internet, allowing them to collect and exchange data. This development has given rise to smart homes, wearable technology and advances in fields like agriculture and manufacturing; however, IoT has given rise to new concerns over privacy, ownership and control, which is a topic for a different study.[15] The internet has also enabled and enhanced the development of high-speed and broadband networks like 5G, platforms

[13] Ibid.

[14] Ibid.

[15] Sharma et al. (2019).

like augmented reality (AR) and virtual reality (VR) and, of course, the wide use of AI.[16]

2.2 Competing Historical Developments of the Internet

As the short historical overview in Sect. 2.1 has shown, the internet is a largely American project. But, what about other great powers like Russia or China? Have they not developed their own technologies? They did indeed try, but they failed to a great extent—at least, until the twenty-first century. Natalia Konradova describes how the prehistory of the Russian internet began in 1957 with the launch of the *Sputnik 1* satellite, which relied on radio communication. The evident success of this long-distance radio communication, and this historical technological achievement in general, prompted American President Dwight D. Eisenhower to found DARPA in 1958, and by 1969, ARPANET had been launched to connect computers across the United States. However, a decade before the launch of ARPANET, in 1959, the first unsuccessful attempt at networking was made by military engineer Anatoly Kitov in the Soviet Union. In 1962, a second attempt was made in the Soviet Union: OGAS, the National Automated System for Computation and Information Processing (from Russian ОГАС: Общегосударственная автоматизированная система учёта и обработки информации). This was an attempt to create a Soviet national information network, and just like the success of Sputnik 1, it pressured the Americans to further invest in ARPANET. OGAS was denied funding by the Soviet government in the 1970s and did not progress.[17]

In the 1980s and 1990s, the Soviet Union joined the USENET network and began corresponding with the Americans. Newsgroups related to the Soviet Union began to emerge, such as *talk.politics.soviet* and *soc.culture.soviet*. During the 1990s, and after the collapse of the Soviet Union, as web pages started to become widespread, shifting internet users from USENET to web pages (websites), the domain *.ru* emerged—Russia received its TLD on April 7, 1994. Russia also registered some official second-level domains like *.ac.ru*, *.gov.ru*, *.mil.ru* and others. The Coordination Center for TLD RU was the official registry. From that point on, the Russian Institute for Public Networks allowed the registration of Russian web addresses, essentially giving birth to the Russian World Wide Web.[18]

The 2000s saw a shift in the relationship between the Russian government and the internet. While the internet continued to grow and thrive, the government began asserting more control over it, as it had done with radio, print and television. In 2012, the Russian Parliament adopted a law boosting governmental control over the internet. The law was introduced as a means to battle child pornography and illegal content, but it granted the power to create a blacklist of censored websites and

[16] Kennedy et al. (2023).

[17] Konradova (2020).

[18] Ibid.

services. In 2014, the Russian government adopted a law requiring bloggers with large followings to register with the authorities, signaling the beginning of increased government oversight.[19] This is discussed in more detail in Chap. 6.

In the third emerging power, China, the internet was developed during the late 1980s and emerged during the 1990s. Although the first email from China was sent in 1987, it was not sent on the TCP/IP network and thus does not technically count as internet communication. Nevertheless, it was a successful attempt that paved the way for internet use, and on November 28, 1990, China registered the *.cn* TLD via its China Internet Network Information Center (CNNIC). China officially gained full internet functionality on April 20, 1994, and by January 1995 the Ministry of Posts and Telecommunications had started providing internet services to the public. By 1996–7 China had enacted its first laws criminalizing online activities—these, and the Russian case, are discussed in later chapters.[20]

2.3 The Structure of the Internet—Cyberspace

By the 1990s and 2000s, the internet as developed by the United States had been made available to many countries. Interestingly, this American-funded project was not only made available to close allies but was made available globally, even to adversaries. The United States hoped that this would break down barriers and allow for the free flow of information to and from each country. The First Amendment was projected outwards—an idea not every country was enthusiastic about, particularly regimes like those of Russia and China.

As described in the short history of the internet in Sect. 2.1, the internet is a network of networks, designed to allow people to communicate and share information. A user with a computer device can connect to another user with such a device, and many devices and interactions together create cyberspace. But how do they all really connect? What is cyberspace? The technical structure can be described using the TCP/IP structure that was developed as part of the ARPANET project and using the Open System Interconnection (OSI) developed by software engineer Hubert Zimmerman, among others, during the 1970s and published by the International Organization for Standardization (ISO) in 1980. Essentially, as described in Table 2.1, these models divide the structure of networks into a physical layer, a logical layer, an application layer and a user layer.[21]

How is the technical structure of cyberspace relevant to this book, which focuses on international relations and international security? The structure of cyberspace is very important in later chapters where I demonstrate how countries control, manipulate and restrict each of the layers.[22] Countries can control the physical connections,

[19] Ibid.; Topor and Tabachnik (2021).

[20] Yang (2012) and Economy (2018).

[21] Russel (2013).

[22] Ibid.

Table 2.1 OSI model and the TCP/IP model: a comparison

	OSI model	TCP/IP model	Explanation
Layer	Application	Application	Human–computer interaction layer
	Presentation		Data presentation and data encryption
	Session		Establishment and management of sessions
Layer	Transport	Transport	Transmission of data
Layer	Network	Internet	Network routing
Layer	Data link	Network	Organization of data into frames
	Physical		Transmission of bits through cables

Table 2.2 Social and technical models of cyberspace

	Four-layer model	OSI model	TCP/IP model	Explanation
Layer	User and information layer	Application	Application	Human–computer interaction layer
		Presentation		Data presentation and data encryption
		Session		Establishment and management of sessions
Layer	Logical layer	Transport	Transport	Transmission of data
Layer		Network	Internet	Network routing
Layer	Physical layer	Data link	Network	Organization of data into frames
		Physical		Transmission of bits through cables

which are explained and in Tables 2.1 and 2.2, countries can control data routing, such as by blocking selected connections or shutting down entire areas, countries can control users by defining when, where and how they use the internet, and, finally, countries can even control encryption. For instance, Russia requires many services like Apple, Google, Yandex and others to provide the Russian federal security agencies with their encryption keys.[23] The free United States of America has also sought access to the keys for encrypted applications and devices—such cases are explained in the following chapters.[24]

Essentially, as Yochai Benkler or Nazli Choucri and David D. Clark explain, cyberspace is made up of four layers: the physical layer, the logical layer, the information layer, and the layer of users. This is outlined in a comparative manner in Table 2.2. The physical layer is the actual physical infrastructure, and it includes fiber-optic cables, nodes, satellites, servers, computers and any other type of hardware. Next is the logical layer, which is built upon the infrastructure and acts as

[23] Moscow Times (2019).

[24] Rimer (2016) and Smith (2021).

the central nervous system of the cyber domain—it is in charge of data routing. It routes information to and from clients and servers. The information layer is the actual data that is either permanently or temporarily stored on the servers and made accessible to users; this layer includes text, video, audio, pictures and any other data format. The last layer is the layer of users—regular and harmless users who create, consume, socialize and work in cyberspace but also users who may be malicious and dangerous, like cybercriminals, state agents or agents of propaganda. Conceptually, these four layers can be divided into two main layers: the physical and logical layers are technical, and the information and user layers are social.[25]

Most of the data in cyberspace passes through submarine fiber-optic cables, while satellites are reserved mainly for research and military use. Just as early ARPANET connections connected one computer device to another, the internet is, by now, the connection of many such devices. A map created by the ITU, provided in Fig. 2.1, shows the physical infrastructure that connects the world, including land cables and submarine fiber-optic cables. To make a point about the importance of physical infrastructure to sovereignty—or control—one can examine North Korea. Figure 2.2 shows that North Korea is not very well connected to cyberspace, thus its population is not connected to the global arena.[26] As Haber and I have argued, some countries may be labeled "internet bubbles" simply due to the fact that they are not connected to the outside world in a way that allows mass consumption and use of the internet.[27]

2.4 Who Runs the Internet?

Although cyberspace is global, the United States was the one to develop and launch it. It developed and spread the physical infrastructure, the routing, ports and protocols, as well as general networking standards, and it has educated, to some extent, the users, who have all used mainly Western-designed hardware and software and who have used—and still use—mainly Western websites, search engines and social media platforms. Furthermore, the Western companies Microsoft, Google, Meta (Facebook) and Amazon own or lease most of the undersea cables.[28] This might answer the question of who places all these cables (see Fig. 2.1). As of 2023, Russia, China and others are working to challenge the status quo. However, in an effort to make cyberspace truly global, some international organizations have emerged under American pressure or by international and mutual decision.

Such organizations include ICANN, IETF and IAB, ITU, Regional Internet Registries (RIRs), the Internet Society (ISOC), the World Wide Web Consortium (W3C), the Network Information Center (NIC) and Country Code Managers, Content

---

[25] Benkler (2006: 23) and Choucri and Clark (2019: 33–65, 101–122).

[26] Maps provided by the International Telecommunication Union (ITU) and updated to early 2023. See an interactive map with more information: https://bbmaps.itu.int/bbmaps/.

[27] Haber and Topor (2023).

[28] Brock (2023) and Satariano (2019).

Table 2.3 Internet ecosystem—governing entities (acronyms explained in text)

Role	Entities
Naming and addressing	ICANN, RIRs, IANA/PTI, gTLDs, ccTLDs
Open standards development	ITU-T, specialized standards bodies (i.e., ISO), IETF, IAB, IRTF
Shared global services and operations	Root servers, network operations, IXP, service creators and vendors, gTLDs, ccTLDs
Local, national, regional and global policy development	Governments, IGOs, private businesses, ISOC and SIGs
Education and capacity building	Governments, internet community and users, universities and NRENs, ISOC
Users	Individual users, civil society, governments, organizations, service creators and vendors

Delivery Networks (CDNs) and Internet Service Providers (ISPs) and, last but not least, governments. Alongside these, state-owned or private companies and even civil society organizations (CSOs) develop websites and web applications. These and others make up cyberspace or, as ISOC refers to it, the internet ecosystem. This ecosystem is presented in Table 2.3, which describes the roles of each of the main internet-related entities. A description of each entity follows at the end of this section.[29]

If a country wants to assume more, or less, control over cyberspace, it has to negotiate with dozens of entities, and this makes operations, regulation and enforcement very difficult. Thus, countries do not control cyberspace—this is an important point that shapes the research and argument of this book since some countries find it more difficult than others to cooperate with dozens of mainly Western-led organizations. Countries like Russia and China have consistently accused organizations like ICANN of serving an American agenda because ICANN itself was an offshoot of the United States government in 1998.[30] For example, Ukraine recently asked ICANN to remove Russian domains from the internet—a request which was not granted but was made to pressure Russia and its society.[31] The Russian case is explained in later chapters.

Since cyberspace is run by dozens of entities, it is indeed distributed, not centralized. However, as many board members of organizations like ICANN, IANA, ITU and others are from the West, it is arguably biased. One interesting case that raised questions of appropriateness was the Columbian appeal to ICANN against Amazon. That is, should the *.amazon* domain belong to the company Amazon.com Inc. or would it be better used to describe the Indigenous Amazonian countries and peoples of Colombia, Bolivia, Brazil, Ecuador, Guyana, Peru, Suriname and Venezuela?

[29] Internet Society (2022).

[30] Klein (2002), ICANN (n.d.) and Selyukh (2014).

[31] Javers (2022) and Rieedel (2022).

The Amazon Cooperation Treaty Organization (ACTO) and the Columbian government appealed to ICANN in 2018 and 2019 with official Reconsideration Requests that they reconsider assigning *.amazon* to the American company Amazon.com. In May 2019, however, the company Amazon, through ICANN, managed to overcome ACTO.[32]

The individuals, groups, organizations, movements, governments, intergovernmental organizations (IGOs) and other entities that all together govern and design cyberspace are[33]:

- Internet Corporation for Assigned Names and Numbers (ICANN): responsible for managing and overseeing the coordination of the internet's domain name system (DNS) and its unique identifiers, such as internet protocol (IP) addresses. It is a non-profit public benefit corporation with a global community of participants and oversees the Internet Assigned Numbers Authority (IANA).
- Internet Assigned Numbers Authority (IANA): responsible for the administrative functions concerning the domain name system (DNS) root, internet protocol addressing, and other internet protocol resources. Functions are carried out by Public Technical Identifiers (PTI), a subsidiary of the Internet Corporation for Assigned Names and Numbers (ICANN).
- Internet Engineering Task Force (IETF): an internet standards body that engages a global community of network designers, operators, vendors, and researchers to develop open standards through open processes. IETF adopts technical and organizational notes and specifications about the internet in the form of the RFC document series. The Internet Society supports IETF through a variety of programs and the establishment of the IETF LLC—the administrative entity that supports the IETF, the Internet Architecture Board (IAB), and the Internet Research Task Force (IRTF).
- International Telecommunication Union (ITU): a United Nations specialized agency for telecommunications. The ITU allocates global radio spectrum and satellite orbits (ITU-R), develops the technical standards that ensure that telecommunication networks and technologies seamlessly interconnect (ITU-T), and strives to improve access to ICTs to underserved communities worldwide (ITU-D).
- Internet Research Task Force (IRTF): promotes research relevant to the evolution of the future internet by creating focused and long-term research groups working on topics related to internet protocols, applications, architecture and technology. The IRTF complements the work of the Internet Engineering Task Force (IETF).
- Internet Society (ISOC): a non-profit organization empowering people to keep the internet a force for good: open, globally connected, secure and trustworthy. Through members, chapters, special interest groups and partners, they are the hub of the largest global network of people and organizations working to build an internet for everyone.

[32] See ICANN (2018, 2019) and Ho (2019).

[33] Internet Society (2022).

- Regional Internet Registries (RIRs): oversee the registration and allocation of internet number resources within a particular region. Each RIR is a member of the Number Resource Organization (NRO), which acts as a coordinating body for the RIRs. The five RIRs are the African Network Information Centre (AFRINIC), the Asia-Pacific Network Information Centre (APNIC), the American Registry for Internet Numbers (ARIN), the Latin America and Caribbean Network Information Centre (LACNIC), and the Réseaux IP Européens Network Coordination Centre (RIPE NCC).
- World Wide Web Consortium (W3C): a global community where member organizations, a full-time staff, and the public work together to develop open standards for the web.
- Internet Exchange Points (IXPs): provide physical infrastructure at regional and national levels that allows network operators to exchange internet traffic between their networks through mutual peering agreements. IXPs improve network resilience, stability, efficiency and quality.
- Content Delivery Networks (CDNs): geographically distributed servers and data centers, placed as nodes over the global internet backbone (cables). The aim of CDNs is to deliver content to users as quickly and reliably as possible by avoiding the bottlenecks often created by extensive data traffic through cables.
- Country Code Top-Level Domains (ccTLDs) are operated according to the policies of the country or territory involved.
- Generic Top-Level Domains (gTLDs): registries operate sponsored and unsponsored gTLDs according to ICANN policies.
- Infrastructure Providers: they invest in and build the physical internet infrastructure that allows network operators to provide users access to the internet. They include companies, organizations and consortiums that build and operate submarine cables, terrestrial networks, satellite networks, cellular towers, internet exchange points (IXPs), content delivery networks (CDNs) and data centers.
- Internet Architecture Board (IAB): chartered as a committee of the Internet Engineering Task Force (IETF) and as an advisory body of the Internet Society (ISOC). Its responsibilities include architectural oversight of IETF activities, internet standards process oversight and appeal, appointment of the Request for Comments (RFC) Editor, and management of IETF protocol parameter registries.
- Internet Governance Forum (IGF): convened by the United Nations Secretary-General in 2006, is a global multistakeholder forum for dialogue on internet governance issues. The IGF functions as a year-long process with annual meetings and intersessional activities. This process is coordinated by the Multistakeholder Advisory Group and the IGF Secretariat. The IGF has spawned several national, regional and youth IGF initiatives. Their collective work and cooperation are facilitated by the IGF Secretariat.
- Public Technical Identifiers (PTI): began performing functions of the Internet Assigned Numbers Authority (IANA) in October 2016. PTI is responsible for the operational aspects of coordinating the internet's unique identifiers, including the

domain name system (DNS) root and internet protocol (IP) addressing, and maintains many of the codes and numbers used in internet protocols in coordination with the Internet Engineering Task Force (IETF).

- Other policy discussion forums: include, but are not limited to, the European Internet Forum (EIF) and World Economic Forum (WEF), as well as national consultative forums and initiatives led by industry associations and civil society.
- Root servers: publish the content of one small file called a root zone file to the internet. This file is at the apex of a hierarchical distributed database called the domain name system (DNS), which is used by almost all internet applications to translate human-readable names like www.internetsociety.org into machine-readable names. The web, email and other internet services use DNS.
- Intergovernmental organizations (IGOs) include, but are not limited to, the United Nations, regional bodies like the African Union, Asia-Pacific Telecommunity, Caribbean Telecommunications Union, European Union, and Organization of American States, as well as policy forums like the Asia-Pacific Economic Cooperation and the Organisation for Economic Co-operation and Development. Respective member governments coordinate policies related to telecommunication and the internet through these organizations.
- Internet community organizations and initiatives promote, deliver, and invest in internet education and capacity building. Organizations include, but are not limited to, the Regional Internet Registries (RIRs), Internet Corporation for Assigned Names and Numbers (ICANN), Network Startup Resource Center (NSRC), internet exchange points (IXPs), network operators, vendors and technology companies. Initiatives include, but are not limited to, the EQUALS Digital Skills Fund and Mutually Agreed Norms for Routing Security (MANRS).
- Multilateral development banks and international financial institutions provide funding and technical assistance to member states to promote access to and use of the internet for socioeconomic development. This includes supporting internet-related education and capacity-building initiatives.
- Network operators are individuals and entities that manage the network infrastructure, which provides users access to the internet. Regional and national network operator groups (NOGs) provide collaboration and consultative opportunities for operators.
- Specialized standards bodies focus on specialized standards; some play key roles in the internet. These organizations include, but are not limited to, the 3rd Generation Partnership Project (3GPP), the European Telecommunications Standards Institute (ETSI), Identity Commons, the IEEE Standards Association (Institute of Electrical and Electronics Engineers), ISO and ANSI (American National Standards Institute), the Liberty Alliance Project, the Organization for the Advancement of Structured Information Standards (OASIS), Open-Source Communities and W3C.
- Universities, academic institutions and national research and education networks (NRENs) play a critical role in educating students, business executives and policymakers about the internet. They also prototype and demonstrate hardware and software solutions that benefit the internet.

- Service creators/vendors provide software applications and platforms that enable the delivery of content and services on the internet. They include, but are not limited to, mobile app development platforms, social media platforms, e-commerce and payment platforms, cloud service providers and cybersecurity companies.
- Governments at national, state and local levels, and their regulators, have roles in setting policies related to the internet, including infrastructure development and access, digitalization of the economy and society, cybersecurity, and data and privacy protection.
- Users include people and organizations that use the internet or provide content and services to others on the internet.

2.5 Who Owns the Internet?

The internet was developed by the United States and has since been adopted by essentially all countries and people worldwide. As described in the previous section, it is regulated and controlled by international organizations like ICANN, IANA, ITU and many others. However, there is another layer of control that makes the entire project economically valuable—the private sector—and this is an essential part of the internet ecosystem. Companies, whether entirely independent or state-backed, are the ones who actually run the internet, operating as ISPs, infrastructure providers, platforms providers and service providers. Companies are the ones that managed to scale up the internet, for profit, and to make it cheap enough for almost everybody (in the West) to use. It is not the aim of this book to provide an exhaustive list of companies or a robust analysis of the impact of private companies on the internet. Nevertheless, understanding the role of the companies that lay down the cables, launch the satellites and operate social media and e-commerce is an essential step in understanding the structure of the internet: developed by one country, adopted and regulated by many, and operated by private businesses.

Some of the major American companies include Amazon, Microsoft, Google (Alphabet), Meta (Facebook), IBM, Apple, Lumen Technologies, Cogent Communications, AT&T, Starlink (SpaceX) and many others. However, not only the United States displays a capitalist approach to the internet. Russia has giant technology companies as well, though they operate under the watchful eye of the Kremlin. Some of these include Yandex, Rostelecom, Sberbank and VK (Mail.Ru). In China, domestic affairs might be more communist, but businesses are capitalist in nature, with companies like Tencent, Alibaba, Baidu, JD.com, TikTok (ByteDance), China Telecom, China Unicom and many others. In Germany, Deutsche Telekom is the largest telecommunications company, one of the largest in the European Union. Orange is a French multinational telecommunications company, and BT Group, a British multinational telecommunications company, is the largest fixed-line telecommunications company in the United Kingdom and one of the largest in Europe.

These companies own and operate a range of internet infrastructure, including the internet backbone of undersea cables, satellites, IXPs, data centers, cloud infrastructure and platforms, services, social media and more. These companies play a vital role in the operation of the internet, and their infrastructure is essential for delivering content and services to users around the world. While the internet is often seen as a public utility, the reality is that it is largely owned and operated by private companies. These companies play a huge role in shaping the internet and its impact on society. Private companies have had a profound impact on the global internet. They have invested heavily in its infrastructure, developed new technologies and created innovative services that have made the internet accessible to billions of people around the world. For instance, almost every internet user in the West has a social media account, and most computers globally run on Microsoft operating systems.[34] In addition, private companies have played a key role in shaping the internet's governance and regulation by facilitating the spread of opinions that impact policymakers (like public influence campaigns). They are also essential to the continued growth and development of the internet. They provide the necessary financial resources, technical expertise and innovative thinking to keep the internet up to date and address the challenges of the future.[35]

How do companies impact international security? Countries facilitate companies and use them as proxies. For instance, the entire world uses Microsoft's operating systems, Facebook's and TikTok's social media platforms, Telegram's and WhatsApp's SMAs and many more companies. Even the most popular Dark Web—TOR, a product of the United States Navy—now operates as a non-profit company. Some examples of nations' use and abuse of companies on the internet are provided in Chaps. 4 and 5; however, one prominent example is the interference in the 2016 United States elections. In this case, Russia used social media platforms like Facebook, Twitter, YouTube, Instagram and more to spread propaganda and damage Hillary Clinton's electoral campaign while simultaneously strengthening Donald Trump's campaign. This example poses a key question for American democracy in the twenty-first century: who elects a president—the people or foreign influencers?[36]

Another example, also presented in more detail later in this book, is the SMA Telegram. This messaging application was developed by two Russian brothers—Nikolai and Pavel Durov—and quickly gained popularity for its security features. Nowadays, however, Telegram is also popular among drug dealers, arms dealers, other sorts of criminals and also terrorists, racists and anti-Semites. A significant example is the use of Telegram by both far-right extremists and foreign influencers to organize the January 6, 2021, Capitol riot in the United States. These groups used Telegram, the Dark Web and many other secure and anonymous platforms to plan the Capitol riot, mainly in order to avoid the watchful eye of law enforcement agencies. Thus, a foreign company and application—Telegram—was used by both domestic

[34] GlobalStats (n.d.).

[35] European Commission (2022).

[36] Abrams (2019).

extremists and foreign influencers (presumably from the largest adversaries of the United States).[37]

Companies are a significant part of the internet ecosystem. The global nature of the internet means that the actions of companies in one region can have far-reaching implications. Cross-border data flows, data localization requirements and differing regulatory frameworks present challenges for companies and policymakers alike. Issues such as data security, privacy and competition are of paramount importance in this interconnected landscape. The dominance of a few major players, particularly in the United States, China, Russia and the European Union, raises concerns about the concentration of power and potential anti-competitive practices—as well as concerns about the way such companies and their services may be used as proxies to influence and intervene in the global political sphere.[38]

2.6 Threats, Vulnerabilities and the Socio-political Impact: A Brief Socio-political Overview

Cyberspace is run by dozens of entities and is not entirely controlled by governments, at least not equally. It is decentralized, and private businesses often have the upper hand over governments and local laws or norms. In addition, users are very free in cyberspace. They can choose to be anonymous or impersonate or pose as others. They can spread malicious information or files, and they can evade local regulations and laws since governments do not entirely control global cyberspace. Before we come to the next chapters, which are oriented more toward the international relations discourse and perspective, it is important to understand the main dangers of cyberspace. Cyber warfare strategies and tactics are presented in detail in Chap. 4; however, a brief overview of the main conceptual threats of cyberspace is provided here. The internet, while a technological marvel, is not immune to societal and political implications and includes, as Haber and I or Robinson and Jones, among others, describe[39]:

- **Cybersecurity threats**: The interconnected nature of cyberspace exposes individuals, businesses and governments to various cyber threats, including hacking, data breaches and malware attacks. Cyberattacks can compromise personal information, disrupt critical infrastructure and lead to financial losses. These vulnerabilities stem from the internet's openness and the challenges of maintaining robust security measures across a vast and complex network.
- **Privacy concerns**: The ability to collect, store and analyze massive amounts of personal data through cyberspace raises significant privacy concerns. Online platforms and services often gather user data for targeted advertising, profiling and

[37] Schwirtz (2021).

[38] Haber and Topor (2023).

[39] Ibid.; Robinson et al. (2015), Andress and Winterfeld (2013) and Benkler (2006).

other purposes, potentially infringing on individuals' privacy rights. The proliferation of surveillance technologies and government monitoring further exacerbates these concerns.

  - **Governmental surveillance**: Mass surveillance programs can infringe on citizens' rights to privacy and free expression, having a chilling effect on online speech.

- **Disinformation and misinformation**: Cyberspace has enabled the rapid spread of disinformation and misinformation, often leading to the distortion of facts, polarization, and the undermining of public trust. The ease of sharing information online, combined with echo chambers and algorithmic biases, contributes to the spread of false narratives and conspiracy theories.
- **Online harassment and cyberbullying**: The anonymity and distance inherent in cyberspace can lead to online harassment, cyberbullying and other forms of digital abuse. The lack of face-to-face interaction and accountability in online spaces can exacerbate such behaviors, negatively affecting individuals' mental health and well-being.
- **The digital divide**: The digital divide refers to the unequal access to and use of cyberspace among different socioeconomic groups and regions. This divide can hinder individuals' opportunities for education, employment and civic participation, exacerbating existing inequalities.
- **Platform manipulation and algorithmic bias**: Online platforms use algorithms to curate content and tailor user experiences. However, these algorithms can inadvertently reinforce existing biases, leading to content polarization and the reinforcement of extremist views. Additionally, the manipulation of platforms for political or commercial purposes can distort public discourse.
- **Government censorship**: Governments around the world may censor cyberspace content and restrict access to information for political or ideological reasons.
- **Spread of extremist content and radicalization**: Cyberspace provides a platform for the dissemination of extremist ideologies and propaganda. Online spaces can be exploited by extremist groups for recruitment, radicalization and the planning of violent acts.
- **Election interference and political manipulation**: The internet's vast reach makes it susceptible to use for election interference and political manipulation. Foreign actors can exploit social media platforms to spread disinformation, sow discord and influence public opinion in other countries.
- **Ethical dilemmas of emerging technologies**: As emerging technologies like AI, biotechnology, and VR become more integrated with the internet, new ethical dilemmas emerge. Questions about algorithmic accountability, digital surveillance and the potential for technological discrimination need to be addressed.

Addressing these vulnerabilities requires a multistakeholder approach involving governments, tech companies, civil society organizations and individuals. Striking a balance between openness and security, privacy and innovation, and free expression and responsible speech is a complex and ongoing challenge that requires collaborative efforts and adaptable solutions. It is important to remember that some countries are more biased toward openness and freedom and others more biased toward security.

2.7 Conclusion

This chapter has provided a comprehensive overview of the internet, including its structure, operation and vulnerabilities, from a semi-technical and socio-political perspective. The internet has evolved significantly since its origins in the ARPANET project of the 1960s. It has grown from a small network of interconnected computers to a global network that connects billions of people and devices. The internet has revolutionized the way we communicate, learn, work and play. It is a powerful tool that has transformed the world in many ways. However, it is important to be aware of the internet's vulnerabilities and the challenges it poses. By understanding these vulnerabilities and challenges, we can work to make the internet a safer and more equitable place for everyone.

So, how does the internet really work? In the simplest sense, an individual or entity sends some sort of data and connects to an ISP, whether local or national, which is connected to an IXP and/or to land cables and/or submarine fiber-optic cables (or satellites), which connect to other countries via a similar route in reverse—a user's data travels from the cables and/or IXP to an ISP, or several, and finally reaches its endpoint: another user. In summary, the internet works by connecting thousands of individual networks through various means, and the path a user's data takes to reach a user in another country involves different networks and infrastructure, facilitated by IXPs (which coordinate and mitigate between ISPs and CDNs).

The structure of the internet, which I will describe as "cyberspace" from this chapter on, can be illustrated technically using the TCP/IP or OSI models; however, to examine the socio-political aspects and implications, the four-layer model is more appropriate and will, therefore, be employed in the following chapters. In this model, cyberspace is made up of four layers: the infrastructure layer, the logical layer, the information (data) layer and the user layer. Each layer has its own vulnerabilities and challenges. The infrastructure layer is the physical foundation of the internet. It includes the cables, routers and other devices that connect computers and networks. The infrastructure layer is vulnerable to physical attacks, such as cable cuts and power outages, as well as cyberattacks such as denial-of-service attacks. The logical layer is responsible for routing traffic across the internet. It includes the protocols and software that allow devices to communicate with each other. The logical layer is vulnerable to routing attacks, which can disrupt or redirect traffic. The information (data) layer is where data is stored and transmitted. It includes the servers, databases and other systems that store and process data. The information layer is vulnerable to data breaches, malware attacks and other cyberattacks. The user layer is where users interact with the internet. It includes the applications and devices that users use to access the internet, such as web browsers, email clients and social media platforms.

The user layer is vulnerable to phishing attacks, social engineering attacks and other attacks that exploit user behavior.

In addition to these challenges, the internet is also facing a number of new challenges, such as the rise of AI. AI is being used to develop new and more sophisticated cyberattacks, as well as to manipulate public opinion and spread misinformation. The growth of the IoT also presents novel challenges. The IoT is a network of interconnected devices that collect and share data, and its rapid expansion is creating new opportunities for cyberattacks. Moreover, a handful of big tech companies control an increasingly large share of the internet ecosystem. This concentration of power raises concerns about competition and innovation. Finally, there are concerns about satellite constellations like Starlink that can bypass geographical borders and make the internet more reachable. It is important to address all these new challenges to ensure that the internet remains a safe and open platform for everyone.

In conclusion, countries developed cyberspace. Through international organizations, it became global, and companies were the ones to scale it up and bring it to the masses. Now, the internet is in everybody's palm. But do countries want the global influence of the internet on their domestic soil? The following chapters will answer this question.

References

Abrams, Abigail. 2019. Here's what we know so far about Russia's 2016 meddling. *TIME*, April 18. https://time.com/5565991/russia-influence-2016-election/.

Andress, Jason, and Steve Winterfeld. 2013. *Cyber warfare: Techniques, tactics and tools for security practitioners*. Elsevier.

Bedos-Rezak, Brigitte Miriam. 2000. Medieval identity: A sign and a concept. *The American Historical Review* 105 (5): 1489–1533.

Benkler, Yochai. 2006. *The wealth of networks: How social production transforms markets and freedom*. New Haven, CT: Yale University Press.

Brock, Joe. 2023. U.S. and China wage war beneath the waves—over internet cables. *Reuters*, March 24. https://www.reuters.com/investigates/special-report/us-china-tech-cables/.

Choucri, Nazli, and David D. Clark. 2019. *International relations in the cyber age: The co-evolution dilemma*. MIT Press.

DataReportal. 2023. Digital around the world. https://datareportal.com/global-digital-overview.

Economy, Elizabeth C. 2018. The great firewall of China: Xi Jinping's internet shutdown. *Guardian*, June 29. https://www.theguardian.com/news/2018/jun/29/the-great-firewall-of-china-xi-jinpings-internet-shutdown.

European Commission. 2022. Digital Economy and Society Index (DESI), July 28. https://digital-strategy.ec.europa.eu/en/library/digital-economy-and-society-index-desi-2022#:~:text=The%20Digital%20Economy%20and%20Society,country%27s%20official%20language(s).

GlobalStats. n.d. Desktop operating system market share worldwide. https://gs.statcounter.com/os-market-share/desktop/worldwide/#monthly-202208-202209-bar.

Haber, Eldar, and Lev Topor. 2023. Sovereignty, cyberspace, and the emergence of internet bubbles. *Journal of Advanced Military Studies* 14 (1): 144–165.

Hauben, Michael, and Ronda Hauben. 1997. *Netizens: On the history and impact of Usenet and the internet*. IEEE Computer Society Press.

Ho, Tara. 2019. Amazon wins '.amazon' domain name, aggravating South American region and undermining digital commons. *The Conversation*, June 21. https://theconversation.com/amazon-wins-amazon-domain-name-aggravating-south-american-region-and-undermining-digital-commons-118186.

ICANN. 2018. Request 18-10: The Amazon Cooperation Treaty Organization. *ICANN*, November 5. https://www.icann.org/resources/pages/reconsideration-18-10-acto-request-2018-11-29-en.

ICANN. 2019. Request 19-1: Colombian Government. *ICANN*, June 15. https://www.icann.org/resources/pages/reconsideration-19-1-colombian-request-2019-06-18-en.

ICANN. n.d. The history of ICANN. https://www.icann.org/history.

Internet Society. 1997. A brief history of the internet. https://www.internetsociety.org/wp-content/uploads/2017/09/ISOC-History-of-the-Internet_1997.pdf.

Internet Society. 2022. The internet ecosystem, July 2022. https://www.internetsociety.org/wp-content/uploads/2022/07/2022-Internet-Ecosystem-EN.pdf.

Javers, Eamon. 2022. Ukraine asked the internet's governing body to remove Russian sites. *CNBC*, March 1. https://www.cnbc.com/2022/03/01/ukraine-asked-icann-to-revoke-russian-domains-shut-dns-servers.html.

Kennedy, Brian, Alec Tyson, and Emily Saks. 2023. Public awareness of artificial intelligence in everyday activities. *Pew Research Center*, February 15. https://www.pewresearch.org/science/2023/02/15/public-awareness-of-artificial-intelligence-in-everyday-activities/.

Klein, Hans. 2002. ICANN and internet governance: Leveraging technical coordination to realize global public policy. *The Information Society* 18 (3): 193–207.

Kleinrock, Leonard. 2019. The first message transmission. *ICANN*, October 29. https://www.icann.org/en/blogs/details/the-first-message-transmission-29-10-2019-en.

Konradova, Natalia. 2020. The rise of Runet and the main stages of its history. In *Internet in Russia: A study of the Runet and its impact on social life*, 39–61.

Leiner, Barry M., V.G. Cerf, D.D. Clark, R.E. Kahn, L. Kleinrock, D.C. Lynch, J. Postel, L.G. Roberts, and S. Wolff. 2009. A brief history of the Internet. *ACM SIGCOMM Computer Communication Review* 39 (5): 22–31.

Moscow Times. 2019. Russia's Yandex pushes back against pressure to share encryption keys. *Moscow Times*, June 4. https://www.themoscowtimes.com/2019/06/04/russias-yandex-pushes-back-against-pressure-to-share-encryption-keys-2-a65870.

Pfaffenberger, Bryan. 2003. A standing wave in the web of our communications: Usenet and the socio-technical construction of cyberspace values. In *From Usenet to CoWebs: Computer supported cooperative work*, ed. C. Lueg and D. Fisher. London: Springer.

Rajaraman, Vaishnavi. 2022a. A concise history of the internet—I. *Resonance* 27 (11): 1841–1856.

Rajaraman, Vaishnavi. 2022b. A concise history of the internet—II. *Resonance* 27 (12): 2045–2068.

Rieedel, Ann Cathrin. 2022. ICANN rejects Ukraine's request to block Russian Internet domains. *Friedrich Naumann Foundation*, March 28. https://www.freiheit.org/taiwan/icann-rejects-ukraines-request-block-russian-internet-domains.

Rimer, Sara. 2016. Will unlocking Apple's iPhone unlock a Pandora's box? *The Brick* (Boston University), March 15. https://www.bu.edu/articles/2016/unlocking-terrorist-iphone-cybersecurity/.

Robinson, Michael, Kevin Jones, and Helge Janicke. 2015. Cyber warfare: Issues and challenges. *Computers & Security* 49: 70–94.

Russel, Andrew L. 2013. OSI: The internet that wasn't. *IEEE Spectrum*, July 29. https://spectrum.ieee.org/osi-the-internet-that-wasnt.

Ryan, Johnny. 2010. *A history of the internet and the digital future*. Reaktion Books.

Satariano, Adam. 2019. How the internet travels across oceans. *New York Times*, March 10. https://www.nytimes.com/interactive/2019/03/10/technology/internet-cables-oceans.html.

Schwirtz, Michael. 2021. Telegram, pro-democracy tool, struggles over new fans from far right. *New York Times*, January 26. https://www.nytimes.com/2021/01/26/world/europe/telegram-app-far-right.html.

Selyukh, Alina. 2014. ICANN chief: Russia, China will not hijack Internet oversight. *Reuters*, April 2. https://www.reuters.com/article/ctech-us-usa-internet-domainnames-idCABREA311SE20140402.

Sharma, Neha, Madhavi Shamkuwar, and Inderjit Singh. 2019. The history, present and future with IoT. In *Internet of things and big data analytics for smart generation*, 27–51.

Smith, Adam. 2021. FBI can gain 'limited' access to private WhatsApp and Apple iMessage conversations, document claims. *Independent*, November 30. https://www.independent.co.uk/tech/fbi-whatsapp-apple-imessage-icloud-access-b1966933.html.

Topor, Lev. 2022. *Phishing for Nazis: Conspiracies, anonymous communications and white supremacy networks on the Dark Web*. Routledge.

Topor, Lev, and Alexander Tabachnik. 2021. Russian cyber information warfare: International distribution and domestic control. *Journal of Advanced Military Studies* 12 (1): 112–127.

Yang, Guobin. 2012. A Chinese Internet? History, practice, and globalization. *Chinese Journal of Communication* 5 (1): 49–54.

Chapter 3
Sovereignty, Power, International Security and a Lack of International Law

Who controls cyberspace? In Chap. 2, which dealt with the structure of cyberspace, it became apparent that while the West, specifically the United States, developed and nurtured cyberspace, it is now controlled by many entities. There are international organizations that are in charge of naming and addressing, such as ICANN and IANA, and others that are in charge of standardizations, like the ITU's Telecommunication Standardization Sector and the IEFT. Such organizations consist of members from many countries, or of many member countries; thus, in theory, countries control the organizations that make and regulate cyberspace. However, if we consider every county as sovereign—and the starting point of this book is that countries strive to be sovereign—then we can conclude that a situation in which other countries can intervene in a country's sovereignty is problematic.

In this chapter, I present a theoretical and practical review of sovereignty and its European history in terms of international relations and international security, viewing the exercise of power from historical and contemporary perspectives. While the concept of sovereignty has existed since time immemorial, and every tribe, village, kingdom and empire has strived to be sovereign, the modern practice of sovereign countries can be traced back to the 1648 Treaty of Westphalia and, before that, to the theory of sovereignty presented by French philosopher Jean Bodin in his work "The Six Books of the Republic" in 1572. Bodin and others, like seventeenth century English philosophers John Locke and Thomas Hobbes, were inspired by the sovereignty of city-states in ancient Greece.

Next, this chapter outlines and explains the reasons for war, based on the six main reasons put forward by Fredric S. Pearson. Subsequently, the use of proxies in warfare is explained and elaborated into the concept of cyber proxy wars, which allow countries to undermine others' sovereignty and indirectly engage in aggressive actions and conflicts. I present the problems and limitations of international law regarding cyberspace while also discussing domestic laws on cyberspace and its regulation. The concept of power in international relations is also explained and employed to further explain how hard, soft, smart and sharp powers are used and abused through cyberspace.

L. Topor, *Cyber Sovereignty*, Global Power Shift,
https://doi.org/10.1007/978-3-031-58199-1_3

This chapter is written as an international relations review, and its central purpose is to explain to readers, especially those who do not have a background in international relations, politics and history, the core concept that has driven our world for hundreds of years: sovereignty. As this chapter evolves, I also integrate examples from and discussions about cyberspace, specifically how it can harm sovereignty, for instance through cyber proxy warfare, a situation in which a country can lose sovereignty but have difficulties attributing the attacks on it. The main portion of these explanations, however, is presented in Chaps. 4 and 5, which delve into the strategies and tactics of cyber warfare and consider global trends.

3.1 Sovereignty in International Relations

Before we proceed to the concept of sovereignty in international relations, let me tell you an anecdote. This anecdote is about every family that is fortunate enough to live in their own apartment or house. The story goes like this:

> John was a proud man. He loved his family and was fiercely protective of his home. He was also a bit of a control freak, and he did not like anyone telling him what to do, especially in his own house.
>
> One day, John's neighbor, Charles, came over to visit. Charles was a kind and well-meaning man, but he was also a bit of a busybody. He liked to give people advice, even when they did not ask for it.
>
> As Charles was walking through John's house, he noticed that John had a lot of clutter in his garage. He could not help but comment on it.
>
> "John," he said, "you really should clean up this garage. It's a mess."
>
> John did not appreciate Charles' unsolicited advice. He frowned and said, "This is my garage, Charles. I will clean it up when I am ready."
>
> Charles was taken aback by John's tone. He had not meant to offend him.
>
> "I am just trying to be helpful," he said.
>
> "I appreciate that, Charles," John said. "But I am perfectly capable of taking care of my own garage."
>
> Charles realized that he had overstepped. He apologized to John and left.
>
> John was glad to see Charles go. He did not like anyone telling him what to do in his own home. He was the sovereign of his castle, and he would run it his way.
>
> The moral of the story is that every family has its own way of doing things. It is important to respect the sovereignty of families in their own homes. Just because you do not agree with how someone else is doing things does not mean you have the right to tell them how to do it.

What does this short anecdote teach us? That individual entities want or need to be able to make decisions and act as they wish. Thus, to put it simplistically, if individuals are sovereign, and countries consist of people of similar origins, nationalities or religions, then countries are sovereign.

The concept of sovereignty is a foundational and enduring principle in politics and international relations. It represents the authority and power vested in a political entity, typically a country, to govern itself without external interference. The idea of sovereignty in international relations is as follows: there is an ultimate and final ruler, an overseer or authority, that has an independent decision-making process and a monopoly on the use of force. The development of the concept of sovereignty can be traced through centuries of political thought and evolving global dynamics shaped by war and peace. Sovereignty, as described in more detail below, is a fundamental concept in the constant reshaping of the international system. The idea of sovereignty can be traced back to medieval and early modern Europe, a time marked by the dominance of monarchies and empires.[1]

Even before Europe's Age of Absolutism in the seventeenth and eighteenth centuries, sovereignty was practiced. Sovereignty stretches back to time immemorial. Tribes and tribe leaders were sovereign; kingdoms, empires and even city-states within empires (like in ancient Greece) had sovereignty. In some periods of human history, God was considered sovereign, and thus his agents, whether clergy or rulers with a "divine right" ruled as sovereigns. During this period, political authority was largely centralized in the hands of absolute rulers. Two key developments laid the groundwork for the idea of sovereignty: the divine right of kings and, later, the Treaty of Westphalia. Thus, the international arena can be historically and conceptually divided into periods before and after the Treaty of Westphalia.[2] Although scholars like Andreas Osiander have quite rightly argued that globalization and industrialization have created great interdependence between countries and detracted from the Westphalian model of sovereignty, countries still act to maintain their sovereignty, especially when other countries attempt to undermine it.[3]

The first idea of sovereignty one should understand is the divine right of kings. The idea that monarchs derived their authority directly from divine sources, particularly from God, was a central feature of ancient and medieval political thought. The concept of the divine right of kings asserted that rulers held absolute authority and were accountable only to God. This belief legitimized the power of monarchs and laid the foundation for the concept of sovereignty as the ultimate authority in a state/country.[4]

A good example of the divine right in action is European Absolutism, particularly French absolutism, which was a form of government in France from the sixteenth to the late eighteenth centuries characterized by the supreme authority of the French monarch. The French monarchs claimed to rule by divine right, meaning that their authority came from God and was not subject to any human laws. French absolutism reached its height under the reign of Louis XIV (1643–1715). Louis XIV was known as "Louis the Great" or the "Sun King" because he believed that he was the center of the universe and that all other things revolved around him. Louis XIV centralized power in his own hands and created a lavish court at Versailles where he could control the nobility and display his wealth and power.[5]

[1] Hinsley (1986: 1–26, 27–44).

[2] Ibid.

[3] Osiander (2001).

[4] Sommerville (2015).

[5] See, generally, Hatton (1976).

Several factors contributed to the rise of French absolutism. One factor was the religious wars that plagued France in the sixteenth century. These wars weakened the French monarchy and led to a desire for a strong central government that could restore order and stability. Another factor that contributed to the rise of French absolutism was the increasing economic power of the French monarchy. French monarchs were able to increase their revenues through taxes and tariffs, which allowed them to build a large army and bureaucracy, further strengthening their power.[6]

The second idea of sovereignty it is necessary to understand is the rights of nations—countries. Once the clergy and the monarchies lost their rights, countries gained them. The Treaty of Westphalia, which concluded the Thirty Years' War (1618–1648), marked a pivotal moment in the development of sovereignty. The war was fought between two main parties. One was the imperial or universalist party, which included the Church (the Holy Roman Empire), the Spanish King and the Habsburg dynasty, led by Ferdinand II, which all sought the right to control Christendom (Christian countries, mainly but not exclusively in Europe). The other party was known as anti-imperialists or particularists and included the monarchies of Denmark, the Netherlands, France, the German principalities and Sweden. While the first party, the imperialists, wanted to have authority over all Christian European monarchies, the second party, the anti-imperialists, rejected this authority and sought independence.[7]

Between May 15 and October 24, 1648, the treaties of Münster and Osnabrück were signed, bringing an end to the religious conflict. During and after the Treaties of Westphalia, known as the "Peace of Westphalia," the powers of the Holy Roman Emperor, by that time Ferdinand III, were stripped and transferred to the anti-imperialists, which were state-like entities. This peace established the principle of territorial sovereignty, affirming that each ruler had the right to govern their territory without external interference, whether from other rulers or from the Church (in the European case). The Westphalian system set the stage for the modern nation-state system, emphasizing the primacy of states/countries in international affairs.[8]

After the Peace of Westphalia, during the Age of Enlightenment in the seventeenth and eighteenth centuries, scholars began to develop the concepts and ideas of modern political thought. Thinkers like Jean Bodin, Thomas Hobbes, John Locke and Jean-Jacques Rousseau introduced new ideas about the social contract, individual rights and the limitations of state power. These concepts had a profound impact on the development of sovereignty. Jean Bodin, a French political philosopher, is often credited with the early formulation of the concept of sovereignty. In his 1576 work "Six Books of the Republic," he argued that sovereignty is the absolute and indivisible power vested in the state, making it the supreme authority in both domestic and international affairs. Bodin's ideas laid the groundwork for the modern understanding

---

[6] Ibid.

[7] See, generally, Parker (2006) and Wilson (2008a).

[8] Gross (1948) and Croxton (1999).

of sovereignty. He argued that in order to be actual and effective, sovereignty must be absolute, perpetual and undivided.[9]

Later, Thomas Hobbes, in his seminal work "Leviathan" (1651), described the state of nature as one of war and chaos. Hobbes proposed a social contract theory in which individuals surrendered some of their natural rights to a sovereign authority (the leviathan) in exchange for security and order. Hobbes' view of the state as the ultimate authority helped solidify the concept of sovereignty as a key element of statehood and portrayed the sovereign country not as one that enslaves but as one that, at least to some extent, provides—it provides security.[10]

In 1689, English philosopher John Locke wrote "Two Treatises of Government," which argued for a social contract in which individuals consented to be governed by a state. He emphasized the importance of individual rights, including life, liberty and property, and contended that the state's authority should be limited to protecting these rights. Locke's ideas contributed to the idea of sovereignty as a power constrained by the rights of individuals.[11] Genevan Jean-Jacques Rousseau built on this philosophical debate. Rousseau's 1762 work "The Social Contract" introduced the concept of popular sovereignty. He argued that true sovereignty resided in the collective will of the people and that the state should be an expression of the general will. This idea, alongside those of Bodin, Hobbes and Locke, challenged the divine right of kings and laid the foundation for modern democratic theory.[12]

Thus, the shift from the divine right of kings, through the Peace of Westphalia, to more enlightened thought about ruling powers brought about a rise in nationalism and sovereignty in Europe from the nineteenth century onwards, as each nation, which had once been a single or a group of monarchies and had possessed similar religious, ethnic and cultural aspects, now perceived itself as having the right to independence and sovereignty among nations. This culminated in the Revolutions of 1848, also known as the Spring of Nations, a series of revolutions across Europe. They were sparked by economic hardship, political repression and a desire for national unification and democratic rights like the people's will for self-rule. The revolutions began in Palermo, Sicily, in January 1848 and quickly spread to France, Germany, Italy, Austria and other parts of Europe. Although these revolutions were met with repression, and many monarchs remained in power, they were a turning point in European history. They led to the spread of (as yet underdeveloped) democracy and nationalism throughout Europe. However, they also showed that the old order was not willing to give up its power without a fight.[13]

As nation-states emerged, sovereignty became a central theme in international relations as each newborn country wanted to be equal to its neighbors and be as sovereign as they were. Nationalism also played a significant role in reshaping political boundaries. The unifications of Italy in 1861 and Germany in 1871, for

[9] Andrew (2011).

[10] Newey (2008: 106–124, 125–141).

[11] Locke (2013).

[12] See, generally, Rousseau (2012: 153).

[13] Breuilly (2000).

example, were driven by nationalist movements seeking to establish independent and sovereign nation-states, now known as countries. Nationalism both enhanced the idea of sovereignty and contributed to conflicts as states competed for territory and power.[14]

The nineteenth and twentieth centuries also marked the crumbling era of European colonialism (which, of course, continued in the form of imperialism, to some extent), and this raised questions about sovereignty in relation to non-European regions. European colonial powers often disregarded the sovereignty of Indigenous peoples, leading to conflicts and resistance movements. This era highlighted the tension between the sovereignty of colonial rulers and the rights of colonized populations. It seemed that Europe sought sovereignty for European nations but not for the rest of the world. This important debate, however, is outside the scope of this book. The Russian Empire collapsed following the Russian Revolution of 1917 and the struggle to abolish its monarchy. In the distant Americas, the United States gained independence in 1776, after it declared itself sovereign and no longer subject to the British Empire. The trend toward independent nations—countries—became popular around the globe.

Another turning point in the concept of sovereignty was the aftermath of World War II, which witnessed the emergence of new international institutions and the further evolution of sovereignty. In 1945, after the end of World War II, the United Nations was established to promote peace and security; it introduced the concept of collective security, where states agreed to work together to prevent conflicts and maintain global peace. While the United Nations upheld the sovereignty of its members—individual countries—it also introduced the responsibility to protect (R2P) doctrine, allowing for intervention in the case of mass atrocities. This was brought about in the wake of the Holocaust by movements such as "Never Again" and individuals like Raphael Lemkin, who pushed for a new society of nations that would protect people. It was globally accepted that sovereignty was limited when countries failed to protect human rights. This doctrine permitted international intervention in such cases.[15]

Thus, in practice, the principle of absolute sovereignty began to erode after World War II. Human rights concerns, environmental issues and the global economy led to an increasing interdependence among states. The notion of "Westphalian sovereignty," with its absolute authority, was challenged as states became more interconnected. In the contemporary world, shaped by globalization, technological advances and changing geopolitical dynamics, the concept of sovereignty faces new challenges and debates. In the twentieth century, and particularly in the twenty-first century, globalization has increasingly blurred the boundaries between domestic and international affairs. Economic interdependence, the spread of information by print, radio, television and, of course, the internet and transnational issues like climate change have raised questions about the extent to which states can exercise sovereignty

[14] Schnee (2001) and Gellner (2015).

[15] Bellamy and Dunne (2016).

in a globalized world. Furthermore, non-state actors such as multinational corporations and international organizations have gained influence in global affairs. Issues like cyber warfare, terrorism and pandemics underscore the need for international cooperation and call traditional sovereignty into question.[16]

To conclude, the concept of sovereignty has evolved significantly over time, from its early roots in the divine right of kings and the Peace of Westphalia to its modern interpretation as a principle that must accommodate global interdependence and humanitarian concerns. While sovereignty remains a fundamental element of international relations, its definition and scope have shifted to meet the challenges of the contemporary world, and they continue to shift and adapt to human needs and technological developments. In this regard, this book seeks to explain yet another shift in the history, or future, of sovereignty. In today's globalized and interconnected world, the tension between state sovereignty and the demands of the global community continues to shape the discourse on international relations. The concept of sovereignty is dynamic and evolving, reflecting the fluid nature of politics and international affairs. As we look to the future, however, it is clear that the concept of sovereignty will remain a central theme in discussions of global governance, security and human rights.[17]

How, then, should we define the evolving term "sovereignty" in the current age? To conclude this summary of sovereignty in (Western) international relations, sovereignty can be defined as the ability of an entity to make independent decisions, considering mainly its own benefit, and to act independently and without interference or intervention of other entities. From this definition, we can derive a definition of what may be considered altering the sovereignty of an entity, and this, of course, is largely built on Robert A. Dahl's definition of power. Power, as Dahl notes, is the ability to do things and control others, to get others to do what they otherwise would not.[18] Thus, if an entity—an international actor—is powerful enough, then it is sovereign. But this brings us to the next question: what exactly is power?

3.2 Power and Foreign Interventions

Power, as mentioned in the previous section, is the ability of A to influence B and make B act or do what it otherwise would not. If a country is sovereign, it can, to some extent, resist influence from other countries and international actors. It is when countries attempt to harm the sovereignty and integrity of others that conflicts and wars break out. However, not all countries are equal in capabilities, wealth, size, military might and influence.[19] Not all countries are equal in power. But what then is power exactly, and how does it relate to sovereignty? We must differentiate

---

[16] Krasner (1999) and Bull (2012).

[17] See, in general, Keohane (2002).

[18] Dahl (1957).

[19] Ibid.

between the power of a country, specifically its ruling party or parties, to control and govern its people and the power of a country to maintain its sovereignty and alter the sovereignty of other countries. Although I explain domestic power and international power as two different concepts in this section, in reality, they are interconnected, and in the following chapters, I will explain how.

First, there is a difference between a country's despotic power and its infrastructural power. Despotic power is the ability of a state to coerce its citizens into compliance. It is based on the threat or use of force, and it can be used to suppress dissent, punish disobedience and maintain order. Examples of despotic power are a police state that uses torture and intimidation to silence its critics, a military dictatorship that enforces curfews and restricts freedom of movement, or a totalitarian regime that censors the media and controls all aspects of public life.[20] As described and explained in more detail in the following chapters, countries use the internet to exercise despotic power. For instance, some censor online content, and others may shut down the internet connectivity of entire regions.

Infrastructural power is the ability of a state to penetrate society and implement its policies. It refers to a country's capacity to govern and influence its society through the development and management of infrastructure. It determines the state's ability to collect taxes, provide services and regulate economic activity. In other words, despotic power is about control, while infrastructural power is about influence. Examples of infrastructural power can include cases where a government builds roads and schools, provides healthcare and social services, and regulates businesses, where a country collects taxes and uses the revenue to fund public programs, or where a government enforces laws and contracts and provides security for its citizens.[21] Thus, as will be further explained in subsequent sections and chapters, the internet is also used to exercise infrastructural power when countries employ it to influence citizens and provide services.[22]

How are these terms relevant to the concept and arguments of this book? It is worth mentioning here that some countries, like China, Russia, North Korea and Iran, utilize despotic power in cyberspace. They implement censorship and coerce their citizens to think twice about everything done online and whether it might offend the state. Other countries, like the United States, Israel, the United Kingdom and many European countries, exercise infrastructural power in cyberspace. That is, they develop and manage internet services and other technological services, in many cases by providing an open platform for businesses. Of course, countries may utilize both despotic and infrastructural powers in cyberspace, particularly within their own cyber borders, by non-intervention or by regulation and censorship. In most cases, this is not a dichotomous scale but a greyscale, and some cases are presented in Chaps. 5, 6 and 7.

It is thus worth emphasizing that states do not utilize only despotic or only infrastructural power. The two types of power can coexist within a state. For example, a

---

[20] Mann (2008) and Lucas (1998).

[21] Ibid.

[22] Ibid.; Soifer and Hau (2008).

totalitarian regime may have a great deal of despotic power, but it may also have a significant degree of infrastructural power, as it needs to be able to penetrate society in order to control it. Weak countries tend to have less infrastructural power than strong states. This means that they have difficulty implementing their policies and providing services to their citizens. As a result, weak countries are more likely to rely on despotic power to maintain control. Stronger and, in general, democratic countries tend to have a higher degree of infrastructural power than authoritarian states. This is because democratic countries typically have a strong bureaucracy and a well-developed system of public services. As a result, democratic countries are more likely to be able to implement their policies and provide services to their citizens without resorting to despotic power. The balance between despotic and infrastructural power can vary depending on the type of regime and the political context. However, it is important to understand the distinction between the two types of power in order to analyze and understand how countries operate.[23]

Moreover, power is a central concept in the field of international relations. Power is the ability to influence the behavior of others, and it is essential for countries to achieve their foreign policy goals. We can distinguish four types of power that countries use to influence, impact or intervene in others: hard power, soft power, smart power and sharp power. As described and explained in Chap. 4, on the global trends of cyber warfare, all these types of power are currently employed not only through traditional means but also through novel cyber warfare strategies and tactics.

Hard power is the ability to coerce others to do what you want. It is based on military might, economic resources and other tangible assets. Hard power is often used to deter aggression, resolve conflicts and protect national interests. For example, the United States uses its hard power to maintain a global military presence and to project its influence around the world. Hard power is a critical tool in statecraft, and its effectiveness is often quantifiable—generally in terms of military and economic might. A nation's military strength is a quintessential element of hard power. Military force serves as both a deterrent and an active instrument of state power. Countries with robust military capabilities have the means to defend their interests, project their influence abroad and exert pressure on others. In many ways, military strength and economic might continue to define the global pecking order. Economic power is generally measured by a nation's economy (mainly its gross domestic product (GDP)) and economic policies. Economic leverage allows international actors to impose sanctions, provide aid or engage in trade to further their strategic objectives. China's economic ascent and its use of economic power to influence neighboring countries exemplify the significance of this form of hard power.[24]

Soft power is the ability to persuade others to do what you want. It is based on intangible assets such as culture, values and ideas. Soft power is often used to build relationships, promote cooperation and shape international norms. Unlike hard power, soft power operates through attraction and persuasion rather than coercion. For instance, the United States uses its soft power to promote democracy and

[23] Ibid.

[24] Wilson III (2008b), Nye (1990) and Keohane (2002).

human rights around the world. One example of soft power is culture. Cultural diplomacy, through media, education and the arts, serves as a vital component of soft power. Hollywood's influence on global pop culture and the allure of American higher education institutions are examples of how culture can shape a nation's global image and soft power. Another example is ideational power—the power of ideas. Ideational soft power stems from a nation's ability to promote its ideas, values and political systems. The global appeal of democracy and human rights, often championed by Western democracies, showcases the impact of such soft power.[25] In addition, economic power can also be soft. Economic soft power can be exerted through foreign aid, trade relationships and development assistance. Humanitarian efforts and economic cooperation can enhance a country's reputation and foster positive international perceptions.[26]

Smart power, a concept developed by Joseph S. Nye, is the ability to combine hard and soft power to achieve foreign policy goals. It is a more nuanced approach to power that recognizes the importance of both coercion and persuasion. Smart power is often used to build coalitions, resolve complex problems and promote global cooperation. Countries often seek to combine their military capabilities with soft power elements, such as diplomacy, cultural exchanges and economic incentives, to achieve their goals. For example, the United States used smart power to build a coalition of countries to invade Iraq in 2003. In another example of hybrid warfare—the Russo-Ukrainian conflict—Russia used both hard military power and offensive cyber operations. In the larger context of the conflict between Russia and NATO, Russia also spread mis/disinformation to complement its hard military power.[27]

Sharp power is the ability to manipulate information and public opinion to influence the behavior of others. This relatively new concept has emerged in recent years with the rise of social media and other digital technologies. As I have argued (with Tabachnik and Haber and Shuker), sharp power is often used to undermine democracy, sow discord and advance authoritarian interests in the form of "fake news"—mis/disinformation campaigns. For example, Russia was accused of using sharp power to interfere in the 2016 United States presidential election. Sharp power is most effective when used by less democratic and less open regimes that can disseminate mis/disinformation to more open societies but can protect themselves from similar actions.[28]

The four types of power described here are not mutually exclusive. Countries can use all four to achieve their foreign policy goals. The best type of power to employ will vary depending on the specific situation. Hard power is most effective when dealing with adversaries or trying to deter aggression. However, it can also be counterproductive, as it can generate resentment and hostility. Soft power is most effective when building relationships and promoting cooperation. However, it can be less effective when dealing with adversaries or trying to resolve complex problems.

[25] Nye (2004, 2008). Also see Mearsheimer (2014).

[26] Ruggie (1982).

[27] Nye (2023) and Shuker and Topor (2021).

[28] Topor and Tabachnik (2021), Haber and Topor (2023) and Shuker and Topor (2021).

Smart power is the most flexible and adaptable approach to power, but it can also be the most difficult to implement effectively. Sharp power can be very effective in influencing public opinion and undermining democracy, but it can also backfire and damage the country's reputation.

The distribution of power in the international system is constantly changing. The rise of China, India and other emerging powers, as well as the continuing efforts by Russia to hold its ground, is challenging the dominance of the United States, leading to a more multipolar world order, in which there are multiple centers of power. This is making it more difficult for any one state to achieve its foreign policy goals through hard power alone.[29] In this changing world order, countries are increasingly turning to soft power and smart power to achieve their foreign policy goals. Soft power is essential for building relationships and promoting cooperation with other states. Smart power is essential for navigating the complex challenges of the twenty-first century. Even hard power is often used through cyberspace, as further exemplified in Chap. 4, to allow a state of vagueness and to alter, or strengthen, deterrence.[30]

3.2.1 Why Do Countries Go to War?

Understanding why countries go to war is a critical aspect of international relations. The study of the motivations and justifications of countries that go to war is not only a subject of academic research but also crucial for policymakers seeking to prevent or manage conflicts. There are various perspectives on this question. In the early 1990s, after the collapse of the Soviet Union and the, at least *de jure*, end of the Cold War, Samuel Huntington and others argued that future conflicts between people would be due to cultural differences. Because there are, undeniably, cultural and religious differences between various civilizations.[31] Although Huntington has a strong case, and I do, to some extent, agree with his arguments, it is important to know why countries went to war before the end of the Cold War and how their reasons mesh with Huntington's predictions.

What is a *casus belli*—an act provoking or justifying war? Countries go to war to defend themselves against a real or perceived threat. Some reasons are altruistic, like humanitarian aid and the R2P doctrine. Other reasons for conflict and war are more egoistic or realistic, like the need for more resources or land or to reshape the regional or global balance of power in a scenario in which another country, which may or may not be an adversary, has gained too much power. Countries go to war for control, and, as further elaborated in Chap. 4, they want to control resources, actors and outcomes (the three measurements of power). There are, of course, just

[29] See Kaplan (2019) and Radulescu et al. (2014).

[30] Nye (2016).

[31] Huntington (1993).

and unjust wars, as Hugo Grotius noted. However, this short review does not deal with the question of the moral justification of war but rather with the question of why countries go to war in practice.[32]

In this regard, Frederic S. Pearson suggested six key reasons for war and for foreign intervention in general. In the context of sovereignty, countries go to war or intervene in others' affairs and effectively harm others' sovereignty when they conquer or compete over land or resources, when they want to protect people outside their borders, when they wish to protect their economic interests, when they wish to protect or advance military/diplomatic interests, when they wish to impose their ideology/religion and when they wish to adjust the balance of power. Thus, war breaks out when sovereignty is altered.[33]

In the context of this book, as will be further explained in Chap. 4, cyber actions can also lead to war and conflicts as all Pearson's reasons can be achieved by cyberattacks and/or cyber influence campaigns, even though a virtual/cyberattack falls outside the United Nations Charter's definition of an armed attack. For this very reason, countries often use cyber warfare to attack adversaries without the use of force, leaving the attacked party without a just cause for retaliation.[34] They also use proxy wars to avoid direct conflicts and retaliation. Although the internet exploded in use and popularity in the 1990s, as of writing (2023), the largest international collective, the United Nations, has not been able to use existing international law to oversee this issue. There is no international law applicable to cyberspace and cyber warfare, setting aside the fact that for retaliation to be considered just, one first needs to prove an attack's origin, something that is extremely difficult to achieve in the current structure of cyberspace.

3.2.2 *Cyber Proxy Warfare*

When countries do not wish to engage in combat directly, mainly nuclear powers that want to avoid mutual assured destruction (MAD), they fight with proxies. Proxy wars are international conflicts between two countries, often global or regional powers, fought on the soil of a third country and disguised as a conflict over the internal issues of that third country or as a war between two or more such parties. That is, global powers often fight using smaller and weaker countries in an attempt not to harm the sovereignty of the other directly. The manpower and resources of the third country are used by the powers to promote their own objectives and strategies.[35] Proxy warfare is not only conducted by using and abusing a third country but by using international organizations like terror groups, groups of hackers, groups of criminals and so on.

---

[32] See, in general, Brunstetter and O'Driscoll (2017) and Walzer (2015).

[33] Pearson (1974). In this regard, see also Coyne and Mathers (2011).

[34] See Article 51, United Nations Charter.

[35] Deutsch (1964) and Mumford (2013: 1–10, 11–29).

Indirect engagement can be considered a preferred strategic choice in most recent conflicts since this kind of proxy conflict allows global powers to avoid the consequences of a direct engagement. When countries consider their interests, ideology and risks, they tend to use a proxy strategy.[36] Countries in conflict, seeking to alter another's control or gain more control themselves, can meddle in the domestic affairs of other countries or international actors, affecting the sovereignty of those actors and avoiding a direct and riskier conflict.

The Cold War can be regarded as a series of proxy wars. During the Cold War, the United States and the Soviet Union, both superpowers with nuclear capabilities, wanted to gain more power and influence globally while also avoiding a MAD nuclear war. For instance, the Korean War (1950–1953) serves as a good example of a proxy war as the United States supported the South Korean government, while the Soviet Union supported the North Korean government. During the Vietnam War (1955–1975), the United States supported the South Vietnamese government, while the Soviet Union and China supported the North Vietnamese government. During the Angolan Civil War (1975–2002), the United States supported the UNITA (National Union for the Total Independence of Angola; from the Portuguese *União Nacional para a Independência Total de Angola*) rebel group, while the Soviet Union and Cuba supported the MPLA government (People's Movement for the Liberation of Angola; from the Portuguese *Movimento Popular de Libertação de Angola*). Also, during the Soviet-Afghan War (1979–1989), the United States and Pakistan trained and armed the Afghan *Mujahedeen*, while the Soviet Union supported the Afghan government.[37]

More recently, post-Cold War, prominent examples of proxy wars include the Syrian Civil War (2011–present), in which Iran, a regional power, and Russia support the Syrian government, while the United States and its allies support the Syrian opposition; the Yemeni Civil War (2014–present), in which Iran supports the Houthi rebels, while Saudi Arabia and its allies support the Yemeni government; the First Libyan Civil War (2011), in which NATO-backed rebels overthrew the government of Muammar Gaddafi, who was supported by Russia and China; the Russian invasion of Ukraine (2022–present), in which NATO, the United States and their allies support Ukraine, while China and Iran support Russia (the preamble of this proxy war dates back to early 2014).[38] The devastating 7/10 terrorist attack by Hamas terrorists on Israel, the largest terrorist attack in a Western country since 9/11, was also a part of Iran's proxy warfare against Israel and, indirectly, the United States.[39]

Proxy wars by regional or global powers are also fought in cyberspace—it is a third domain, but it also allows an attack to go virtually undetected. Thus, cyber proxy wars are conflicts between two or more foreign powers fought on or using the cyber domain, disguised as actions by unrelated international actors or entities and pursued in an attempt to influence an international actor or its strategic decisions. Of

---

[36] Ibid.

[37] Berman and Lake (2019).

[38] Ibid.

[39] Wintour (2023).

course, both the attacker and the victim can be proxies. Specifically, in cyber warfare, a country's victim can also be a proxy—a social media platform, a hosting company or an entertainment company.[40] The attacking proxy can be another country or just its IP, a hacker group, financed or not, by a country, or a company used to spy on those that use its services, software or hardware.

One prominent example of a cyber proxy is the Lazarus hacker group, known to be financed by North Korea and employed against Western and American agencies and businesses. Another infamous group is the Sandworm group, a hacker group linked to the Russian GRU intelligence unit (the Main Intelligence Directorate of the Armed Forces of the Russian Federation; from the Russian Гла́вное управле́ние Генера́льного шта́ба Вооружённых сил Росс´ийской Федера́ции).[41] Another well-known group is the GhostSec group, linked mainly to Western countries. It has fought against radical Islamist websites, mainly after the Charlie Hebdo shooting terrorist attack in January 2015; it later began to attack Russian and Iranian targets, following Russia's aggression toward Ukraine.[42] It is important to note that it can be difficult to definitively identify which hacker groups are foreign proxies. This is because hacker groups often operate anonymously and use sophisticated technological techniques to cover their tracks. However, evidence suggests that a growing number of hacker groups are being used by foreign governments to achieve their strategic goals.

The use of cyber proxies by foreign governments poses a number of challenges to cybersecurity. First, it makes it more difficult to attribute cyberattacks to specific actors, thus making it harder to justify retaliation against a proxy's "boss" or operator. This can make it difficult to hold governments accountable for their actions and to deter future attacks. Second, cyber proxies can be used to launch attacks that are below the threshold of armed conflict. This can make it difficult for governments to respond to the attack without escalating the conflict. This situation, in which no one can be held accountable, creates an incentive for countries to create more sophisticated cyber tools to hide the attacks carried out by their proxies.[43]

3.3 (A Lack of) International Law

There are two main problems with cyberspace and acts of cyber warfare: there are no international laws and norms applicable to cyber warfare, and there are limited ways to attribute an attack to a country. Unless proven otherwise, an attacker remains virtual, while the victim is real. As of writing, international law, such as Article 51 in the United Nations Charter, only determines which physical actions justify physical responses. There is a challenge in determining when a cyber action would amount

[40] Maurer (2018: 3–28), Krieg and Rickli (2018) and Schmitt and Vihul (2014).

[41] See, in general, Greenberg (2019).

[42] Poireault (2023).

[43] Nye (2016).

to a physical action so as to justify and make legitimate a response. What would be a legitimate response to espionage or data leaks? What would be a legitimate response to spreading disinformation? What would be a *jus ad bellum*?

To fully understand the lack of international law regarding cyber warfare, one needs to understand the nature of international law. International law is a body of laws and norms that govern the relations among countries and other international actors. It is based on the principle of sovereignty, which means that all countries are equal and independent, as explained in the first section of this chapter. International law is developed through treaties, customary international law and general principles of law. Regarding war and conflict, several key principles have been developed over time. First, countries are prohibited from using force against other countries other than in self-defense. Of course, as history tells us, this United Nations international law is often broken. Second, countries need to distinguish between civilians and combatants. Third, military attacks must be proportional to the military objectives being pursued and, fourth, they must be necessary to achieve the military objectives being pursued (principle of necessity).[44]

When it comes to physical warfare, there are several existing international laws (treaties, conventions, resolutions, etc.). For each example of international law, each country signed and agreed to the principles as an independent and sovereign country. These legal instruments are designed to prevent and regulate armed conflicts, protect civilians and promote global peace and security. Some of the most significant ones include (stated dates are effective, not dates of drafts):

1. **United Nations Charter (1945)**: The United Nations Charter is the foundational document of modern international law. It prohibits the use of force in international relations, except in self-defense or when authorized by the Security Council. It establishes the United Nations as the central institution for maintaining international peace and security. Virtually all recognized sovereign countries in the world are members of the United Nations.[45]
2. **Geneva Conventions (1949)**: The Geneva Conventions consist of four treaties that set standards for the treatment of wounded and sick combatants, prisoners of war and civilians during armed conflicts. They also establish the distinctive emblems of the Red Cross and the Red Crescent. In 1977 and 2005, additional protocols were added. Virtually all recognized sovereign countries in the world signed these conventions.[46]
3. **Hague Conventions (1899 and 1907)**: The Hague Conventions address the laws and customs of war. They regulate issues like the treatment of prisoners of war and the use of certain types of weaponry. These laws began the era of arms control. Thirteen countries (out of 193 United Nations members) have not

[44] Greenwood (1987).

[45] United Nations Charter, 1945. https://www.un.org/en/about-us/un-charter.

[46] The Geneva Conventions and their Commentaries, International Committee of the Red Cross, 1949. https://www.icrc.org/en/war-and-law/treaties-customary-law/geneva-conventions.

signed these conventions, including countries like Afghanistan, Chad, Eritrea and North Korea.[47]

4. **Chemical Weapons Convention (1997)**: This treaty bans the production, stockpiling, acquisition and use of chemical weapons and their precursors. It aims to eliminate these inhumane weapons and their potential use in warfare. This convention was signed by most United Nations members. Israel has signed but not ratified this convention, and Egypt, North Korea and South Sudan have not signed it at all.[48]
5. **Biological Weapons Convention (1972)**: The Biological Weapons Convention has 109 signatures, and it prohibits the development, production, acquisition and stockpiling of biological weapons. It seeks to prevent the use of biological agents as weapons of mass destruction.[49]
6. **Non-Proliferation Treaty (NPT; 1970)**: The NPT aims to prevent the spread of nuclear weapons and promote nuclear disarmament. It has three pillars: preventing the spread of nuclear weapons, promoting disarmament and facilitating peaceful nuclear cooperation. Israel, India, Pakistan and South Sudan have not signed this treaty.[50]
7. **Convention on Certain Conventional Weapons (CCW; 1983)**: The CCW is a series of agreements regulating the use of specific conventional weapons, including landmines, incendiary weapons, blinding laser weapons and explosive remnants of war. The CCW's protocols address each of these categories. Over 100 countries have signed most of its protocols.[51]
8. **Rome Statute of the International Criminal Court (ICC; 1998 and 2002)**: The Rome Statute established the ICC, which has jurisdiction over individuals for the most serious international crimes, including war crimes, crimes against humanity and genocide. This statue was signed by 123 countries.[52]
9. **The Arms Trade Treaty (2014)**: This treaty aims to regulate the international trade in conventional arms, including small arms and light weapons, to prevent

[47] Convention (II) with Respect to the Laws and Customs of War on Land and its annex: Regulations concerning the Laws and Customs of War on Land. The Hague, 29 July 1899. https://ihl-databases.icrc.org/en/ihl-treaties/hague-conv-ii-1899; Convention (IV) respecting the Laws and Customs of War on Land and its annex: Regulations concerning the Laws and Customs of War on Land. The Hague, 18 October 1907. https://ihl-databases.icrc.org/en/ihl-treaties/hague-conv-iv-1907. Also see Hudson (1931).

[48] Chemical Weapons Convention, Organisation for the Prohibition of Chemical Weapons, 1997. https://www.opcw.org/chemical-weapons-convention.

[49] Biological Weapons Convention, United Nations Office for Disarmament Affairs. https://disarmament.unoda.org/biological-weapons/.

[50] Treaty on the Non-Proliferation of Nuclear Weapons (NPT). United Nations Office for Disarmament Affairs. https://disarmament.unoda.org/wmd/nuclear/npt/.

[51] The Convention on Certain Conventional Weapons. https://disarmament.unoda.org/the-convention-on-certain-conventional-weapons/#:~:text=It%20was%20adopted%20on%2010,or%20to%20affect%20civilians%20indiscriminately.

[52] The Rome Statute of the International Criminal Court. https://www.icc-cpi.int/sites/default/files/RS-Eng.pdf.

their diversion to the illicit market and to reduce human suffering resulting from their misuse. Over 100 countries have signed this treaty.[53]

10. **The Convention on Cluster Munitions (2008 and 2010)**: This convention prohibits the use, stockpiling, production and transfer of cluster munitions, which can have severe humanitarian consequences, particularly for civilians. This convention was ratified by 112 countries and signed by another 12 countries.[54]
11. **United Nations Security Council Resolutions**: The United Nations Security Council regularly passes resolutions related to international security, including authorizing military interventions, imposing sanctions and establishing peacekeeping missions.
12. **International Court of Justice (ICJ; 1945)**: The ICJ is a part of the United Nations Charter, and all countries are automatically party to this statute. It is the principal judicial organ of the United Nations. It is the only permanent international court with jurisdiction to hear disputes between countries and handle disputes over issues such as the use of force and territorial, maritime and diplomatic disputes, among others.
13. **United Nations Convention on the Law of the Sea (UNCLOS; adopted 1982, effective from 1994)**: UNCLOS is an international treaty that defines the rights and responsibilities of nations concerning the use of the world's oceans. It was adopted in 1982 and came into force in 1994. UNCLOS establishes guidelines for various activities in the oceans, including territorial seas, economic zones, navigational freedom and more. It also governs the actions and movement of warships.[55] This convention also deals with submarine cables in the part regarding continental shelves (Part VI) and in the part regarding the High Seas (Part VII).

The above non-exhaustive list deals with war, human rights and arms control, and most sovereign countries have signed most of these treaties and conventions. In addition to these treaties and conventions, several other international laws are applicable to war and international security. These laws include customary international law, which is law that has developed through the consistent practice of states, and general principles of law, such as the principle of proportionality and the principle of necessity. However, although the above treaties and conventions deal with conventional and nuclear weapons, they do not address cyber weapons or cyberattacks.

The only convention that is indirectly, but significantly, associated with cyberspace is UNCLOS. Since approximately 95% of the global internet connections run through submarine fiber-optic cables, the question of who lays them, as well as when and how, is of great importance. For instance, Article 79 of the convention notes that: "All States are entitled to lay submarine cables and pipelines on the continental

---

[53] The Arms Trade Treaty (ATT). https://thearmstradetreaty.org/treaty-status.html?templateId=209883.

[54] The Convention on Cluster Munitions. https://www.clusterconvention.org/states-parties/.

[55] The United Nations Convention on the Law of the Sea. https://www.un.org/depts/los/convention_agreements/texts/unclos/unclos_e.pdf.

shelf, in accordance with the provisions of this article." Article 112 goes even further, dictating that "All States are entitled to lay submarine cables and pipelines on the bed of the high seas beyond the continental shelf." Thus, excluding near-coast economic zones, countries can lay cables wherever they want, including between archipelagic countries (blocs of islands). In our context, as is expanded upon in Chaps. 6 and 7, China can thus lay cables near Europe and the United States and vice versa. Leaving the issue of submarine cables to one side for now, however—what exactly is the status of international law regarding cyber warfare?

3.3.1 International Law: The State of Cyber Warfare

Cyber warfare is a new and emerging form of warfare that poses significant challenges to international law. Traditional international law was developed to regulate warfare in the physical world. It does not explicitly address cyber warfare, which takes place in the cyber domain. However, some scholars, policymakers and groups argue that existing principles of international law can be applied to cyber warfare. For example, the prohibition on the use of force under Article 2(4) of the United Nations Charter could be applied to cyberattacks that cause significant damage to a country's infrastructure or economy or that cause injuries and loss of human life. However, this example is unique as kinetic damage can be easily seen.

Existing international law is inadequate to address the challenges posed by cyber warfare as cyberattacks are often difficult to attribute to a specific country, and there is no clear consensus on what constitutes a prohibited cyberattack. In recent years, there has been some progress in developing new international laws, norms and agreements to address cyber warfare. For example, the Tallinn Manual on the International Law Applicable to Cyber Operations, published in 2013, provides a set of non-binding guidelines for the application of international law to cyber operations. In 2017, this manual was updated and published as the Tallinn Manual 2.0. This manual, while important, is non-binding as it is an academic (and policy-oriented) study by legal experts of how international law applies to cyberspace and cyber warfare.[56]

Several international treaties and agreements address specific aspects of cyber warfare. The most notable is the 2001 Budapest Convention on Cybercrime (effective from 2004), which seeks to harmonize national laws on cybercrime and enhance international cooperation in investigating and prosecuting cybercriminals. Cyber powers like the United States, Israel, Estonia, the United Kingdom, Germany, France and others have signed and agreed to it, although countries like Russia, China and Iran have not.[57]

---

[56] See, in general, Schmitt (2017).

[57] Budapest Convention on Cybercrime. https://www.coe.int/en/web/cybercrime/the-budapest-convention.

In 2010, the United Nations General Assembly (UNGA) established the Group of Governmental Experts (GGE) to study the implications of information and telecommunications technologies in security. The GGE was tasked with developing recommendations for the United Nations on how to address cyber threats. In 2013, the GGE released a report identifying a number of common elements of responsible state behavior in cyberspace. In July 2015, the GGE report affirmed that international law, particularly the United Nations Charter, applies to cyberspace. The group of twenty experts in the 2015 GGE, which included experts from the United States, Russia, China, Germany, the United Kingdom, France, Israel, Japan and others suggested norms of responsible behavior regarding cyberspace, which they refer to as the field of information and communication technology (ICT) in the context of international security.[58] They developed eleven key recommendations, which were later interpreted by NATO's Cooperative Cyber Defence Centre of Excellence (CCDCOE). They agreed that countries are sovereign, that sovereignty is equal, that settlement of disputes should be done by peaceful means, and that countries should refrain from the use of force and respect human rights. They also agreed that there was a need for non-intervention in the internal affairs of other countries—something many of the countries were guilty of (i.e., the Russian interference in the 2016 United States presidential elections). They divided their suggestions into two categories: limiting norms and good practice/positive duties.[59]

Limiting Norms

1. Countries should not knowingly allow their territory to be used for internationally wrongful acts using ICTs.
2. Countries should not conduct or knowingly support ICT activity that intentionally damages critical infrastructure.
3. Countries should take steps to ensure supply chain security and should seek to prevent the proliferation of malicious ICT and the use of harmful hidden functions.
4. Countries should not conduct or knowingly support activity to harm the information systems of another state's emergency response teams (CERT/CSIRTS) and should not use their own teams for malicious international activity.
5. Countries should respect the United Nations resolutions that are linked to human rights on the internet and to the right to privacy in the digital age.

Good Practices and Positive Duties

1. Countries should cooperate to increase stability and security in the use of ICTs and to prevent harmful practices.
2. Countries should consider all relevant information in case of ICT incidents.

---

[58] UN General Assembly, A/70/174 Session. https://documents-dds-ny.un.org/doc/UNDOC/GEN/N15/228/35/PDF/N1522835.pdf?OpenElement.

[59] See 2015 UN GGE Report: Major Players Recommending Norms of Behaviour, Highlighting Aspects of International Law. NATO's Cooperative Cyber Defence Centre of Excellence (CCDCOE). https://ccdcoe.org/incyder-articles/2015-un-gge-report-major-players-recommending-norms-of-behaviour-highlighting-aspects-of-international-law/.

3. Countries should consider how best to cooperate to exchange information, to assist each other, and to prosecute terrorist and criminal use of ICTs.
4. Countries should take appropriate measures to protect their critical infrastructure.
5. Countries should respond to appropriate requests for assistance by other states whose critical infrastructure is subject to malicious ICT acts.
6. Countries should encourage responsible reporting of ICT vulnerabilities and should share remedies to these.

The 2015 GGE thus did not establish any binding laws or norms but merely produced a few suggestions about how countries should avoid using cyberspace for warfare. In 2017, the GGE was unable to agree on a final consensus report or make clear suggestions about how to create and regulate international law regarding cyberspace. In particular, China, Russia and Cuba did not agree to proceed with any effective measures.[60]

Following the failure of the GGE on cyber regulation, the United Nations passed Resolution A/RES/73/27 in December 2018 and initiated the Open-Ended Working Group (OEWG) on developments in the field of information and telecommunications in the context of international security. It is important to note that Resolution 73/27 is not legally binding.[61] The OEWG is a forum for intergovernmental dialogue and cooperation on cybersecurity issues. It was established by the UNGA to further develop international norms, rules and principles of responsible state behavior in cyberspace. The OEWG is open to all United Nations member countries, and its work is informed by the views of a wide range of stakeholders, including industry, academia and civil society. It meets annually to discuss and negotiate on a range of cybersecurity issues. Currently in its second stage (2021–2025), the OEWG has agreed to suggest that countries should not knowingly allow their territory to be used for internationally wrongful acts in cyberspace, should not intentionally damage critical infrastructure belonging to others and should cooperate in responding to cybersecurity incidents. Thus, the OEWG has copied what the GGE had already agreed upon and produced nothing of a normative and binding nature.

The main GGE related to cybersecurity started work in 2015, the OEWG was decided upon in late 2018, and in 2019 the UNGA (A/RES/73/266) established yet another, sixth, GGE. It was composed of 25 member countries, including global powers like the United States, Russia, China, the United Kingdom, Germany, France and India, among others.[62] The sixth GGE recommended that countries should refrain from using cyber means to intentionally damage infrastructure or essential services, should cooperate for cybersecurity and against cybercrime, should respect human rights and should aid developing countries in the field of cybersecurity. Thus, again, the 2019 GGE was no different from the 2018 OEWG or the 2015 GGE, and none of these were binding.

---

[60] Henriksen (2019).

[61] See UN A/RES/73/27. https://documents-dds-ny.un.org/doc/UNDOC/GEN/N18/418/04/PDF/N1841804.pdf?OpenElement.

[62] See UN A/RES/73/266. https://documents-dds-ny.un.org/doc/UNDOC/GEN/N18/465/01/PDF/N1846501.pdf?OpenElement.

Next, the Global Commission on the Stability of Cyberspace (GCSC), established in 2017 with the support of the Hague Centre for Strategic Studies, was an independent, international commission to develop proposals for norms, rules and principles to enhance international security and stability and guide responsible state and non-state behavior in cyberspace. The GCSC published its final report in November 2019 and concluded its activities after the publication of the CyberStability Paper Series in December 2021.[63] The GCSC was composed of dozens of experts from around the world, including government officials, academic researchers, business leaders and civil society representatives. It held a series of meetings and workshops to consult with a wide range of stakeholders on its proposals, and in its final report it concluded that:

1. State and non-state actors must adopt and implement norms that increase the stability of cyberspace by promoting restraint and encouraging action.
2. State and non-state actors, consistent with their responsibilities and limitations, must respond appropriately to norms violations, ensuring that those who violate norms face predictable and meaningful consequences.
3. State and non-state actors, including international institutions, should increase efforts to train staff, build capacity and capabilities, promote a shared understanding of the importance of the stability of cyberspace and take into account the disparate needs of different parties.
4. State and non-state actors should collect, share, review and publish information on norms violations and the impact of such activities.
5. State and non-state actors should establish and support Communities of Interest to help ensure the stability of cyberspace.
6. The GCSC recommends establishing a standing multistakeholder engagement mechanism to address stability issues, one where states, the private sector (including the technical community) and civil society are adequately involved and consulted.

The GCSC provided a better framework than those suggested by the United Nations GGEs and OEWG because it addressed, at least to some extent, the use of proxies in international affairs. It recommended that not only countries (states) should agree to cyber-related international norms but also non-state actors, which might include international organizations, companies, civil society and even hacker groups and terrorist groups.[64]

Following initiatives and calls for a political commitment on cyberspace, both international and country-led like the ones mentioned above, as well as by private stakeholders like the president of Microsoft's original call for a "Digital Geneva Convention," Microsoft partnered with the French government to build a legally non-binding instrument focused on elaborating a core set of cyber norms for all stakeholders, including countries, industry, civil society and academia. Thus, the

[63] Global Commission on the Stability of Cyberspace (2019).

[64] Eggenschwiler (2020).

Paris Call was launched in November 2018, at the opening of the Internet Governance Forum and one day after the centennial observation of the end of World War I. By the time of the conference, the Paris Call had garnered signatures from over 67 countries, 358 companies and 139 civil society organizations. It is also worth noting that this initiative overshadowed the German initiative—the Siemens Charter of Trust of November 2018. By November 2023, the Paris Call was supported by 81 countries, 36 public authorizers, 390 organizations and 706 companies and private sector entities.[65] The Paris Call produced nine key principles regarding cyberspace, which, again, were not binding. Countries, businesses, organizations and other entities that support the Paris Call agree to:

1. Protect individuals and infrastructure: Prevent and recover from malicious cyber activities that threaten or cause significant, indiscriminate or systemic harm to individuals and critical infrastructure.
2. Protect the internet: Prevent activity that intentionally and substantially damages the general availability or integrity of the public core of the Internet.
3. Defend electoral processes: Strengthen our capacity to prevent malign interference by foreign actors aimed at undermining electoral processes through malicious cyber activities.
4. Defend intellectual property: Prevent ICT-enabled theft of intellectual property, including trade secrets or other confidential business information, with the intent of providing competitive advantages to companies or the commercial sector.
5. Non-proliferation: Develop ways to prevent the proliferation of malicious software and practices intended to cause harm.
6. Lifecycle security: Strengthen the security of digital processes, products and services throughout their lifecycle and supply chain.
7. Cyber hygiene (refers to an array of "best" practices to minimize security risks): Support efforts to strengthen advanced cyber hygiene for all actors.
8. No private hack-back: Take steps to prevent non-state actors, including the private sector, from hacking back for their own purposes or those of other non-state actors.
9. International norms: Promote the widespread acceptance and implementation of international norms of responsible behavior as well as confidence-building measures in cyberspace.

The Paris Call's chief strength lies in its multistakeholder orientation. It is supported by a broad base, including all levels of government, industry and civil society. Like the GCSC, and unlike the United Nations GGE and OEWG initiatives, it also focuses on non-state actors, hinting to countries that they are not to use proxies for international influence campaigns in cyberspace. In November 2021, the European Union and the United States joined the Paris Call,[66] whereas Russia, China and Iran, among others, do not currently support the Paris Call.

[65] See the Paris Call: https://pariscall.international/en/. Also see Ruhl et al. (2020).

[66] "The United States Supports the Paris Call for Trust and Security in Cyberspace," U.S. Department of State (November 10, 2021). https://www.state.gov/the-united-states-supports-the-paris-call-for-trust-and-security-in-cyberspace/.

While countries have made laws regarding cybersecurity and information security, in the form of local laws and regulations and by developing dedicated organizations (i.e., the United States Digital Millennium Act, California Consumer Privacy Act (CCPA), the European Union's GDPR, establishment of the United States National Institute of Standards and Technology (NIST), Russian Sovereignty Law, Chinese Cyberspace Law, etc.), they find it difficult to achieve an international consensus for several reasons: the difficulty of attribution, the fuzzy threshold for the use of cyber tools and force and the lack of enforcing mechanisms. Other problems, as explained below, include issues like the digital divide between developed and less developed countries.

The attribution problem is one of the key challenges in the realm of cyber warfare. Determining the origin of a cyberattack is often complex, as attackers can hide their identities using various techniques. This makes it difficult to hold countries or individuals accountable under international law. For example, the 2017 WannaCry ransomware attack, which affected numerous countries, was attributed to North Korea only after extensive investigation (further explained in Chap. 4).

Another problem is the lack of a clear threshold. The traditional threshold for the use of force in international law is ill-suited to the subtleties of cyber warfare. Countries are increasingly engaged in cyber operations that fall below the threshold of armed conflict, such as espionage or economic espionage, data leaks and the dissemination of mis/disinformation. This creates ambiguity in applying the concept of self-defense, as seen in the 2015 United States–China agreement not to engage in cyber-enabled economic espionage. United States President Barack Obama and Chinese leader Xi Jinping agreed that neither of their governments would conduct or condone economic espionage in cyberspace in a deal that sought to address a major source of friction in the bilateral relationship. In this regard, governments will not conduct cyber espionage themselves, but proxy hacker groups probably will.[67]

Finally, international law lacks effective enforcement mechanisms for cyber violations. While the United Nations Security Council can authorize sanctions or other measures in response to cyberattacks, it often faces political deadlock as the global powers, permanent members of the Security Council, Russia, China, the United States, France and the United Kingdom, have veto power to block decisions each of them regards as unfit. Additionally, countries may be reluctant to take legal action against cyber actors due to concerns about revealing their own cyber capabilities. For instance, the United States has revealed some material about the alleged Russian interference in the 2016 presidential election but did not act against Russia fiercely or openly. In the example of the 2020 SolarWinds cyberattack, which the United States blamed on Russia, there was a problem directly attributing the attack to Russia and, again, the United States did not take any fierce actions against Russia in the open (such cyberattacks and others are detailed in Chap. 4).

[67] Nakashima and Mufson (2015).

3.3.2 Successful Regulation Attempts: European GDPR, DMA, DSA

The European Union has been at the forefront of regulating the digital sphere, particularly in the realms of data privacy, cybersecurity and fair competition. The European Union's cyber laws have evolved over time, reflecting the ever-changing digital landscape and the growing importance of data and technology. It is challenging to establish international norms and laws regarding cyberspace due to the global nature of the internet and the diversity of legal systems and cultures. While there have been efforts to develop international agreements on cybersecurity and data protection, these efforts have faced a number of obstacles, as explained above. Yet, in the absence of international norms and laws, the European Union has taken the lead in developing its own cyber laws, such as the General Data Protection Regulation (GDPR), the Digital Markets Act (DMA) and the Digital Services Act (DSA). These laws have had a significant impact on the global digital landscape, and they are likely to continue to do so in the years to come.

The European Union is a political and economic union of 27 members with shared history, values and aims. It managed to successfully develop cyber laws, despite individual European Union members—countries—being sovereign and having different laws, for several reasons. First, the European Union has a strong legal tradition and a commitment to upholding fundamental rights, as well as a shared culture. This has provided a foundation for the development of cyber laws that protect the privacy and security of European citizens. Second, the European Union is a large and powerful market, and its laws have a significant impact on businesses that operate in the European Union. This has given the European Union a strong bargaining chip in international negotiations on cyber governance. Its laws impact not only the European Union but also those collaborating and trading with the European Union, and these laws also establish a regime of sanctions, hinting at a possible future development in the field of international cyber law. Third, the European Union has been willing to cooperate with non-European Union countries on cyber issues, even when there is no consensus on norms and principles. This has helped to build trust and cooperation between the European Union and non-European Union countries. Fourth, and most important, is that the European Union is a working union of countries based on established treaties.[68]

The European Union began regulating cyberspace when the internet was significantly developing and spreading worldwide, as early as the 1990s. In 1995, it adopted the European Union Data Protection Directive (95/46/EC), a landmark piece of legislation that established the framework for data protection in the European Union. It aimed to safeguard individuals' privacy by regulating the collection, processing and storage of personal data. The directive introduced key principles such as data minimization, purpose limitation and consent, which remain cornerstones of data protection law today. In 2016, almost two decades after the Data Protection Directive, the

[68] Buzan and Diez (1999) and Hodson et al. (2022).

European Union adopted the GDPR (2016/679). The GDPR represented a significant overhaul of data protection law, reflecting the growth of the digital economy and the increasing complexity of data flows. The GDPR introduced stricter requirements for data controllers, enhanced individual rights and established a more harmonized approach to data protection across the European Union.[69]

Next, the DMA and DSA were introduced in response to the growing power of large online platforms. The European Union proposed the DMA and DSA in December 2020, and the rules came into force in November 2022. The DMA aims to address the gatekeeper power of large online platforms, such as Google, Amazon and Meta, by imposing obligations that prevent them from abusing their market dominance. The DSA, on the other hand, aims to regulate online intermediaries, such as social media platforms and online marketplaces, by making them more accountable for the content and activities on their platforms.[70]

These regulations are expected to have a significant impact on the digital landscape, shaping the behavior of large online platforms and protecting the rights of internet users. The evolution of European cyber laws reflects the European Union's commitment to safeguarding the privacy, security and rights of its citizens in the digital age. From the Data Protection Directive to the GDPR, DMA and DSA, the European Union has sought to regulate the digital sphere in a way that promotes innovation but protects consumers and upholds fundamental values.[71] The European cyber laws are a significant step in the emergence of either an as-yet-unseen regime of international norms and laws or of cyber blocs.

Another piece of legislation worth mentioning after discussing the European laws is the Californian CCPA, which was enacted in 2018. It is a unique and landmark legislation that grants California residents significant control over their personal information collected by businesses. Although it is not specifically directed toward the cyber domain, it might prompt other states in the United States to follow its example on issues relating to (personal) cyber privacy. Generally, the CCPA grants Californians the right to know what information is/has been collected about them, the right to delete such information and more.[72]

---

[69] Li et al. (2019).

[70] See Digital Markets Act (DMA), European Commission. https://digital-markets-act.ec.europa.eu/legislation_en; Digital Services Act (DSA), European Commission. https://digital-strategy.ec.europa.eu/en/policies/digital-services-act-package.

[71] Albrecht (2016), Blankertz and Jaursch (2021) and Ryan-Mosley (2023).

[72] See California Consumer Privacy Act (CCPA), Office of the Attorney General, State of California Department of Justice (2018). https://oag.ca.gov/privacy/ccpa#:~:text=This%20landmark%20law%20secures%20new,them%20(with%20some%20exceptions)%3B.

3.4 Conclusion

Cyberattacks are on the rise as countries utilize proxies to indirectly attack or influence other countries or international organizations. The cybersecurity company CheckPoint suggested that there were approximately 38% more global cyberattacks in 2022 than in 2021. However, since cyberattacks are difficult to trace, it is probable that the actual increase was even larger. There are currently no applicable international norms or laws on cyberspace accepted by most countries, that is to say, by most UN members. There is, however, a cyber bloc of 27 countries, the European Union, that has adopted the GDPR, the DMA and the DSA to restrain giant technology companies and protect their citizens.

International law faces significant challenges in effectively regulating cyber warfare. While existing legal principles are adaptable to the cyber domain, gaps and ambiguities persist. The need for clear rules regarding attribution, the threshold for the use of force and effective enforcement mechanisms is evident. As some global powers benefit from the lawlessness of cyberspace, making international treaties and sanction regimes will be extremely difficult. This has only been successful within existing international establishments like the European Union. Addressing these challenges is essential to ensure that international law remains relevant in an increasingly interconnected and digitized world.

As cyber warfare continues to evolve, states must work together to develop and strengthen the legal framework governing this domain. Cooperation, transparency and the development of cyber-specific treaties and agreements are critical steps toward establishing a more comprehensive and enforceable system of international law for cyber warfare. The international community needs to develop new strategies to address the threat posed by cyber proxies. These strategies should include the improvement of attribution. Governments and cybersecurity companies need to invest in new tools and techniques to improve their ability to attribute cyberattacks to specific actors. This will help to hold governments accountable for their actions and to deter future attacks. However, not all governments want to be exposed.

International norms must be developed further. The international community needs to develop new norms and agreements to govern the use of cyber proxies. These norms and agreements should aim to reduce the risk of cyberattacks escalating into armed conflict. But, again, not all countries seek such international norms and laws. Those with the most cyber power, mainly the United States, Russia, China and a few others will probably oppose international treaties and sanction regimes. Such developments will not only pose a threat to countries' sovereignty—as they will need to accept others' requirements—they will also weaken countries' power and ability to control the measurements of power: resources, actors and outcomes.

References

Albrecht, Jan Philipp. 2016. How the GDPR will change the world. *European Data Protection Law Review* 2: 287.

Andrew, Edward. 2011. Jean Bodin on sovereignty. *Republics of Letters: A Journal for the Study of Knowledge, Politics, and the Arts* 2 (2): 80.

Bellamy, Alex J., and Tim Dunne. 2016. R2P in theory and practice. In *The Oxford handbook of the responsibility to protect*, ed. Alex Bellamy and Tim Dunne, 3–17. Oxford University Press.

Berman, Eli, and David A. Lake (eds.). 2019. *Proxy wars: Suppressing violence through local agents*. Cornell University Press.

Blankertz, Aline, and Julian Jaursch. 2021. What the European DSA and DMA proposals mean for online platforms. *Brookings Institute*, January 14. https://www.brookings.edu/articles/what-the-european-dsa-and-dma-proposals-mean-for-online-platforms/.

Breuilly, John. 2000. The revolutions of 1848. In *Revolutions and the revolutionary tradition—In the West 1560–1991*, ed. David Parker, 109–131. Routledge.

Brunstetter, Daniel R., and Cian O'Driscoll (eds.). 2017. *Just war thinkers: From Cicero to the 21st century*. Routledge.

Bull, Hedley. 2012. The anarchical society: A study of order in world politics. Bloomsbury Publishing

Buzan, Barry, and Thomas Diez. 1999. The European Union and Turkey. *Survival* 41 (1): 41–57.

Coyne, Christopher J., and Rachel L. Mathers (eds.). 2011. *The handbook on the political economy of war*. Edward Elgar Publishing.

Croxton, Derek. 1999. The peace of Westphalia of 1648 and the origins of sovereignty. *The International History Review* 21 (3): 569–591.

Dahl, Robert A. 1957. The concept of power. *Behavioral Science* 2 (3): 201–215.

Deutsch, Karl W. 1964. External involvement in internal war. In *Internal war, problems and approaches*, ed. Harry Eckstein. New York, NY: Free Press of Glencoe.

Eggenschwiler, Jacqueline. 2020. Expert commissions and norms of responsible behaviour in cyberspace: A review of the activities of the GCSC. *Digital Policy, Regulation and Governance* 22 (2): 93–107.

Gellner, Ernest. 2015. Nations and nationalism. In *Conflict after the Cold War*, 378–389. Routledge.

Global Commission on the Stability of Cyberspace. 2019. *Advancing CyberStability*. https://hcss.nl/wp-content/uploads/2019/11/GCSC-Final-Report-November-2019.pdf.

Greenberg, Andy. 2019. *Sandworm: A new era of cyberwar and the hunt for the Kremlin's most dangerous hackers*. Anchor.

Greenwood, Christopher. 1987. The concept of war in modern international law. *International & Comparative Law Quarterly* 36 (2): 283–306.

Gross, Leo. 1948. The peace of Westphalia, 1648–1948. *American Journal of International Law* 42 (1): 20–41.

Haber, Eldar, and Lev Topor. 2023. Sovereignty, cyberspace, and the emergence of internet bubbles. *Journal of Advanced Military Studies* 14 (1): 144–165.

Hatton, Ragnhild Marie. 1976. *Louis XIV and absolution*. Macmillan Press.

Henriksen, Anders. 2019. The end of the road for the UN GGE process: The future regulation of cyberspace. *Journal of Cybersecurity* 5 (1): 1–9.

Hinsley, Francis H. 1986. *Sovereignty*, 2nd ed. Cambridge University Press.

Hodson, Dermot, Uwe Puetter, John Peterson, and Sabine Saurugger (eds.). 2022. *The institutions of the European Union*. Oxford University Press.

Hudson, Manley O. 1931. Present status of the Hague Conventions of 1899 and 1907. *American Journal of International Law* 25 (1): 114–117.

Huntington, Samuel. 1993. The clash of civilizations. *Foreign Affairs* 72 (3): 22–49.

Kaplan, Robert D. 2019. *The return of Marco Polo's world: War, strategy, and American interests in the twenty-first century*. Random House.

Keohane, Robert Owen. 2002. *Power and governance in a partially globalized world*. Psychology Press.

Krasner, Stephen D. 1999. Globalization and sovereignty. In *States and sovereignty in the global economy*, 34–52.

Krieg, Andreas, and Jean-Marc Rickli. 2018. Surrogate warfare: The art of war in the 21st century? *Defence Studies* 18 (2): 113–130.

Li, He., Lu Yu, and Wu He. 2019. The impact of GDPR on global technology development. *Journal of Global Information Technology Management* 22 (1): 1–6.

Locke, John. 2013. Two treatises of government, 1689. In *The anthropology of citizenship: A reader*, ed. Sian Lazar, 43–46. Wiley.

Lucas, John. 1998. The tension between despotic and infrastructural power: The military and the political class in Nigeria, 1985–1993. *Studies in Comparative International Development* 33: 90–113.

Mann, Michael. 2008. Infrastructural power revisited. *Studies in Comparative International Development* 43: 355–365.

Maurer, Tim. 2018. *Cyber mercenaries*. Cambridge University Press.

Mearsheimer, John. 2014. *The tragedy of great power politics*, updated ed. W. W. Norton & Company.

Mumford, Andrew. 2013. *Proxy warfare*. Cambridge: Polity Press.

Nakashima, Ellen, and Steven Mufson. 2015. U.S., China vow not to engage in economic cyberespionage. *Washington Post*, September 25. https://www.washingtonpost.com/national/us-china-vow-not-to-engage-in-economic-cyberespionage/2015/09/25/90e74b6a-63b9-11e5-8e9e-dce8a2a2a679_story.html#.

Newey, Glen. 2008. *Routledge philosophy guidebook to Hobbes and Leviathan*. Routledge.

Nye, Joseph S. 1990. Soft power. *Foreign Policy* 80: 153–171.

Nye, Joseph S. 2004. *Soft power: The means to success in world politics*. Public Affairs.

Nye, Joseph S. 2008. Public diplomacy and soft power. *The Annals of the American Academy of Political and Social Science* 616 (1): 94–109.

Nye, Joseph S. 2016. Deterrence and dissuasion in cyberspace. *International Security* 41 (3): 44–71.

Nye, Joseph S. 2023. Get smart: Combining hard and soft power. In *Soft power and great power competition: Shifting sands in the balance of power between the United States and China*, 63–66. Singapore: Springer Nature.

Osiander, Andreas. 2001. Sovereignty, international relations, and the Westphalian myth. *International Organization* 55 (2): 251–287.

Parker, Geoffrey. 2006. *The thirty years' war*. Routledge.

Pearson, Frederic S. 1974. Foreign military interventions and domestic disputes. *International Studies Quarterly* 18 (3): 259–290.

Poireault, Kevin. 2023. Hacker group GhostSec unveils new generation ransomware implant. *InfoSecurity Magazine*, October 19. https://www.infosecurity-magazine.com/news/hacker-ghostsec-unveils-new/.

Radulescu, Irina Gabriela, Mirela Panait, and Catalin Voica. 2014. BRICS countries challenge to the world economy new trends. *Procedia Economics and Finance* 8: 605–613.

Rousseau, Jean-Jacques. 2012. *The major political writings of Jean-Jacques Rousseau: The two discourses and the social contract*. Translated and edited by John T. Scott. University of Chicago Press.

Ruggie, John Gerard. 1982. International regimes, transactions, and change: Embedded liberalism in the postwar economic order. *International Organization* 36 (2): 379–415.

Ruhl, Christian, Duncan Hollis, Wyatt Hoffman, and Tim Maurer. 2020. *Cyberspace and geopolitics: Assessing global cybersecurity norm processes at a crossroads*. Carnegie Endowment for International Peace.

Ryan-Mosley, Tate. 2023. The internet is about to get a lot safer. *MIT Technology Review*, March 6. https://www.technologyreview.com/2023/03/06/1069391/safer-internet-dsa-dma-eu/.

Schmitt, Michael N. (ed.). 2013. *Tallinn manual on the international law applicable to cyber warfare*. Cambridge University Press.
Schmitt, Michael N. (ed.). 2017. *Tallinn manual 2.0 on the international law applicable to cyber warfare*. Cambridge University Press.
Schmitt, Michael N., and Liis Vihul. 2014. Proxy wars in cyberspace: The evolving international law of attribution. *Fletcher Securities Review* 1: 53.
Schnee, Walter. 2001. Nationalism: A review of the literature. *Journal of Political & Military Sociology* 29 (1): 1–18.
Shuker, Pnina, and Lev Topor. 2021. Russian influence campaigns against NATO in the Baltic region: Spread of chaos and divide et impera. In *The Russian Federation in global knowledge warfare*, 295–314. Cham: Springer.
Soifer, Hillel, and Matthias Vom Hau. 2008. Unpacking the strength of the state: The utility of state infrastructural power. *Studies in Comparative International Development* 43: 219–230.
Sommerville, Johann P. 2015. Early modern absolutism in practice and theory. In *Monarchism and absolutism in early modern Europe*, 117–130. Routledge.
Topor, Lev, and Alexander Tabachnik. 2021. Russian cyber information warfare: International distribution and domestic control. *Journal of Advanced Military Studies* 12 (1): 112–127.
Walzer, Michael. 2015. *Just and unjust wars: A moral argument with historical illustrations*. Hachette UK.
Wilson, Peter H. 2008a. The causes of the thirty years war 1618–48. *The English Historical Review* 123 (502): 554–586.
Wilson III, Ernest J. 2008b. Hard power, soft power, smart power. *The Annals of the American Academy of Political and Social Science* 616 (1): 110–124.
Wintour, Patrick. 2023. How Iran uses proxy forces across the region to strike Israel and US. *Guardian*, November 1. https://www.theguardian.com/global/2023/nov/01/how-iran-uses-proxy-forces-across-the-region-to-strike-israel-and-us.

Chapter 4
Cyber Warfare: Global Trends and Proxy Wars

"The United States is certainly less powerful at the end of the twentieth century than it was in 1945."[1] Moreover, as Joseph S. Nye put it in 1990, the definitions and perceptions of power and even security had begun to shift from the classical use of hard power toward softer, yet at times much more effective uses of power. Now, in the twenty-first century, power is also projected through cyberspace, sometimes in a soft manner but, at other times, in a hard or sharp manner. Following the overview on sovereignty in international relations in Chap. 3, in this chapter, I examine the following question: how is power projected with and through the cyber domain in international relations? The findings of this chapter confirm that the power utilized in cyber warfare, and cyberspace in general, is not only softer but also more dynamic, non-bound to distinct size and strengths, and can be used to complement traditional soft and hard powers alike. Furthermore, if power once lay in military force, and later in traditional diplomacy and currency, now it lies in an innovative currency: in cyber diplomatic, information, military and economic (DIME) warfare. Cyber DIME is a term used to describe the expression and reflection of diplomatic, information, military, or economic measures through the cyber domain.

To answer the research question and reflect properly on the situation in reality, a mixed methodology is used. Qualitative analyses of six cyberattacks (case studies) are performed alongside a quantitative analysis of 500 significant cyber incidents. The case studies include the Russian meddling in the 2016 United States presidential election, Russian disinformation campaigns in Sweden around 2017, the Russian cyberattack on the Ukrainian power grid in 2015 and the North Korean WannaCry ransomware attack of 2017, as well as the 2020 cyberattack, allegedly by a Russian hacker group, on the company SolarWinds. They also include the infamous Stuxnet cyber weapon, allegedly deployed by the United States and Israel against Iran (discovered in 2010). Descriptive statistics and cross-tabulations are then used to analyze 500 significant cyber incidents. This is done to uncover the connections among cyber

[1] Nye (1990, 153, para. 3).

L. Topor, *Cyber Sovereignty*, Global Power Shift,
https://doi.org/10.1007/978-3-031-58199-1_4

warfare tactics, measures of power in international relations, types of perpetrators and types of victims.

The analysis makes clear that traditional powers like the United States, the United Kingdom, Russia and China are not only less powerful than they were during the shift from hard power to soft power, but their military and economic capabilities are, to some extent, dissolving in the face of the potential of cyberspace and cyber warfare. Powerful nations are becoming more vulnerable and losing their international influence since other states, non-state actors and even individuals are utilizing cyber DIME to multiply their power.

4.1 DIME: Elements of Power

Power is the ability to do things and control others, to get others to do what they otherwise would not.[2] This ability is often associated with the possession of certain resources: territory, population, natural resources, economic size and strength, military force and political stability. A neo-realistic approach to power emphasizes hard power, especially the hard power of states—such as military power—while a neo-liberal approach to power emphasizes softer power, such as diplomatic, economic and cultural influence. In more recent studies, smart power has been praised as the ability of an actor to combine elements of hard and soft power.[3] Additionally, sharp power was defined by the National Endowment for Democracy in 2017 and by Christopher Walker and Jessica Ludwig as a type of power that non-democracies like Russia or China use to project their influence, in terms of international security, by taking advantage of the asymmetry between true democracies and less or non-democracies.[4] In the context of cyberspace, as further elaborated in the next section and in this chapter in general, cyber power is the struggle to control and influence others through cyberspace.[5]

In cyberspace, less or non-democratic countries can utilize soft power, such as influence campaigns, or hard power, such as cyberattacks on infrastructures, against their adversaries while keeping themselves secure against similar attempts. That is, true democracies with free political platforms are more vulnerable to foreign manipulations and influence, whereas non or less-democratic countries can close their cyber borders or censor content and websites.[6] Indeed, Russia and China are one step ahead of the West in terms of both cyber influence and cybersecurity.[7]

Traditionally, states have tested their powers during times of war—using hard power. For instance, all the mentioned resources were put to the test during World

[2] Dahl (1957).

[3] Nye (2023), Wilson III (2008).

[4] National Endowment for Democracy (2017).

[5] Klimburg and Faesen (2020).

[6] Lutscher et al. (2020).

[7] Topor and Tabachnik (2021).

War I and World War II in the first half of the twentieth century. Subsequently, during the second half of the twentieth century, the definition, expression and exercise of power shifted toward a softer stance, emphasizing technology, education and economic growth.[8] Similarly, in many parts of the world, softer power has been gaining significance over traditional hard power as the norms of using brute force decline. As Thomas Ward put it, "Moderation is not alien to war."[9] Nevertheless, in other parts of the world, such as the Middle East, military power is still perceived as vital in international affairs. Moreover, whereas states were once traditionally the main actors with significant influence in international relations and international security, with organizations having less influence and individuals almost none, in the twenty-first century, individual actors and other non-state actors have the potential to significantly influence international relations, international security and even a state's domestic security status. The actions of Edward Snowden,[10] who disclosed many classified American surveillance programs and related files, and Julian Assange,[11] founder of WikiLeaks, prove that even a few mouse clicks and leaks by individuals can have a tremendous impact on politics.

DIME is power. As defined in the 2019 Department of Defense (DoD) Dictionary of Military and Associated Terms, national power is exerted through DIME.[12] Different variations or ratios between diplomatic, information, military and economic influence can yield different types of power. Generally, diplomacy and information are associated much more with softer power, whereas military and economy are terms associated with hard power.[13]

There are three main approaches to measuring power in international relations: control over resources, control over actions, and control over events and outcomes. Traditionally, control over resources, such as military size and number of weapons, energy and food reservoirs and even financial resources, is indicative of a more physical and empirical power.[14] As Rudolph J. Rummel suggested in the early 1970s,

---

[8] Nye (1990).

[9] Ward (2001, 1).

[10] Edward Snowden is an American "whistle-blower." He leaked highly classified information from the National Security Agency (NSA), including information on several classified national surveillance programs, in 2013. The United States brought criminal charges against Snowden that year, while he fled to other countries such as Hong Kong and Russia. As these lines are written, Snowden's residence remains an unknown location in Russia. For more information see Snowden (2019).

[11] Julian Paul Assange is an Australian investigative journalist who founded the leaking platform WikiLeaks in 2006. The platform became internationally recognized and sought after when it published leaks on the American war in Afghanistan and Iraq. In November 2010, the United States opened a criminal investigation into the leaks under the Espionage Act of 1917. For more information on the case see Leigh and Harding (2013).

[12] U.S. Department of Defense (2019, 106).

[13] Nye (2008).

[14] Hart (1976).

dimensions of states can be assessed, and this measure is consistent over time. Unless a state collapses,[15] it is likely to maintain similar physical resources and abilities.[16]

Control over actions is simply another way of stating Robert Dahl's definition of power as the ability of A to get B to do something he otherwise would not. The scope of power and influence of one actor over another is limited, and if A can indeed influence B, it does not mean he can influence C, D and so on. Interestingly, in the context of smart power and asymmetrical conflicts, A might be able to influence B with hard power, but B can potentially influence A with softer or smarter power.[17] That is how the weak win wars and how big nations can lose small wars.[18]

The third main measure of power in international relations is control over events and outcomes. Under the logic of the rational choice theory, actors in international relations might want to control other actors or resources to achieve certain outcomes. A desired outcome for an actor might strengthen this actor in several aspects related to international relations and international security, such as security, economy, society and governance. Actors connect their actions to certain events they want to control. The events are then connected to a preferred outcome or goal. It is thus unlikely that an actor will achieve a desired outcome without first achieving control over events.[19] Several refuting examples are given in the next sections; cyber DIME, specifically the smart utilization of diplomacy and information, can help an actor achieve outcomes without controlling actual events—through propaganda or fake news, for example.

4.2 Diplomacy, Information, Military, Economy: Theoretical and Operational Definitions

Diplomacy is defined as an essential political activity in international relations with the purpose of securing an actor's objectives without the use of force, propaganda or applicable law—that is, in a peaceful manner using methods of negotiation and international deals, treaties and advocacy.[20] Alongside military and economic strength, diplomacy was an essential driver of the American victory in the Cold War. Now, in the age of information, diplomacy does not just consist of negotiations between the officials of two or more states, but it is operationally public and executed in cyberspace. In current times, diplomacy is public; it is an attempt to win and shape the hearts and minds of others—other states, other legislatures and other societies.[21]

[15] For this chapter and concept, a collapsing state is regarded as one which has lost a significant war, been conquered, or experienced an internal national or natural disaster, causing its political and institutional structure to completely collapse.

[16] Rummel (1972).

[17] Dahl (1957).

[18] Hart (1976), Arreguin-Toft (2001), Mack (1975).

[19] Hart (1976).

[20] Berridge (2015, 1), Barston (2014, 1–13).

[21] Neumann (2003).

Moreover, while there is a tremendous amount of information available worldwide due to the spread of communication methods such as the internet, the real fight in the arena of public diplomacy is the fight for attention. Cyber diplomacy is an emerging international practice that attempts to construct a cyber-international society, bridging the national interests of states with world society dynamics.[22]

Both global actors and the business world now regard attention as a form of currency. Diplomacy and information, which are defined and discussed in the next paragraph, both thrive on attention. Those who get public and global attention will achieve their goals, while those with larger issues or problems but with no public and global attention will not.[23] Lanham and Merkoski suggest that "Increasingly, attention is a form of capital. Some economists argue that attention in fact constitutes a parallel economy run on a virtual currency."[24]

Information is defined as the resolution of uncertainty. James Gleick defines information as letters, messages, sounds, images, news, instructions, figures, facts, signals and signs—almost all the things in our lives that provide us with certain knowledge. In their contemporary operational form, ICT such as the internet, emails, satellites, television, mobile phones and even the IoT are all significant mechanisms that provide each of us with the basics of information.[25] Through websites, phone calls and more, we receive letters, messages, sounds, images, news, instructions, figures, facts, signals, signs and many more types of information. Our brains can even extract information from smells.[26]

However, in the international arena, it is the responsibility of each side to use information wisely. That is, the side that spreads information must adapt it to suit its strategic goals, such as in the case of Russian propaganda and fake news, which is discussed later. The side that consumes and makes its decisions based on incoming information must fact-check and verify it. Otherwise, foreign powers could affect the receiving side's security. All the mentioned methods and platforms can spread information, be it true, false or vague.[27] Diplomacy and information, specifically the control over these terms and the ability to adapt them, are critical to a state's ability to influence international relations and international security.[28]

Military affairs and activities, or warfare, are traditionally defined using Clausewitz's definition of war: "War is thus an act of force to compel our enemy to do our will."[29] Moreover, Clausewitz asserts that the aim of war is to disarm the enemy.[30] Quincy Wright and Louise Leonard Wright argue that war is a conflict between political groups, especially sovereign states, carried out by armed forces of considerable

[22] Nye (2008), Barrinha and Renard (2017).

[23] Teixeira (2014).

[24] Lanham and Merkoski (2008, 2).

[25] Gleick (2012, 7).

[26] Eriksson and Giacomello (2006), Porter et al. (2005).

[27] Carson (2019).

[28] Larson et al. (2009), U.S. Department of Defense (2019, 154).

[29] Clausewitz (1975, 75).

[30] U.S. Department of Defense (2019, 77).

magnitude for a considerable period.[31] Although the discussion of what war is can be quite interesting, as Yehoshafat Harkabi discusses and explains in his *War and Strategy* manual, the modern operational definition can be very obscure.[32]

One operational definition of war and warfare is the use of force, any force, regardless of the weapons employed.[33] A more specific definition involves the prohibition of the threat or use of force. Article 2(4) of the United Nations Charter states that "All members [of the United Nations] shall refrain in their international relations from the threat or use of force against the territorial integrity or political independence of any State, or in any other manner inconsistent with the Purposes of the United Nations."[34] However, the *Tallinn Manual on the International Law Applicable to Cyber Warfare* specifically states that cyber operations by states or their agents are also defined as the use of force. It does not, however, include private individuals or organizations.[35] The second version of the Tallinn Manual states that cyber operations and espionage are not a clear violation of international law, though it is very vague: "Although peacetime cyber espionage by States does not per se violate international law, the methods by which it is carried out might do so."[36]

The Tallinn Manual also notes that while the use of force is an elusive term, some criteria can be applied to determine whether force (or threat) was used. These criteria are severity, immediacy, directness, invasiveness, measurability of effects, military character, state involvement and presumptive legality. Although these criteria are neither exhaustive nor binding, they are very useful for defining cyber military force in this chapter and for those dealing with cyber warfare in general.[37] Nevertheless, the various case studies presented in the next sections of this chapter prove that even these eight criteria are often inadequate.

Lastly, economy is traditionally defined as "the system of trade and industry by which the wealth of a country is made and used."[38] This definition avoids the eternal debate between capitalist and socialist economic systems. The economy this chapter refers to is mostly political—the methodology of economics applied to the analysis of political behaviors and institutions.[39] A state and a market exist in parallel with mutual interactions; this combination creates and defines modern political economies.[40] The operational definition of an economy is a hierarchical structure composed of a dominant core and a dependent periphery.[41] Interestingly, the theory of the dual

---

[31] Wright and Wright (1983, 3–4, 103–105).

[32] Harkabi (1990).

[33] United Nations (1996, para. 39).

[34] United Nations (1945, Chap. 1, Article 2).

[35] Schmitt (2013, 45–52).

[36] Schmitt (2017, 168).

[37] Ibid.

[38] Cambridge Dictionary, "Economy" (n.d.), https://dictionary.cambridge.org/dictionary/english/economy.

[39] Weingast and Wittman (2008, 3).

[40] Gilpin (2016, 8).

[41] Ibid, 93.

economy presents itself in reverse when addressing cyber DIME issues. While the first type of the dual economy theory, the modern and progressive economy, drives much of the world, it is in fact far more vulnerable to cyberattacks and influences than the second, traditional, non-modern type of local self-sufficient economy. Less developed, simple, economies and markets are thus less subject to cyberattacks and influences.[42]

Further, while classical realists would probably classify economy as a soft power, so-called currency wars are very concrete and hard.[43] Since the beginning of the twenty-first century, states have accused each other of engaging in currency wars, violation of trade deals and other types of economic aggression. In 2010, Brazil's finance minister, Guido Mantega, accused the United States of launching currency wars through quantitative easing and a lower dollar. During the American-Chinese trade blows of 2018–2020, China's leaders stated that the Chinese currency could be used as a weapon in the trade war. China's leader, Xi Jinping, threatened to weaken the Chinese currency to damage Western and American imports and exports.[44] Ray Dalio, the founder of the world's largest hedge fund, Bridgewater Associates, claimed in August 2019 that China could weaponize its massive United States Treasury debt holdings of approximately $1.11 trillion. The trade war may thus increase in complexity and danger since China and the United States have a debtor-creditor relationship, both in the governmental sphere and the private sphere.[45]

Another worrisome example is cybercrime. The Center for Strategic and International Studies (CSIS), in partnership with McAfee, concluded that nearly one percent of the global GDP, about $600 billion in 2018, was lost to cyber criminals.[46] By late 2020, cybercrime had stolen almost $1 trillion. Furthermore, cybercrime does more than just financial damage; efficiency, productivity, brand image and personal morale are also lost.[47] Cybercrime, converted to and manipulated by governmental cyberattacks, influence and exploitation, could potentially disrupt financial services capabilities, especially payment systems and stock exchange markets around the world.[48]

---

[42] Ibid, 66–67.

[43] Jervis (1994).

[44] Perlez and Stevenson (2019).

[45] Lee (2019).

[46] Lewis (2018).

[47] Smith and Lostri (2020).

[48] Mee and Schuermann (2018).

4.3 Cyber Warfare and Cyber DIME

Cyber warfare is the use of cyber weapons and other cyber systems and means to cause injury, death, damage, destruction, or influence of international actors and/or objects. Acts of cyber warfare can be executed by individuals, organizations, companies, states, state proxies and even AI entities.[49] Cyber warfare is now an integral part of wider national security strategies, and states aim to strengthen their homeland cyber security and secure their cyber capabilities in international relations and international security. Regarding cyber warfare strategy, there are two main approaches: a revolutionary approach and an evolutionary approach. The revolutionary approach sees cyber weapons such as malicious code attacks as a "revolution in military affairs" in the same way sailors once viewed the development and widespread use of air power—as something that could transform the strategy and power of states. The evolutionary approach sees cyber weapons as a tactical development. That is, military affairs and strategy have not changed in any dramatic way—states still long for power and influence in international relations and are willing to fight over it. In this view, the main change of cyber warfare is thus not strategic but tactical and technological: a conflict is a conflict, no matter the weapons—whether guns, bombs or malicious code.[50]

The United States National Cyber Strategy from September 2018 exemplifies the evolutionary approach.[51] In its goals and objectives, it is very similar to the United States National Security Strategy from December 2017.[52] Both emphasize four main pillars of strategy: (1) protect the American people, the homeland and the American way of life, (2) promote American prosperity, (3) preserve peace through strength, and (4) advance American influence.

Though the tactics, methods and innovations of cyberwarfare can be revolutionary, even the cyber nation of Israel is taking an evolutionary approach. In September 2017, the National Cyber Directorate of the Prime Minister's Office published a strategic brief on cyber security. Just as the American national cyber strategy, it focuses on offense and defense, on homeland security and on influence in matters of international relations and international security. There are three Israeli strategic pillars, and they are more obscure than the American ones. They aim to aggregate cyber robustness and develop systemic cyber resilience and national cyber defense.[53]

China and Russia, which have the potential to pose a strategic threat to the United States, Europe, East Asia, the Middle East and the rest of the world, have also emphasized and amplified their cyber capabilities in recent years.[54] The United Kingdom, through its National Cyber Security Strategy, has made similar suggestions to those

---

[49] Andress and Winterfeld (2013, 1–14).

[50] Valeriano et al. (2018, 1–21).

[51] The White House (2018).

[52] The White House (2017).

[53] National Cyber Directorate (2017).

[54] Coats (2019).

of the United States and other key actors regarding capabilities and security aspects.[55] In mid-2019, the European Union announced that it would run cyber war games to prepare for Russian and Chinese cyberattacks in light of a series of incidents of alleged Russian and Chinese cyberattacks on European Union member states.[56] Iran is a key affiliate of the Russo-Sino cyber initiatives as it is one of the most anti-Western states in the West Asia and Middle Eastern region. In July 2019, Iran and China agreed to cooperate against "U.S. unilateralism and hegemony in the field of IT."[57] Moreover, Iran, Russia and China continue their collaborations to prepare for a cyber war, each with its own unique strategic interests that contrast with American and Western international relations and international security interests.[58]

The Russian Federal Council, in a document titled "The Concept of the Cyber Security Strategy of the Russian Federation" (Russian: Концепция Стратегии Кибербезопасности Российской Федерации), has emphasized the growing importance of cyber warfare, ICT, and the utilization of cyber-related actions to accommodate and complement other acts in the international relations arena.[59] Russian officials are convinced that Moscow is locked in an ongoing existential international relations struggle. Russian military officials do not use the term cyber warfare. Instead, they conceptualize cyber warfare within the broader framework of information warfare, a holistic concept that includes computer network operations, electronic warfare, psychological operations and information operations.[60]

Daniel Ray Coats, the former director of United States intelligence, argues that Russia poses a very significant cyber threat, specifically in the form of espionage, influence and attacks through the cyber domain.[61] In August 2020, the United States Global Engagement Center (GEC), suggested that Russia has created an entire "ecosystem" of disinformation and propaganda platforms. Moscow uses bots, trolls, and official and non-official websites to spread chaos in the United States and Europe through disinformation.[62] Furthermore, Russian cyber warfare strategies include legal and practical limitations such as domestic internet regulations, monitoring and control. This puts Russian cyber sovereignty one step ahead of its Western opponents as the less regulated, more democratic nature of countries like the United States, the United Kingdom or Germany makes them more susceptible to cyberattacks.[63]

According to the NATO Cooperative Cyber Defence Centre of Excellence (CCDCOE) in Tallinn, Estonia, the arsenal of cyber warfare tactics includes several

---

[55] Dawda (2021).

[56] Bofey (2019).

[57] Doffman (2019).

[58] Coats (2019), Lindsey (2019).

[59] Committee of the Federation, n.d.

[60] Connell and Vogler (2016).

[61] Coats (2019).

[62] U.S. Department of State (2020).

[63] Topor and Tabachnik (2021).

actions: espionage, propaganda, denial of service (DoS), data modification and infrastructure manipulation or sabotage.[64] These threats are not directed merely against governmental databases or personal computers; they can effectively harm every connected item (i.e., IoT), including airplanes, ships, cars and critical infrastructure.[65] In effect, flying airplanes can be shot down without missiles, and ships can be sunk without torpedoes. Moreover, an airplane passenger with a laptop or even a tablet or smartphone can hijack an airplane without any weapons. It can even be done remotely. Airport security does not screen for malicious code, just for bombs and other harmful items.[66]

As mentioned, cyber DIME is a dynamic currency. Though it can theoretically qualify as a softer or smarter power, compared to traditional hard power, the fact that the United States, the European Union, Russia, China and even other smaller states, such as Israel, regard cyber DIME as an innovative extension of traditional international relations and international security strategies proves that cyber DIME is dynamic enough to be both soft and hard. Furthermore, as shown in the following sections of this chapter, it can complement traditional hard power utilizations. The different tactics mentioned by the CCDCOE can be measured using the Tallinn Manual's criteria: severity, immediacy, directness, invasiveness, measurability of effects, military character, state involvement and presumptive legality.[67] Thus, it can be assumed that any of the tactics (espionage, propaganda, DoS, data modification and infrastructure manipulation) can be regarded as the exercise of both soft power and hard power.

4.4 Significant Cyber DIME Incidents

It can often be challenging to understand the behavior of adversaries in cyber warfare; for that reason, several significant cyber DIME incidents are presented here before the global trends are analyzed. The tactics, methods and variations of cyber DIME operations (attacks and influences) are myriad. Significant examples, perpetrated by the competitors and opposers of the United States and other liberal Western states, from Russia to North Korea, have been chosen. However, it is not only non-Western countries that utilize cyberspace, and one can assume that those that developed cyberspace in the first place, particularly the United States, are also heavily invested in cyber warfare. Therefore, a case of Western origin is also examined. The significant incidents were chosen from a pool of 500 worldwide cyber operations collected and published by the Center for Strategic and International Studies

---

[64] Geers (2008).

[65] Maple (2017).

[66] National Business Aviation Association (2016), Perez (2015).

[67] See, generally, Schmitt (2013).

(CSIS)[68] with the input of three Israeli cyber warfare specialists.[69] The incidents are presented, analyzed and assessed using the theories and measures mentioned earlier in this chapter, and they include cases that represent different parts of DIME, such as a diplomacy and information-related incident, a military incident and an economic incident. The analyses show that each incident is both a stand-alone operation and a complementary action to other acts in international relations.

Throughout the analysis of the incidents and the global trends, questions are asked regarding measurements, criteria and tactics: Who initiated the cyber act and why—was it a state, a state's proxy, an organization, a company or an individual? Who is the victim? What did the incident achieve—was it control over resources, actions or outcomes and events? Was the incident severe, immediate, direct and invasive, did it have a measurable effect, a military character, and state involvement, and was it presumptively legal? Lastly, what type of incident was it in general—an act of espionage, propaganda, DoS, data modification or sabotage? It is also important to note that the measurements, criteria and tactics that are discussed in this section are neither entirely exhaustive nor binding for other cyber DIME incidents. Nevertheless, the most significant measurements, criteria and tactics are isolated and analyzed.

4.4.1 Russian Fake News and Influence Operations in Sweden

A significant example of cyber diplomacy, the promotion of values and the struggle for online attention is the Russian effort to influence Swedish politics and internal decision-making using information warfare, propaganda and fake news. This fake cyber diplomacy is directly related to Russia's geopolitical objective of keeping Sweden apart from NATO (and Finland, in this regard, which did join in 2023), thus minimizing the Western presence and influence in the Baltic region, Russia's backyard. Information is critical for any act in international relations and international security—soft, hard and smart power acts alike. Information can be true, false and even debatable. In that regard, information and disinformation are effective tools in pursuing a country's international relations and international security strategic goals. As presented below, Russia's information warfare is both a stand-alone operation as well as an operation that complements more traditional approaches, such as submarine reconnaissance and intimidation.[70] Furthermore, it is not internationally binding, not illegal, to spread fake news.

[68] "Significant Cyber Incidents," Center for Strategic and International Studies, https://www.csis.org/programs/technology-policy-program/significant-cyber-incidents

[69] A set of interviews was conducted in August and September 2020 in Tel Aviv, Israel, with a retired Intelligence branch officer from the Israeli Defense Force and a senior competitive intelligence consultant. Both interviewees were presented with the research findings of this chapter and the CSIS cyber operations pool. They mentioned several significant incidents from the pool, as well as several others that are mentioned briefly throughout the chapter.

[70] Henley (2017).

The Baltic region follows the geographical borders of Denmark, Sweden, Finland, Germany, Poland, Estonia, Lithuania, Latvia and Russia. Of the mentioned states, excluding Russia (as NATO was established to counter the Soviet Union in the first place), only Sweden is not a NATO member. In this case, Russia sought to keep the status quo of isolating Estonia, Latvia and Lithuania from other NATO members in Europe. This division weakens NATO; thus, maintaining the status quo helps Russia in its international relations and international security strategies.[71]

In January 2017, the Swedish Institute of International Affairs accused the Russian Federation of using fake news, false documents and disinformation as part of a coordinated propaganda campaign to influence public opinion and decision-making in Sweden. According to the report by the Swedish Institute of International Affairs, Russia was guilty of forging documents and interviews, spreading false information on mainstream Swedish, Russian, and international media using Russian news agencies RT and Sputnik, and operating an army of internet and social media trolls and bots that targeted Swedish journalists and academics.[72] It had also allegedly hacked several influential Twitter accounts. All these efforts, the majority of which took place as cyber operations, were meant to portray a more positive image of Russia and a more negative image of the West to the Swedish people and decision-makers.[73] Sweden's prime minister, Stefan Löfven, claimed that he "cannot rule out" Russia trying to influence the 2018 elections and control the outcome in its strategic favor.[74]

As a precaution, five of Sweden's largest media platforms created a fact-checking collaborative to increase fact-checking efforts.[75] In January 2018, ahead of the Riksdag elections in September 2018, Anders Thornberg, former head of Sweden's security service, argued that the largest threat to Sweden's security was Russia, which lies just across the Baltic Sea. He noted that in recent years, Russian submarines had also been spotted in Sweden's territorial waters in the Baltic Sea, an attempt to intimidate Sweden and other Baltic countries. In this case, the actions of submarines and web bots complemented each other. Mr. Thornberg noted that one of his top priorities was to protect the Swedish election from Russian influence and from Russian attempts to spread chaos in the Swedish political arena. The Russian influence operations included, for instance, forged letters about arms deals with Ukraine, fake news articles about former ministers, fake accusations of immigrants vandalizing a church and so on. Most of this fake propaganda was spread on social media by web bots and trolls. As Thornberg noted, the aim was not to push a particular viewpoint or political candidate but to spread chaos.[76] Thus, Russia sought to control outcomes in Sweden in a sophisticated manner by not allowing Sweden to have its own control over domestic issues.

---

[71] Blank (1998).

[72] Helmus et al. (2018).

[73] Kragh and Åsberg (2017).

[74] Henley (2017).

[75] Cederberg (2018).

[76] Corera (2018).

By the Tallinn Manual's standards, the Russian propaganda campaign in Sweden was not very invasive and was mostly indirect. The measurability of the effects is very problematic—how can one effectively measure fake news? Moreover, even though Russia was behind the campaign, Sputnik and RT News are independent organizations, even though they operate under Russia's direction and finance. A propaganda campaign is immoral but legal. That is, it is not against international law to spread fake news, which some might even call competing narratives.

4.4.2 The Russian Cyberattack on the Ukrainian Power Grid

The Russian cyberattack on the Ukrainian power grid on December 23, 2015, is a very significant example of the utilization of cyber warfare to compel an enemy to do your will, as defined by Clausewitz. This case study is important due to its sophistication and because many tactics were involved: espionage, DoS, data modification and sabotage. It is also considered the largest known successful cyberattack on a nation's power grid.[77] Approximately, a quarter of a million Ukrainians were left without electricity for several hours. The Russian cyberattack can be regarded as both a stand-alone operation due to its severity and immediacy as well as an operation that aided and complemented other, hard power-related operations, as Russia had invaded Eastern Ukraine in early 2014 utilizing "hybrid warfare" strategies.[78] The Russian cyberattacks continued throughout the years and included another significant ransomware attack, named NotPetya, on Ukrainian banks, its power grid, government offices and more.[79]

The Russian cyberattack on the Ukrainian power grid was an advanced persistent threat (APT)[80] that aimed to jump the air-gapping security measures (an independent network, not connected to the internet) that protect operational technologies (OT) like power stations. It consisted of two main phases: the reconnaissance, preparation and development phase (Phase 1) and the execution phase (Phase 2).[81] Together, the phases represent a basic cyber kill chain, which generally comprises reconnaissance, intrusion, exploitation, privilege escalation, lateral movement, obfuscation or anti-forensics, DoS and exfiltration.[82] The main goal of the cyber operation by Russian intelligence was to effectively establish control over the Supervisory Control and Data Acquisition (SCADA) systems of the power grid in Ukraine, which they did.

---

[77] Kostyuk and Zhukov (2019).

[78] Greenberg (2017).

[79] Dawda (2021), Farmer (2018).

[80] An advanced persistent threat (APT) is a sophisticated and prolonged cyberattack in which an intruder gains undetected access to a network with the intention of stealing highly sensitive data, conducting espionage or causing disruption. APT attacks are characterized by their continuous and clandestine nature, as well as their use of sophisticated hacking techniques to evade existing security measures. These attacks are mainly carried out by countries (states) or state-supported groups.

[81] Lee et al. (2016).

[82] Buckbee (2018).

It is widely believed that both NotPetya and the BlackEnergy malware were used in this attack.[83]

Their control over SCADA allowed the hackers to sabotage, manipulate and deny proper treatment. The hackers established control over the Ukrainian Kyiv Oblast power company, a regional electricity distribution company and thirty other substations. They sabotaged the electricity distribution, which caused outages. Then they manipulated the user interface into presenting different information. That is, problems were affecting internal OT systems, but the external graphical presentation presented different information to the engineers of the power company. To put it simply, imagine that somebody put potatoes in the oven and set the timer for 45 min at 180 °C, but the actual time was doubled, and it heated to 230 °C —resulting in burnt potatoes. This manipulation caused a lot of confusion and delayed the response time of the repair. They also manipulated the schedule of the uninterruptible power supply (UPS) systems. More confusion was caused by another simple but smart move. The hackers flooded the Ukrainian company's customer support telephone lines, meaning that customers could not reach the line and report their outages. Lastly, the hackers used a KillDisk method to erase the master boots of the systems and sabotaged the communications between the power stations and the substations, making the issues even harder to resolve.[84] Weeks before the cyberattack, the European Union had extended sanctions on Russia, while the Ukrainian resistance and rhetoric against the Russian annexation and aggression was growing stronger. The attack fits extremely well within that timeline and chain of events. Russia's response was a cyber DIME.[85]

By the Tallinn Manual's standards, the Russian cyberattack was severe as it affected hundreds of thousands of Ukrainians. It was immediate, and the effect could be measured instantaneously—Ukrainians either had power or not. The act was military in character and was complementary to Russia's hybrid warfare in Ukraine. The cyberattack could be interpreted as an illegal act if Ukraine could prove, with solid evidence, that Russia was behind it.

4.4.3 The North Korean WannaCry Ransomware Attack

Cyberattacks on financial institutions, both those carried out by international relations adversaries and by cyber criminals, are often motivated by financial incentives. States usually seek to alter the economies of other international relations actors, while cyber criminals seek to gain profit. Banks, stock exchanges, other financial corporations and even automated teller machines (ATMs) and individuals can all be affected. A significant financial cyberattack was the mid-2017 WannaCry ransomware attack attributed to the North Korean Lazarus hacking group. This North Korean-led attack

[83] Lee et al. (2016).

[84] Ibid.

[85] Center for Strategic and International Studies (n.d.)

was thought to be general and not specifically aimed at any of North Korea's adversaries. States and large IT systems were the main targets. It was also quite small in financial scale (or gain) and limited in its direct impact.[86] Still, it was chosen for analysis since it has some unique characteristics that are important for the further understanding and analysis of cyber DIME incidents: it was carried out by a state-led proxy, a hacking group, and its purpose was to fund other North Korean resistance activities and to test cyber capabilities and global reactions.[87]

The initial outbreak of the WannaCry ransomware attack was in May 2017, and the malware is still spreading.[88] Computers running older versions of Microsoft Windows were targeted. The WannaCry ransomware is essentially a computer worm[89] that spreads and encrypts devices. To decrypt a device, victims were asked to pay a ransom of around $300 to $600. The ransomware uses the EternalBlue exploit and the DoublePulsar backdoor tool, which were both initially used by the National Security Agency (NSA) and were later leaked by the Shadow Brokers hacking group. Following the May 2017 attack, Microsoft issued a security patch aimed at tackling the exploits and preventing the ransomware from taking hold. In August 2017, intelligence agencies around the world found out that more than $140,000 had been withdrawn from Bitcoin accounts associated with the WannaCry attack.[90] The North Koreans' sophistication managed to turn a cyber DIME into an actual dime.

The ransomware was seemingly indiscriminate; it affected private users, corporations and governments. The ransomware affected outdated operating systems as they were not maintained by users or IT managers. However, it was thoughtfully planned and was in fact targeted. The attackers knew beforehand that private users tend to update their devices more often than big organizations and governmental IT systems. Large IT systems need to be updated and maintained all at once to function properly, and the maintenance work can slow down business or governmental operations. Since private users commonly own only one or two Windows devices, they update them whenever needed. In addition, organizational licenses are expensive, and many governments worldwide use the operating systems without contract renewal. With these facts in mind, the attackers knew exactly who they were after. Governmental, financial and healthcare information cannot be held encrypted as it is too crucial. The attackers made a safe bet.[91] One of the most severe cases of infection was in the United Kingdom where the National Health Service (NHS) was criticized for using outdated IT systems, including Windows XP, then a seventeen-year-old operating system, that could be vulnerable to cyberattacks. The impact was severe and saw thousands of life-saving appointments canceled. The IT update would have

[86] Perlroth (2017).

[87] Bossert (2017), Carlisle (2017).

[88] Winder (2019).

[89] A computer worm is a standalone malware program that replicates itself to spread to other devices through networks.

[90] Gibbs (2017).

[91] This logical process was described by the interviewees mentioned earlier in this chapter.

been expensive, but surely not as expensive as the estimated damage of over $100 million.[92]

By the Tallinn Manual standards, the North Korean ransomware attack was severe as it denied people access to their own data. The same point is relevant to the question of measurability of effect. It was immediate. As for directness, it could be interpreted either way, although the analysis suggests that the ransomware was indirect only to masquerade its direct objectives. Finally, the ransomware attack was illegal as it denied people access to their own data.

4.4.4 The SolarWinds Cyberattack: Was It Russia?

The SolarWinds cyberattack, discovered in December 2020, was one of the largest and most significant and complex breaches in recent cybersecurity history. This attack, also known as SUNBURST or Solorigate, emerged as a sophisticated supply chain attack that targeted SolarWinds, a prominent information technology (IT) management software provider. It compromised SolarWinds' Orion platform, a widely used network management tool. Cyber attackers gained unauthorized access to SolarWinds' software build system, embedding malicious code into software updates distributed to its customers. The attack was orchestrated by stealthily inserting a malicious backdoor within the software build process, leading to the deployment of tainted updates to SolarWinds' Orion customers, which included very large companies like Microsoft and Deloitte as well as governmental agencies in the United States and around the world. The attackers, believed to be Russian proxy hacker groups known by the names of APT29, Cozy Bear, and the Dukes disguised their actions to avoid detection, enabling the compromised software to operate undetected for an extended period. The backdoor allowed threat actors to infiltrate numerous high-profile organizations and government agencies.[93]

The hackers likely studied the source code and customer data to select their target. Orion was the perfect choice as it was the crown jewel of SolarWinds' products, accounting for approximately 45% of the company's revenue and occupying a privileged place in customer network—it connected to and communicated with a lot of other servers. The hackers could hijack those connections to jump to other systems without arousing suspicion. SolarWinds was, allegedly, Russia's gateway to many other Western companies and agencies.[94]

The SolarWinds breach had a far-reaching impact, compromising the networks of various organizations, including multiple United States government agencies like the Department of Defense, Department of State, Department of Homeland Security (DHS) and the Treasury. Additionally, private sector entities and multinational

---

92 Field (2018); Carlisle (2017).

93 Zetter (2023), Kumar (n.d.), US Government Accountability Office (2021), Alkhadra et al. (2021), Willett (2023).

94 Ibid.

corporations were affected, leading to concerns regarding the exposure of sensitive data and intellectual property. Companies like cybersecurity company FireEye, the previously mentioned Microsoft and Deloitte, as well as Intel and Cisco were all breached and infected.[95]

The discovery of the SolarWinds cyberattack sent shockwaves through the cybersecurity community, prompting a global response from governments, security firms and affected organizations. The United States Cybersecurity and Infrastructure Security Agency (CISA) issued emergency directives and provided guidance on mitigating the attack's impact. The DHS established a SolarWinds task force to coordinate the response and provide assistance to affected organizations. President Joe Biden signed an executive order to enhance cybersecurity defenses and improve government response capabilities.[96] The SolarWinds cyberattack served as a reminder of the evolving nature of cybersecurity threats and the need for continuous adaptation. Supply chain attacks, where attackers exploit weaknesses in third-party software to compromise downstream targets, have become increasingly sophisticated, requiring a comprehensive approach to risk management and threat mitigation. Organizations have since increased their adoption of zero-trust security models, assuming that all systems and data are potentially compromised, and now implement layered security controls to deter, detect and respond to attacks.

Who did it, and to what end? While initial assessments pointed toward state-sponsored actors, specifically ones associated with Russia, attribution remains a complex and ongoing process in the realm of cybersecurity as it is extremely difficult to gather direct proof and reverse-engineer cyberattacks. Various cybersecurity experts and agencies continue to analyze the attack to identify the precise perpetrators and motives behind the breach. As mentioned, it is believed that a large number of engineers and hackers collaborated to execute this attack, suggesting that it was probably state sponsored. Groups like APT29 (Cozy Bear) have left footprints from ongoing and previous attacks, but no direct and robust evidence connecting this attack to Russia has been published to the public yet. Furthermore, as the attack did not include extensive ransomware requests, the main purpose of this cyberattack is believed to be espionage. The attackers were likely interested in gathering intelligence on a wide range of targets, including government agencies, private corporations and critical infrastructure providers, and attempted to hide malicious code in the compromised companies and agencies for future use. By compromising the Orion software, a network management system used by many of the abovementioned organizations, the attackers gained access to a vast trove of sensitive data, including email communications, financial records and intellectual property.[97]

To conclude, the SolarWinds cyberattack currently stands as a significant moment in the evolution of cybersecurity threats—it was one of the largest cyber espionage attacks known to date. Its impact reverberated across government agencies, businesses and global cybersecurity strategies. The incident emphasized not only the

---

[95] Ibid.

[96] Ibid.; Temple-Raston (2021).

[97] Ibid.

technical challenges of cybersecurity but also the challenges of attribution and retaliation. As with the previous case studies in this section, we might ask what a country can do if it suspects another country has engaged in espionage when there is no kinetic damage. The review of (the lack of) cyber law in Chap. 3 hints at possible solutions—countries can lock their cyber borders, retaliate and risk escalation of the conflict, or enhance their security and respond with similar means: hacking by proxy.

4.4.5 Russian Meddling in the 2016 United States Presidential Elections

The 2016 United States presidential elections saw unprecedented interference from Russian entities, which stirred controversy and raised concerns about the integrity of the democratic process—and even more about the integrity of an electoral system affected by social media. It prompted the simple question—who elects the president? The people or foreign influencers? The intervention consisted primarily of covert operations aimed at influencing public opinion, spreading disinformation and hacking political entities' systems. The Russians exerted their influence through social media manipulations and hacking with the aim of destabilizing the electoral system and presidential campaigns, as well as creating public chaos.

As special counsel Robert Mueller concluded in his investigation, based on his experience as the sixth Director of the Federal Bureau for Investigations (FBI), Russian operatives exploited social media platforms, particularly Facebook, Twitter and Instagram, to disseminate divisive content and mis/disinformation. Entities like the Internet Research Agency, a Russian troll farm posing as a company, led these efforts, reaching millions of Americans with targeted propaganda. Moreover, Russian intelligence agencies, notably the GRU, hacked into the Democratic National Committee's (DNC) and Hillary Clinton campaign's emails. They leaked sensitive information via WikiLeaks and other platforms with the objective of undermining Hillary Clinton's candidacy.[98] Russia's intervention aimed to sow discord, amplify existing political divisions and undermine faith in democratic institutions. It can be assumed that the ultimate goal was to damage Clinton's candidacy and boost Donald Trump's chances of winning the election.[99]

The dissemination of false information and divisive content through social media influenced public opinion, exacerbating political polarization. While debates persist about the direct impact on the election results, the interference led to heightened scrutiny of election security and raised questions about the legitimacy of the electoral process. However, as no international laws made Russia's actions entirely

[98] See Mueller, Robert S. III, Volume I, 2019; Mueller, Robert S. III, Volume II (2019), Badawy et al. (2018).

[99] Ibid.; Abrams (2019).

illegal, as explained in the previous chapters, the United States opted to retaliate using soft means. In response to the interference, the United States government imposed sanctions on Russia, expelled diplomats, and initiated cybersecurity measures to strengthen its governmental cybersecurity and, in particular, the security of the electoral process. It also launched several inquiries and investigations, including the investigations and legal proceedings of special counsel Robert Mueller and congressional inquiries.[100]

Russia used sharp power to try to control the outcome of the 2016 United States presidential election; in doing so, it intervened in the integrity and sovereignty of the United States, particularly its electoral system. However, Russia did not directly violate any international laws, as no such laws exist. Using proxies, Russia disseminated mis/disinformation and sowed chaos in the electoral process, undermining Hillary Clinton and helping to publicize Donald Trump. The American people did indeed elect him, but who brainwashed them—if that did occur—and how can such a connection be proven? To this day, no hard evidence has been provided. Many people, companies and organizations were associated with the 2016 election interference, but they were all proxies, and Russia denied such allegations, regardless. Thus, as no kinetic damage was done, the United States could only retaliate mildly by sanctioning those it considered responsible.[101] Of course, this again raises the question of attribution and deterrence in cyberspace. Can a country retaliate over "fake news"? And can it make itself resilient to such? This question, in particular, is examined in Chap. 5.

4.4.6 Stuxnet: An Attack on Iranian Centrifuges

The Stuxnet case was a pivotal moment in the early years of cyber warfare, marking a paradigm shift in the way countries dealt with conflict in the digital realm. This sophisticated computer worm, first uncovered in 2010, targeted Iran's nuclear program with unprecedented precision and destructive capability. Its success demonstrated the potential of cyberweapons to inflict physical damage on critical infrastructure. Although many details are still unknown, it is estimated that Stuxnet can be traced back to the early 2000s, when Western concerns over Iran's nuclear ambitions prompted a covert operation codenamed Operation Olympic Games—a joint effort between the United States and Israel against Iran's uranium enrichment program. The Iranian program was a crucial step in developing nuclear weapons, an effort that is ongoing to this day. Initially, the sophisticated cyber weapon Stuxnet was deployed to prevent Iran from developing nuclear weapons and undermine the development process, but it also worked as a deterrent, sending a clear message to Iran and other

---

[100] Ibid.

[101] Nye (2016).

countries that the United States and Israel would not hesitate to use any means necessary to prevent such initiatives or developments.[102]

It is assumed that the development of Stuxnet involved a team of highly skilled programmers and cybersecurity experts tasked with creating malware capable of infiltrating Iran's air-gapped industrial control systems (ICS)—networks isolated from the internet to prevent cyberattacks. The worm's complexity was unprecedented, requiring a deep understanding of Siemens software, the control system used in Iran's centrifuges, and the ability to exploit multiple zero-day vulnerabilities—previously unknown software flaws. It spread primarily through infected USB drives, targeting Windows-based systems within Iran's nuclear facilities. Once installed, the worm replicated itself and sought out Siemens control systems, specifically targeting the programmable logic controllers (PLCs) that controlled the centrifuges. The worm's primary objective was to sabotage the centrifuges, causing them to spin erratically and ultimately self-destruct. It achieved this by manipulating the PLC software, altering the centrifuges' operating parameters in subtle but destructive ways. This sabotage caused significant damage to Iran's nuclear program, delaying its progress by an estimated two years.

The attack also raised concerns about the proliferation of cyberweapons, as the technology and expertise used in Stuxnet could fall into the hands of malicious actors. The victim of Stuxnet, Iran, increased its cybersecurity measures and further isolated the networks related to its nuclear program. Interestingly though, while the United States and Israel strived to deter Iran, this cyberattack actually prompted Iran to arm itself with cyber knowledge and cyber means, to develop not only defensive but also offensive capabilities and to strike back. Iranian cyberattacks on Israel and the United States have been on the rise ever since.[103]

The origin of Stuxnet is still unclear, and Iran could not directly connect it to the United States or Israel, although it has accused them publicly. In the case of Stuxnet, as in the case of the Russian hack on the Ukrainian power grid, physical damage was the goal, and it was achieved, although there was no significant loss of human life. Still, such cases raise debates over the threshold of cyberattacks—under which circumstances and after what amount of damage can a country retaliate by kinetic means and shoot or bomb the other side? Although proxy wars in the Gulf area and the Middle East have since been prominent, Iran has made no directly related open attack.[104]

[102] Langner (2011), Kushner (2013), Farwell and Rohozinski (2011), Setton (2023).

[103] Lyngaas (2023).

[104] Sen (2015), Dehghan (2011), Zetter (2015).

4.5 Cyber DIME Trends Worldwide

Cyber DIME warfare is a fluid currency. Moreover, it has grown in capacity and impact over the years. Billions of cyberattacks are conducted by different international relations actors each month. Still, not all of these are accessible and transparent enough for academic analysis. In order to analyze the cyberattacks properly, extensive information is needed. The CSIS' publicly accessible list of over 500 cyberattacks was chosen for analysis for these operational reasons. Below, the incidents are analyzed using descriptive statistics and a cross-tabulation methodology.

Each cyberattack is broken down into different segments: tactics, measurement of power in international relations, perpetrator, victim and date (month and year). First, the key frequencies of cyber warfare incidents are presented. Next, the cross-tabulation analysis presents key trends and addresses which tactics were mostly used by which actors, which tactics were mostly used to control which measurements, and which tactics were mostly used against which actors.

4.5.1 Descriptive Statistics

Tables 4.1, 4.2, 4.3, 4.4 present the frequencies of the tactics, perpetrators, victims, and the measurement of power.[105] As presented, between May 2006 and December 2019, the most frequently used tactic was a general hacking campaign consisting of phishing and targeting methods. The second most frequently used tactic was manipulation/sabotage. The third most frequently used tactic was espionage. Furthermore, of the 500 cyberattacks, 367 were used to control resources and 89 to control actors. Eight cyberattacks were made to control resources, actors and outcomes together.

As for the perpetrators and the victims, 165 cyberattacks were perpetrated by states, almost a third. Individuals were responsible for 113 incidents, and 58 incidents were perpetrated by state proxies. Organizations made 5 cyberattacks. States suffered the vast majority of cyberattacks, with 273 incidents, and companies suffered 136 incidents. Individuals suffered 54 incidents. This finding contributes to the argument that the North Korean WannaCry ransomware attack was not entirely aimed at individuals.

[105] The findings presented in the text are cumulative. The analysis and the way findings are presented in the Tables 4.1, 4.2, 4.3, 4.4 are segmented into sole values and combinations of values for better precision.

Table 4.1 Frequency of tactics in cyber DIME warfare

Tactic	*N*	%
Data modification	1	0.2
Data modification, manipulation/sabotage	3	0.6
Denial of service	12	2.4
Denial of service, manipulation/sabotage	7	1.4
Espionage	120	24.0
Espionage, Denial of service	1	0.2
Espionage, manipulation/sabotage	19	3.8
General hacking campaign	207	41.4
Manipulation/sabotage	117	23.4
Manipulation/sabotage, propaganda	2	0.4
Manipulation/sabotage, propaganda, espionage	1	0.2
Propaganda	7	1.4
valid (no data)	3	0.6
Sum	500	100.0

Table 4.2 Frequency of measurement of power in international relations—control over what

Control over	*N*	%
Actors	21	4.2
Actors, outcomes	15	3.0
Outcomes	8	1.6
Resources	313	62.6
Resources, actors	45	9
Resources, actors, outcomes	8	1.6
Resources, outcomes	1	0.2
Valid (no data)	89	17.8
Sum	500	100.0

Table 4.3 Frequency of perpetrators

Perpetrated by	N	%
Company	1	0.2
Individual	110	22.0
Individual, company	2	0.4
Individual, organization	1	0.2
Organization	4	0.8
State	164	32.8
State proxy	57	11.4
State, state proxy	1	0.2
Valid (no data)	160	32.0
Sum	500	100.0

Table 4.4 Frequency of victim types

Victim type	N	%
Company	115	23.0
Company, individual	2	0.4
Company, state	13	2.6
Individual	44	8.8
Individual, company, state	1	0.2
Organization	43	8.6
Organization, company	1	0.2
State	244	48.8
State proxy	9	1.8
State proxy, company	1	0.2
State, company, organization	3	0.6
State, individual	7	1.4
State, Organization	2	0.4
State, state proxy	3	0.6
Valid (no data)	12	2.4
Sum	500	100.0

4.5.2 *Cross Tabulation*

Tables 4.5, 4.6, 4.7 present the connections between the variables. Table 4.5 presents the connection between tactics and the measurement of power in international relations. It addresses which tactic was mostly used to control which measurement. Table 4.6 presents the connection between tactics and types of perpetrators. Table 4.7 presents the connection between tactics and types of victims.[106]

The tactics most frequently used to control resources were general hacking campaigns, manipulation/sabotage and espionage (Table 4.5). To control actors, perpetrators mostly used general hacking campaigns and espionage. To control both actors and resources, perpetrators used espionage as their main tactic. To control outcomes, DoS and manipulation/sabotage were mostly used. To control all three—resources, actors and outcomes—general hacking campaigns were used.

The various tactics were used by all types of actors (Table 4.6). States conducted 63 out of a total of 207 general hacking campaign incidents. Individuals performed 45 general hacking campaigns. Of the 117 manipulation/sabotage incidents, 40 were carried out by individuals. As for espionage, states used this tactic 58 times out of the total incidence of 120. State proxies mostly used general hacking campaigns and espionage tactics.

[106] The presentation of findings in the text and in Tables 4.5, 4.6, 4.7 differs from the descriptive statistics presented above. They are presented in an isolated manner. Sole values are highlighted rather than combinations of values.

Table 4.5 Connection between tactics and measurement of power in international relations

Control over tactic	Valid (no data)	Actors	Actors, outcomes	Outcomes	Resources	Resources, actors	Resources, actors, outcomes	Resources, outcomes	Sum
Valid (no data)	3	0	0	0	0	0	0	0	3
Data modification	0	0	0	0	0	1	0	0	1
Data modification, Manipulation/ sabotage	0	0	0	0	3	0	0	0	3
Denial of service	2	0	1	0	6	1	1	1	12
Denial of service, Manipulation/ sabotage	0	0	1	3	3	0	0	0	7
Espionage	4	8	1	0	**85**	20	2	0	**120**
Espionage, denial of service	0	0	0	0	0	1	0	0	1
Espionage, manipulation/ sabotage	2	0	0	0	17	0	0	0	19
General hacking campaign	71	8	3	2	**104**	15	4	0	**207**
Manipulation/ sabotage	7	3	3	2	**95**	6	1	0	**117**

(continued)

Table 4.5 (continued)

Control over tactic	Valid (no data)	Actors	Actors, outcomes	Outcomes	Resources	Resources, actors	Resources, actors, outcomes	Resources, outcomes	Sum
Manipulation/ sabotage, propaganda	0	0	1	0	0	1	0	0	2
Manipulation/ sabotage, propaganda, espionage	0	0	0	1	0	0	0	0	1
Propaganda	0	2	5	0	0	0	0	0	7

Table 4.6 Connection between tactics and types of perpetrators

Perpetrated by tactic	Valid (no data)	Company	Individual	Individual, company	Individual, organization	Organization	State	State proxy	State, state proxy	Sum
Valid (no data)	2	0	0	0	0	0	1	0	0	3
Data modification	0	0	0	0	0	0	0	1	0	1
Data modification, manipulation/ sabotage	1	0	0	0	0	1	1	0	0	3
Denial of service	3	0	2	0	0	0	6	1	0	12
Denial of service, manipulation/ sabotage	1	0	2	0	0	0	4	0	0	7
Espionage	26	1	16	0	1	1	**58**	17	0	**120**
Espionage, denial of service	1	0	0	0	0	0	0	0	0	1
Espionage, manipulation/ sabotage	4	0	3	1	0	0	7	4	0	19
General hacking campaign	70	0	**45**	1	0	1	**63**	26	1	**207**
Manipulation/ sabotage	50	0	**40**	0	0	0	20	7	0	**117**

(continued)

Table 4.6 (continued)

Perpetrated by tactic	Valid (no data)	Company	Individual	Individual, company	Individual, organization	Organization	State	State proxy	State, state proxy	Sum
Manipulation/ sabotage, data modification	0	0	1	0	0	1	0	0	0	2
Manipulation/ sabotage, denial of service	0	0	0	0	0	0	1	0	0	1
Manipulation/ sabotage, espionage	2	0	1	0	0	0	3	1	0	7

Table 4.7 Connection between tactics and victim types

Victim type tactics	Valid (no data)	Company	Company, individual	Company, state	Individual	Individual, company, state	Organization	Organization, company	State
Valid (no data)	3	0	0	0	0	0	0	0	0
Data modification	0	1	0	0	0	0	0	0	0
Data modification, manipulation/sabotage	0	1	0	0	0	0	0	0	2
Denial of service	0	5	0	0	0	0	2	0	4
Denial of service, manipulation/sabotage	0	1	0	0	0	0	1	0	5
Espionage	3	**25**	0	3	14	0	15	0	**54**
Espionage, denial of service	0	0	0	0	1	0	0	0	0
Espionage, manipulation/sabotage	0	3	0	1	3	1	2	0	7
General hacking campaign	5	**36**	2	6	18	0	15	1	**111**
Manipulation/sabotage	1	**43**	0	3	6	0	8	0	**53**

(continued)

Table 4.7 (continued)

Victim type tactics	Valid (no data)	Company	Company, individual	Company, state	Individual	Individual, company, state	Organization	Organization, company	State
Manipulation/ sabotage, propaganda	0	0	0	0	0	0	0	0	2
Manipulation/ sabotage, propaganda, espionage	0	0	0	0	0	0	0	0	1
Propaganda	0	0	0	0	2	0	0	0	5

Victim type tactics	State proxy	State proxy, company	State, company, organization	State, individual	State, organization	State, state proxy	Sum
Valid (no data)	0	0	0	0	0	0	3
Data modification	0	0	0	0	0	0	1
Data modification, manipulation/sabotage	0	0	0	0	0	0	3
Denial of service	0	0	0	1	0	0	12
Denial of service, manipulation/sabotage	0	0	0	0	0	0	7
Espionage	3	0	1	1	1	0	**120**
Espionage, denial of service	0	0	0	0	0	0	1
Espionage, manipulation/sabotage	1	0	0	1	0	0	19
General hacking campaign	3	1	2	4	0	3	**207**

(continued)

Table 4.7 (continued)

Victim type tactics	State proxy	State proxy, company	State, company, organization	State, individual	State, organization	State, state proxy	Sum
Manipulation/sabotage	2	0	0	0	1	0	**117**
Manipulation/sabotage, propaganda	0	0	0	0	0	0	2
Manipulation/sabotage, propaganda, espionage	0	0	0	0	0	0	1
Propaganda	0	0	0	0	0	0	7

All victim types suffered all types of tactics (Table 4.7). Of the 207 general hacking campaigns, 111 were aimed at states. They were aimed at companies 63 times. Manipulation/sabotage was aimed at states 53 times and at companies 43 times. Espionage was used against states 54 times and against companies 25 times.

4.6 Conclusion

How is power projected in the global arena through the cyber domain? Cyber DIME power is not only softer and more dynamic than traditional hard and soft powers, but it is also not bound to a particular size or strength and can be utilized by international actors to complement other, more traditional operations. The main findings confirm and extend Herbert Lin and Amy Zegart's argument that offensive cyber operations are becoming increasingly prominent in countries' foreign policies, as well as among other international actors.[107] Furthermore, global powers are becoming more vulnerable and losing their international influence and reach since other states and even non-state actors are utilizing cyber DIME to amplify their power.

Cyber DIME, as a way of exercising power, is not revolutionary but evolutionary. The main aims of international actors, mainly states, have changed little in the last few hundred years. That is, the grand strategy remains the same even while the tactics change and become more up to date with cyber capabilities. International actors now perceive cyber warfare as an integral part of international relations and international security strategies. Theoretically and practically, cyber DIME can be divided into softer power (diplomacy and information) and harder power (military and economy). It can be used as hard power, as exemplified by the Russian cyberattack on the Ukrainian power grid. Another example is the North Korean WannaCry ransom campaign which acted, de facto, both as a forced crowdfunding mechanism and as a targeted financial cybercrime.

The dynamic and illusive nature of cyber DIME means that the attribution of actions is another key issue; it creates a victim without pinpointing a definitive perpetrator. Moreover, of all 500 cyber incidents analyzed, the most frequently used tactic is a general hacking campaign, which usually consists of phishing and targeting methods, the second most common tactic is manipulation/sabotage, and the third is espionage. The Tallinn Manual clearly states that cyber espionage is not a clear violation of international law. Targeting, phishing, espionage and information collection in general are very vague in terms of legality. Moreover, the utilization of diplomacy and information for cyber warfare, propaganda and disinformation is not illegal at all. Bots, trolls and private news agencies can influence global affairs without violating a single international law. However, the findings of the trends analysis do align with the traditional theory of measurements of power in international relations; out of the 500 cyber incidents, 363 were carried out to control resources (some of which also targeted other measurements). Eighty-nine incidents aimed to control actors, and

[107] Lin and Zegart (2019).

only eight cyber incidents attempted to control all three measurements of resources, actors and outcomes.

Cyber operations are increasing, whether purely offensive in nature or as part of softer attempts to influence the global arena. States, non-state actors and even individuals are playing on this virtual ground in an attempt to achieve their strategic goals. Based on the findings and analyses in this chapter, we can conclude that due to the illusive and dynamic nature of cyber DIME measures, actors in the international arena will only increase their cyber capabilities and actions in the near future. States, and international powers in particular, benefit from this situation, which is one reason why there are no international laws or norms that govern cyber operations. However, as Tabachnik and I have also argued, the situation is evolving.[108] While some powers, like the United States, still allow the cyber domain to self-regulate, generally speaking, others like Russia and China control their cyber domains and block cyber DIME measures against them. We can assume that it is only a matter of time before Western states take countermeasures against cyber operations—countermeasures like local cyber regulation and monitoring. For instance, Israel's cyber bill or "Facebook Law" emerged in recent years to prevent online abuse and resist mis/disinformation. Moreover, countries will presumably attempt to block non-state actors and individuals from utilizing cyber DIME by restricting the usage of free, private, secure and anonymous platforms.

References

Abrams, Abigail. 2019. Here's what we know so far about Russia's 2016 meddling. *TIME*, April 18. https://time.com/5565991/russia-influence-2016-election/.

Alkhadra, Rahaf, Joud Abuzaid, Mariam AlShammari, and Nazeeruddin Mohammad. 2021. Solar winds hack: In-depth analysis and countermeasures. In *12th International Conference on Computing Communication and Networking Technologies (ICCCNT)*, 1–7.

Andress, Jason, and Steve Winterfeld. 2013. *Cyber warfare: Techniques, tactics and tools for security practitioners*. Elsevier.

Arreguin-Toft, I. 2001. How the weak win wars: A theory of asymmetric conflict. *International Security* 26 (1): 93–128.

Badawy, Adam, Emilio Ferrara, and Kristina Lerman. 2018. Analyzing the digital traces of political manipulation: The 2016 Russian interference Twitter campaign. In IEEE/ACM international conference on advances in social networks analysis and mining (ASONAM), 258–265. IEEE.

Barrinha, André, and Thomas Renard. 2017. Cyber-diplomacy: The making of an international society in the digital age. *Global Affairs* 3 (4–5): 353–364.

Barston, R.P. 2014. *Modern diplomacy*. Routledge.

Berridge, G.R. 2015. *Diplomacy: Theory and practice*. New York: Palgrave Macmillan.

Blank, S. 1998. Russia, NATO enlargement, and the Baltic States. *World Affairs* 160 (3): 115–125.

Bofey, D. 2019. EU to run war games to prepare for Russian and Chinese cyber-Attacks. *Guardian*, June 27. https://www.theguardian.com/technology/2019/jun/27/eu-war-games-prepare-russia-china-cyber-attacks.

Bossert, T.P. 2017. It's official: North Korea is behind WannaCry. *Wall Street Journal*, December 18. https://www.wsj.com/articles/its-official-north-korea-is-behind-wannacry-1513642537.

[108] Topor and Tabachnik (2021).

Buckbee, Michael. 2018. What is the cyber kill chain and how to use it effectively? *VARONIS Systems*, July 12. https://www.varonis.com/blog/cyber-kill-chain/.

Carlisle, D. 2017. Cybercriminals' finances under the microscope. *RUSI Commentary*, May 17. https://rusi.org/explore-our-research/publications/commentary/wannacry-ransomware-putting-cybercriminals-finances-under-microscope.

Carson, J. 2019. Fake news: What exactly is it – and how can you spot it? *Telegraph*, November 6. https://www.telegraph.co.uk/technology/0/fake-news-exactly-has-really-had-influence/.

Cederberg, G. 2018. Catching Swedish phish—How Sweden is protecting its 2018 elections. *Belfer Center for Science and International Affairs*. https://www.belfercenter.org/sites/default/files/files/publication/Swedish%20Phish%20-%20final2.pdf.

Center for Strategic and International Studies. n.d. The Ukrainian crisis timeline. http://ukraine.csis.org/#301.

Clausewitz, C. 1975. *On war*. New Jersey: Princeton University Press.

Coats, D.R. 2019. *Worldwide threat assessment of the US intelligence community*. Washington, D.C: Office of the Director of National Intelligence. January 29. https://www.dni.gov/files/ODNI/documents/2019-ATA-SFR---SSCI.pdf.

Connell, M. and S. Vogler. 2016. Russia's approach to cyber warfare. Center for Naval Analysis. https://apps.dtic.mil/dtic/tr/fulltext/u2/1019062.pdf.

Corera, G. 2018. Swedish Security Chief warning on fake news. *BBC*, January 4. https://www.bbc.com/news/world-europe-42285332.

Dahl, Robert A. 1957. The concept of power. *Behavioral Science* 2 (3): 201–215.

Dawda, S. 2021. Exploring national cyber security strategies: Policy approaches and implications. *RUSI Occasional Paper*.

Dehghan, Saeed Kamali. 2011. Iran accuses Siemens of helping launch Stuxnet cyber-attack. *Guardian*, April 17. https://www.theguardian.com/world/2011/apr/17/iran-siemens-stuxnet-cyber-attack.

Doffman, Z. 2019. Cyber warfare threat rises as Iran and China agree 'united front' against U.S. *Forbes*, July 6. https://www.forbes.com/sites/zakdoffman/2019/07/06/iranian-cyber-threat-heightened-by-chinas-support-for-its-cyber-war-on-u-s/#1956945c42eb.

Eriksson, J., and G. Giacomello. 2006. The information revolution, security, and international relations: (IR) relevant theory? *International Political Science Review* 27 (3): 221–244.

Field, M. 2018. WannaCry cyber attack cost the NHS £92m as 19,000 appointments cancelled. *Telegraph*, October 11. https://www.telegraph.co.uk/technology/2018/10/11/wannacry-cyber-attack-cost-nhs-92m-19000-appointments-cancelled/.

Farmer, B. 2018. Russia was behind 'malicious' cyber attack on Ukraine, Foreign Office says. *Telegraph*, February 15. https://www.telegraph.co.uk/news/2018/02/15/russia-behind-malicious-cyber-attack-ukraine-foreign-office/.

Farwell, James P., and Rafal Rohozinski. 2011. Stuxnet and the future of cyber war. *Survival* 53 (1): 23–40.

Geers, K. 2008. Cyberspace and the changing nature of warfare. *Cooperative Cyber Defense Centre of Excellence*. https://ccdcoe.org/uploads/2018/10/Geers2008_CyberspaceAndTheChangingNatureOfWarfare.pdf.

Gibbs, S. 2017. WannaCry: Hackers withdraw £108,000 of bitcoin ransom. *Guardian*, August 3. https://www.theguardian.com/technology/2017/aug/03/wannacry-hackers-withdraw-108000-pounds-bitcoin-ransom.

Gilpin, R. 2016. *The political economy of international relations*. New Jersey: Princeton University Press.

Gleick, J. 2012. *The information: A history, a theory, a flood*. New York: Vintage Books.

Greenberg, A. 2017. How an entire nation became Russia's test lab for cyberwar. *WIRED*, July 20. https://www.wired.com/story/russian-hackers-attack-ukraine/.

Harkabi, Y. 1990. *War and strategy*. Ministry of Defense, Israel: Maarachot [Hebrew].

Hart, J. 1976. Three approaches to the measurement of power in international relations. *International Organization* 30 (2): 289–305.

Helmus, T.C., E. Bodine-Baron, A. Radin, M. Magnuson, J. Mendelsohn, W. Marcellino, A. Bega, and Z. Winkelman. 2018. *Russian social media influence: Understanding Russian propaganda in Eastern Europe*. Santa Monica, CA: RAND Corporation. https://www.rand.org/pubs/research_reports/RR2237.html.

Henley, Jon. 2017. Russia waging information war against Sweden, study finds. *Guardian*, January 11. https://www.theguardian.com/world/2017/jan/11/russia-waging-information-war-in-sweden-study-finds.

Jervis, R. 1994. Hans Morgenthau, realism, and the scientific study of international politics. *Social Research* 61 (4): 853–876.

Klimburg, A and L. Faesen. 2020. A balance of power in cyberspace. In *Governing cyberspace*, eds. D. Broeders and B. van den Berg, 145–172.

Kostyuk, N., and Y.M. Zhukov. 2019. Invisible digital front: Can cyber attacks shape battlefield events? *Journal of Conflict Resolution* 63 (2): 317–347.

Kragh, M., and S. Åsberg. 2017. Russia's strategy for influence through public diplomacy and active measures: The Swedish case. *Journal of Strategic Studies* 40 (6): 773–816.

Kumar, Anil. n.d. Analysis of SolarWinds hack. *Cloud Control*. https://www.ecloudcontrol.com/analysis-of-solarwinds-hack/#:~:text=SolarWinds%20hack%20is%20considered%20to,compromised%20remains%20unknown%20even%20today.

Kushner, David. 2013. The real story of Stuxnet. *IEEE Spectrum* 50 (3): 48–53.

Langner, Ralph. 2011. Stuxnet: Dissecting a cyberwarfare weapon. *IEEE Security & Privacy* 9 (3): 49–51.

Lanham, R.A., and D.Merkoski. 2008. The economics of attention. *USC Annenberg School for Communication: The Norman Lear Center*, April 9. https://learcenter.org/pdf/EconofAttention.pdf.

Larson, Eric V., Richard E. Darilek, Daniel Gibran, Brian Nichiporuk, Amy Richardson, Lowell H. Schwartz, and Cathryn Q. Thurston. 2009. *Foundations of effective influence operations: A framework for enhancing army capabilities*. Santa Monica, C.A: RAND Arroyo Center.

Lee, Y.N. 2019. Ray Dalio says he wouldn't rule out China weaponizing its massive US Treasury holdings. *CNBC*, August 16. https://www.cnbc.com/2019/08/16/ray-dalio-china-could-weaponize-us-treasury-holdings-in-trade-war.html.

Lee, R.M., M.J. Assante, and T. Conway. 2016. Analysis of the cyber attack on the Ukrainian power grid. *E-ISAC, SANS*, March 18. https://ics.sans.org/media/E-ISAC_SANS_Ukraine_DUC_5.pdf.

Leigh, D., and L. Harding. 2013. *WikiLeaks: Inside Julian Assange's war on secrecy*. Guardian Faber Publishing.

Lin, Herbert, and Amy Zegart, eds. 2019. *Bytes, bombs, and spies: The strategic dimensions of offensive cyber operations*. Brookings Institution Press.

Lindsey, N. 2019. The rise of the global cyber war threat. *CPO Magazine*, August 5. https://www.cpomagazine.com/cyber-security/the-rise-of-the-global-cyber-war-threat/.

Lewis, J.A. 2018. Economic impact of cybercrime—No slowing down. The Center for Strategic and International Studies. *McAfee*. https://www.csis.org/analysis/economic-impact-cybercrime.

Lutscher, P.M., N.B. Weidmann, M.E. Roberts, M. Jonker, A. King, and A. Dainotti. 2020. At home and abroad: The use of denial-of-service attacks during elections in nondemocratic regimes. *Journal of Conflict Resolution* 64 (2–3): 373–401.

Lyngaas, Sean. 2023. Israel's cyber defense chief tells CNN he's concerned Iran could increase severity of its cyberattacks. *CNN*, November 6. https://edition.cnn.com/2023/11/06/politics/israel-cyber-defense-iran-concerns/index.html.

Mack, A. 1975. Why big nations lose small wars: The politics of asymmetric conflict. *World Politics* 27 (2): 175–200.

Maple, C. 2017. Security and privacy in the internet of things. *Journal of Cyber Policy* 2 (2): 155–184.

Mee, Paul, and Til Schuermann. 2018. How a cyber attack could cause the next financial crisis. *Harvard Business Review*, September 2018. https://hbr.org/2018/09/how-a-cyber-attack-could-cause-the-next-financial-crisis.

Mueller, Robert S. III. 2019a. Report on the investigation into Russian interference in the 2016 presidential election—Volume I of II. US Department of Justice, Washington DC.

Mueller, Robert S. III. 2019b. Report on the investigation into Russian interference in the 2016 presidential election—Volume II of II. US Department of Justice, Washington DC.

National Business Aviation Association. 2016. *Cyber security: Top flight department threats*. July 4. https://nbaa.org/aircraft-operations/security/cyber-security-top-flight-department-threats/.

National Cyber Directorate. 2017. *Israel national cyber security strategy—in brief*. Jerusalem, Israel. http://cyber.haifa.ac.il/images/pdf/cyber_english_A5_final.pdf.

National Endowment for Democracy. 2017. *'Sharp power': Rising authoritarian influence*. December 6. https://www.ned.org/events/sharp-power-rising-authoritarian-influence/.

Neumann, I.B. 2003. The English School on diplomacy: Scholarly promise unfulfilled. *International Relations* 17 (3): 341–369.

Nye, Joseph S. 1990. Soft power. *Foreign Policy* 80: 153–171.

Nye, Joseph S. 2008. Public diplomacy and soft power. *The Annals of the American Academy of Political and Social Science* 616 (1): 94–109.

Nye, Joseph S. 2016. Deterrence and dissuasion in cyberspace. *International Security* 41 (3): 44–71.

Nye, Joseph S. 2023. Get smart: Combining hard and soft power. In Soft power and great power competition: Shifting sands in the balance of power between the United States and China, 63–66. Singapore: Springer Nature.

Perez, E. 2015. FBI: Hacker claimed to have taken over flight's engine controls. *CNN*, May 19. https://edition.cnn.com/2015/05/17/us/fbi-hacker-flight-computer-systems/index.html.

Perlez, J., and A. Stevenson. 2019. In trade war, China's hard-line stance risks economy. *New York Times*, August 6. https://www.nytimes.com/2019/08/06/world/asia/china-xi-jingping-trade.html.

Perlroth, N. 2017. More evidence points to North Korea in ransomware attack. *New York Times*, May 22. https://www.nytimes.com/2017/05/22/technology/north-korea-ransomware-attack.html.

Porter, J., T. Anand, B. Johnson, R.M. Khan, and N. Sobel. 2005. Brain mechanisms for extracting spatial information from smell. *Neuron* 47 (4): 581–592.

Rummel, R.J. 1972. *The dimensions of nations*. Sage Publications.

Schmitt, Michael N. ed. 2013. *Tallinn manual on the international law applicable to cyber warfare*. Cambridge : Cambridge University Press.

Schmitt, Michael N. ed. 2017. *Tallinn manual 2.0 on the international law applicable to cyber warfare*. Cambridge : Cambridge University Press.

Sen, Ashish Kumar. 2015. Iran's growing cyber capabilities in a post-Stuxnet era. *Atlantic Council*, April 10. https://www.atlanticcouncil.org/blogs/new-atlanticist/iran-s-growing-cyber-capabilities-in-a-post-stuxnet-era/.

Setton, Keren. 2023. On the brink: Unpacking Israel's unilateral strike threat against Iran. *The Media Line*, June 6. https://themedialine.org/top-stories/israel-threatens-action-against-irans-nuclear-program-amid-war-drill/.

Smith, Z.M., and E. Lostri. 2020. The Hidden cost of Cybercrime. *McAfee*, December 2020. https://www.mcafee.com/enterprise/en-us/assets/reports/rp-hidden-costs-of-cybercrime.pdf.

Snowden, E. 2019. *Permanent record*. Metropolitan Books.

Teixeira, T.S. 2014. *The rising cost of consumer attention: Why you should care, and what you can do about it*. Harvard Business School, Working Paper No. 14-055.

Temple-Raston, Dina. 2021. Biden order to require new cybersecurity standards in response to SolarWinds attack. *NPR*, April 29. https://www.npr.org/2021/04/29/991333036/biden-order-to-require-new-cybersecurity-standards-in-response-to-solarwinds-att.

The White House. 2017. *National security strategy of the United States of America*. https://www.whitehouse.gov/wp-content/uploads/2017/12/NSS-Final-12-18-2017-0905.pdf.

The White House. 2018. *National Cyber Strategy of the United States of America*. https://www.whitehouse.gov/wp-content/uploads/2018/09/National-Cyber-Strategy.pdf.

Topor, Lev, and Alexander Tabachnik. 2021. Russian cyber information warfare: International distribution and domestic control. *Journal of Advanced Military Studies* 12 (1): 112–127.

United Nations. 1945. *Charter of the United Nations*. New York: United Nations.

United Nations. 1996. *Legality of the threat or use of nuclear weapons. Advisory opinion of 8 July 1996*. New York: United Nations.

U.S. Department of Defense. 2019. *DOD dictionary of military and associated terms*. Washington, D.C.: U.S. Department of Defense https://www.jcs.mil/Portals/36/Documents/Doctrine/pubs/dictionary.pdf.

U.S. Department of State. 2020. Pillars of Russia's disinformation and propaganda ecosystem. *Global Engagement Center*. https://www.state.gov/russias-pillars-of-disinformation-and-propaganda-report/.

US Government Accountability Office. 2021. SolarWinds cyberattack demands significant federal and private-sector response (infographic). April 22. https://www.gao.gov/blog/solarwinds-cyberattack-demands-significant-federal-and-private-sector-response-infographic.

Valeriano, B., B.M. Jensen, and R.C. Maness. 2018. *Cyber strategy: The evolving character of power and coercion*. New York: Oxford University Press.

Ward, Thomas. 2001. *The ethics of destruction: Norms and force in international relations*. Cornell University Press.

Wright, Q., and L.L. Wright. 1983. *A study of war*. Chicago and London: University of Chicago Press.

Weingast, B.R., and D.A. Wittman. 2008. *The Oxford handbook of political economy*. Oxford University Press.

Willett, Marcus. 2023. Lessons of the SolarWinds hack. In *Survival April–May 2021: Facing Russia*, 7–25. London: Routledge.

Wilson III, Ernest J. 2008. Hard power, soft power, smart power. *The Annals of the American Academy of Political and Social Science* 616 (1): 110–124.

Winder, D. 2019. Infection hits French hospital like it's 2017 as ransomware cripples 6,000 computers. *Forbes*, November 20. https://www.forbes.com/sites/daveywinder/2019/11/20/infection-hits-french-hospital-like-its-2017-as-ransomware-cripples-6000-computers/#7c8b09d4576e.

Zetter, Kim. 2015. The NSA acknowledges what we all feared: Iran learns from US cyberattacks. *WIRED*, February 18. https://www.wired.com/2015/02/nsa-acknowledges-feared-iran-learns-us-cyberattacks/.

Zetter, Kim. 2023. The untold story of the boldest supply-chain hack ever. *WIRED*, May 2. https://www.wired.com/story/the-untold-story-of-solarwinds-the-boldest-supply-chain-hack-ever/.

Chapter 5
Mis/Disinformation and National Resilience: Are Countries Immune to Fake News?

National resilience is, generally, a nation's capacity or ability to withstand difficult situations or difficult times and to regain internal balance, stability and function. This regards a nation's ability to regain its function in the economic, political and strategic (military and diplomatic) senses, as well as in the social sense, preventing social rifts from increasing. Such national stability is of crucial importance for democracies since matters that harm a country can lead to a loss of power and drive it into becoming less democratic and less liberal in terms of human rights.[1] However, national stability is also important to authoritarian and less democratic countries: dictators and oppressive governments want to avoid domestic criticism and opposition.

Following the discoveries and insights of Chaps. 3 and 4, mainly the fact that mis/disinformation is not internationally illegal and does not approach the standard international threshold for engaging in direct war, this chapter addresses a simple yet elusive question—what, if anything, is the impact of mis/disinformation, nowadays mainly propagated via cyberspace, on national resilience in democracies like the United States, the United Kingdom, Germany or Israel? Specifically, I focus on certain strategies and tactics of cyber warfare and assess the impact on national resilience in light of various factors. In this chapter, I address only democracies since authoritarian countries often censor any information they consider destabilizing, whether true or false.

This chapter has three main parts, which each help further our understanding of national resilience to cyber warfare in general and to mis/disinformation campaigns, aka "fake news," in particular. First, I elaborate on the concepts and theory of political warfare, influence campaigns and propaganda to set the conceptual stage for the chapter. This is important since nations have been using mis/disinformation campaigns since long before the cyber age. During the Cold War, the

[1] Canetti et al. (2014).

L. Topor, *Cyber Sovereignty*, Global Power Shift,
https://doi.org/10.1007/978-3-031-58199-1_5

Soviet Union spread lies about the West, just as the United States spread such mis/disinformation about the Soviet Union. Before that, during World War II, such strategies and tactics were used by both the Allies and the Axis. Throughout history, deception has been employed in warfare via rumors, radio and print. Now, it is mainly employed in cyberspace.

Second, I focus on the concept of sharp power in international affairs, particularly the way less-open nations strictly control their internal mass media affairs but utilize the openness of their adversaries to spread chaos. In this part, I present several cases from the United States and the United Kingdom, including the 2016 election interference, which was analyzed in Chap. 4, the January 6 Capitol riot, and the issue of Brexit in the United Kingdom. I also include several less-known cases from Germany and the case of Sweden and NATO.

Third, I present the Israeli case in greater depth as Israel is a regional power and a sought-after player in the Middle East. This case is less well known but particularly interesting since Israel is a Western proxy in the Middle East and is under constant kinetic and cyberattack by Middle Eastern and Gulf countries that are proxies of other global powers, mainly Russia and China. I present cases of mis/disinformation and discuss their effects on Israeli national resilience. In the case of Israel, can "fake news" impact decision-making, electoral outcomes and matters of war and peace? Interestingly, mis/disinformation campaigns in the form of social media bots and trolls, fake media stories and publications, and information leaks all influence people's perceptions and thus also directly and indirectly (in times of elections or watershed moments) affect the perceptions and decisions of policymakers and politicians. As in Europe, the United Kingdom and the United States, mis/disinformation campaigns create chaos and even social and political stagnation caused by internal power struggles.

Although it is considered a "cyber-nation," Israel is no exception—mis/disinformation campaigns against Israel cause political struggles and enhance social rifts that, in turn, lead to internal debates, making Israel less influential as a regional power. Israel currently has some internal balance, even considering the ongoing debates over the 2023 judicial reform and the October 7 massacre by the terrorist organization Hamas, which led to the 2023 Israel–Hamas war (known as "Swords of Iron"). Nevertheless, mis/disinformation campaigns weaken its stability and could even lead to chaos that would, inevitably, make Israel less democratic and less powerful. It nudges people into chaos and fear. Foreign influence groups, like Iranian groups, are constantly trying to deepen social rifts in Israel. Even Iran's proxy, Hezbollah, can see the effect—its leader, Hassan Nasrallah, argued in early 2023 that Israel was undergoing its most significant crisis in 75 years.[2]

[2] Gleefully Picking Up On Herzog Warning, Nasrallah Says Israel Tearing Itself Apart (2023).

5.1 Political Warfare, Propaganda and Influence Campaigns

Political warfare, propaganda and influence campaigns are three terms that have much in common, and they might read the same at a glance. However, it is important to understand the differences among them, particularly what term is related to mis/disinformation campaigns, in order to understand why "fake news" is being spread via cyberspace and why this spells bad news for national stability and resilience. In the twenty-first century, in the cyber age, political warfare, propaganda and influence campaigns are conducted via cyberspace with the use of digital mass media, social media and anonymous communication platforms.[3] Before the internet, during the Cold War, the World Wars, and even earlier, political propaganda and mis/disinformation were spread using agents of influence, radio and print publications and, of course, rumors. However, whether online or offline, the strategic aims have always been similar: to exert as much influence as possible on an adversary or adversarial alliance, thereby making them less capable and less powerful.[4] In terms of the measurements of power mentioned in Chaps. 3 and 4, mis/disinformation aims to affect the decisions and actions of actors and the outcomes of events.

How does politics relate to war? War is political—as Carl von Clausewitz famously noted, it is a "continuation of politics by other means." By that logic, if war is a continuation of politics by other means, then [international] politics is the continuation of war by other means. Yet, in the late twentieth and early twenty-first century, wars are no longer directly fought between global powers by conventional kinetic means as they could quickly escalate into full-scale nuclear conflicts and bring MAD down upon us all.[5] Wars are now often fought indirectly, either through proxies, through proxy means like mass communications or cyberspace, or both. Thus, global and regional powers often turn to "political warfare," which, as George F. Kennan wrote in 1948, is:

> ...the employment of all the means at a nation's command, short of war, to achieve its national objectives. Such operations ... range from such overt actions as political alliances, economic measures, and 'white' propaganda to such covert operations as clandestine support of 'friendly' foreign elements, 'black' psychological warfare and even encouragement of underground resistance in hostile states.[6]

Modern political warfare, falling short of war, is very similar to what the Soviets called "active measures" and consists mainly of overt and covert measures designed to destabilize a strategic move by an adversary, whether an international move or a domestic move that could directly affect international affairs. Overt

---

[3] Shuker and Topor (2021), Zimdars (2022).

[4] Graham (2021), Shultz and Godson (1984, 1–5).

[5] Sokolski (2004).

[6] Congressional Research Service (2023).

measures include official and unofficial propaganda channels and diplomatic relations—these can be considered simple propaganda. Covert measures include, mainly, covert propaganda, mis/disinformation, the use of agents of influence to propagate an idea or policy, clandestine radio and print, and the use of international front organizations as proxies.[7]

Propaganda involves the spread of information for a cause, whether for marketing and for-profit purposes, political campaigning or strategic purposes concerning war and peace. At times, the purposes of propaganda interwind. This is why the definition of propaganda is important in this chapter. As defined by Encyclopedia Britannica, propaganda is the spread of biased or misleading information to promote a certain idea; it can take the form of speeches, posters, writings, videos, recordings, social media posts and so on. The messages promoted by propaganda can be true or false; however, the important point to make here is that propaganda is an effort to promote a certain idea. For instance, a commercial for McDonald's or Apple is indeed propaganda.[8]

Next, influence campaigns are defined as the coordinated, synchronized and combined application of diplomatic, informational, military and economic abilities, alongside other national capabilities, in times of peace, war or crises, to strategically influence a certain adversary or entity. Influence campaigns seek to affect the behaviors and decisions of foreign target populations and persuade them to adopt positions that serve the interests of the campaign's initiators. The difference between political warfare and influence campaigns is that influence campaigns focus on information and the perception of it by adversarial crowds—they are a part of the political warfare repertoire.[9]

One good example of an influence campaign was the Soviet anti-Zionist campaign against Israel. During the Cold War, Israel was perceived by the Soviet Union as a Western proxy in the Middle East, thus the Soviet Union turned to its arsenal of active measures to try to influence Israel's adversaries, as well as more neutral and distant nations, to act against the country or at least oppose it under the umbrella of the United Nations. To this purpose, anti-Zionist propaganda, including anti-Semitic propaganda, was created, manipulated and spread in many languages and via many platforms. The Soviets promoted films, lectures, articles, conferences, radio programs and television broadcasts to shape the hearts and minds of others against Israel. After some difficult early years, the existence of the Jewish nation became a hard fact, and the Soviets, seeking to create chaos, massively promoted the Palestinian narrative through the above-mentioned means but also via agents of influence—people or organizations that the covert Soviet forces supported to promote the Palestinian idea at the expense of the Israeli idea.[10] Apart from supporting key Palestinian leaders (like Mahmoud Abbas) and Israeli citizens

[7] Shultz and Godson (1984, 1–5), Robinson et al. (2018).

[8] Smith (2022).

[9] Larson et al. 2009; Shuker and Topor (2021).

[10] See as an example: Solmar (1978). Also see Tabarovsky (2019, 2023), Frankel (1972).

who extensively promoted extreme ideas over the years, the Soviet Union has also supported and promoted terror organizations like the Palestinian Liberation Organization.[11] While it is true that since the creation of the state of Israel in 1948, the Palestinian case has been seen as hybrid—both domestic and international in nature—one cannot overlook its importance in Israeli politics—an importance so great that it led to the assassination of a prime minister (Yitzhak Rabin z"l, assassinated on November 4, 1994) and national chaos during the first and second Intifadas and beyond.

Nowadays, it seems as if the Palestinian case, particularly Palestinian terror, is used as a sort of dimmer switch by foreign powers to spread chaos and shape Israeli political discourse. Turning right increases attacks, and turning left decreases them. For instance, in May 2021, while Israel was fighting a foreign entity—Hamas—anti-Zionist Arab communities and even some Jewish anti-Zionists rioted against the Israeli and Jewish people, institutions and symbols. Such terror was supported by fake videos and pictures of alleged deaths or injuries of Palestinians caused by Israel. Many turned out to be fake or forged, but they nevertheless poured fuel on the fire.[12] More recent examples of propaganda are presented in the following sections, emphasizing the spread of mis/disinformation on digital media and social media.

5.2 Mis/Disinformation Through Cyberspace: Sharp Power

Free and open liberal democratic systems are often good for the people—for human rights and freedom of speech—but not so much for strategic power struggles between global adversaries. In this part, I present the concept of sharp power in cyberspace and explain how less-open nations like Russia, China and Iran use the imbalance between open and restricted mass communication systems to their advantage. I also include several important and well-known cases of the execution of such sharp power, like the 2016 election interference in the United States, which was discussed in Chap. 4, the January 6 Capitol riot in the United States, the Brexit issue in the United Kingdom, the Lisa case in Germany, and NATO-related disinformation in Sweden and the Baltic region as a whole. These cases are then compared to the Israeli case, which I present in more detail afterward.

Sharp power is an approach to global affairs that includes actions to censor or manipulate the integrity of independent institutions and states. This is usually done by authoritarian or less-open regimes to open regimes. The approach takes advantage of the asymmetry between the free systems of liberal democracies and the

[11] Baker (2016).

[12] Shalev (2022), Topor (2021), Creedon (2021).

restricted systems of authoritarian regimes, allowing the latter to harm free expression and distort political integrity and stability in democracies while simultaneously shielding their own domestic public expressions and media from unwanted media and information, such as democratic appeals from abroad.[13]

For instance, Russia created the RuNet project to allow Moscow to unplug Russia from the global internet grid while keeping internal communications and services intact. It also introduced laws against unwanted information, like the Yarovaya law and the "sovereign internet" law, as analyzed by myself and Tabachnik. China created its Great Firewall, which restricts foreign information flow and foreign services like social media. Other countries, like Iran, also restrict their cyber domain. On the other hand, countries like the United States cannot legally censor most foreign information flows due to the First Amendment and Section 230 of the United States Code. Even in the extreme case of the Capitol riot in 2021, when extremists, pushed by conspiracy theories and foreign propaganda, rioted and tried to take over, the United States did not shut down services or the internet, even though evidence suggested that the rioters had organized online, particularly on social media and SMAs like Telegram.[14]

Since print and radio can now, in the twenty-first century, be more easily restricted and manipulated, and since such platforms usually have gatekeepers, countries have discovered that cyberspace is the perfect platform for spreading mis/disinformation and chaos. After all, the internet is widely accessible and open but also under-regulated—there is no applicable international law regarding cyberspace, as described extensively in Chap. 3. The internet, particularly social media, provides nations with a proxy (virtual) ground where they can hide behind a veil of anonymity. Thus, even if an article or video turns out to be fake, or a social media user turns out to be a bot or a troll, attribution is forensically difficult.[15] Deterrence mechanisms for cyberattacks in general and mis/disinformation in particular are slow, blunt and ineffective. To put it simply, it is not internationally acceptable to use hard power against sharp power: It is not internationally acceptable to use a kinetic weapon, let alone start a war, over a tweet.[16]

Mis/disinformation is a form of political warfare, as explained in the introduction to this chapter. One well-known example of mis/disinformation using sharp power was the Russian interference in the 2016 United States elections, in which Russia worked to widen political gaps in the United States and hacked the computers of American citizens and electoral entities. Russia, as the United States concluded, also worked to undermine the public's faith in democratic processes and to weaken Hillary Clinton. This case was detailed in Chap. 4, but it is brought up once again to highlight a dangerous process and to provide a basis for comparison with other cases. The Russian hack of the 2016 United States presidential

[13] Walker (2018), Topor and Tabachnik (2021).

[14] Topor and Tabachnik (2021), Haber and Topor (2023), Jeppesen et al. (2022).

[15] Topor (2022, 20–37).

[16] Nye (2016), Schmitt (2017).

elections raises questions about attribution and deterrence in cyberspace, but it also raises questions about democracy in the cyber age. If no hard direct forensic links to the Kremlin were present, only connections to proxies (and this is still under ongoing investigation), can attribution be achieved? Can the United States retaliate using non-cyber means if no kinetic damage was done? And, in the age of international social media platforms and a global, open internet under the control of technology giants, do we all still have free will to vote?[17]

In another example from the United States, it was suggested that Russia, China and Iran were behind influence campaigns that "weaponized" the QAnon conspiracy theory and other anti-Semitic and racist conspiracy theories that led to the January 6 Capitol riot in 2021.[18] Thus, adversaries of the United States used sharp power to benefit from the borderless American internet. The events of January 6, 2021, marked a pivotal moment in contemporary American history when a violent mob breached the US Capitol, disrupting the certification of the presidential election results and trying to undermine the legitimization of the election of President Joe Biden. This unprecedented incident, instigated by supporters of then-President Donald Trump, unfolded against a backdrop of political polarization and heightened rhetoric.[19]

On the day of the riot, a significant number of individuals, incited by Trump's rhetoric, converged on the Capitol, breaching its security measures. The rioters vandalized property, clashed with law enforcement and disrupted the certification process, causing chaos and posing a threat to the safety of elected officials. The physical breach of the Capitol resulted in multiple injuries, deaths and widespread condemnation. The riots showcased a confluence of physical and cyber dynamics. The role of social media platforms in organizing the riot, disseminating misinformation and amplifying extremist narratives was very significant; the extremists who rioted used fringe social media platforms like Parlor and Gab, as well as SMAs like Telegram and Discord (an instant messaging application) to organize the whole event. Online forums, including but not limited to social media, played a pivotal role in galvanizing and coordinating the actions of those who participated in or supported the riot. Using such online platforms, the rioters managed to evade

---

[17] Kessler (2023).

[18] QAnon is a far-right, conspiracy theory-driven political movement that originated in the US. It centers on the belief that a cabal of Satanic, cannibalistic child molesters is operating a global child sex trafficking ring and conspiring against former President Donald Trump. QAnon followers believe that Trump is secretly fighting this cabal and will eventually bring them to justice. The theory originated in online forums in 2017, when an anonymous poster known as "Q" began sharing cryptic messages that purported to be insider information about Trump's war against the cabal. QAnon followers quickly latched onto these messages and began interpreting them as evidence of a vast conspiracy. See "QAnon" in *Encyclopedia Britannica*, https://www.britannica.com/topic/QAnon; Cohen (2021).

[19] Gambino and Strauss (2021).

surveillance and plan their riot while law enforcement agencies remained almost clueless about the scale of the event.[20]

At first glance, it may seem that the Capitol riot was carried out by domestic extremists who were unhappy with the election results. However, evidence has been uncovered about the role of foreign entities in promoting conspiracy theories on the above-mentioned social media platforms and SMAs. Furthermore, some individuals who played key roles in organizing the riots received over $500,000 from foreign individuals, specifically to support their extreme ideologies and plans. Although the individuals paying to support the rioters were traced to Europe, it is widely believed that they were extended proxies of Russia, China and Iran.[21]

The case of foreign influence and the use of cyberspace in the Capitol riot is interesting, and it makes the debate about international laws applicable to cyberspace more difficult because in this case, physical damage, injuries and even deaths occurred. In previous cases of foreign influence online, like in the campaign to influence the 2016 United States presidential elections, foreign propaganda did indeed influence the American people, but no physical damage, injuries or deaths occurred. In the case of the Capitol riot, however, foreign powers influenced those who were later charged with murder, among other charges.[22] Can such a case be considered an act of aggression under the Charter of the United Nations? Can this be the threshold that, once breached, justifies retaliation? And, if the United States were to eventually retaliate, would it be by kinetic, cyber or hybrid means? As there is no international law governing cyberspace, there is no clear answer. In the case of the 2016 presidential elections, foreign forces undermined the very beginning of the electoral process, and in the case of the Capitol riot, foreign forces undermined the end of the electoral process—the final certification.

Additionally, the Capitol riot had a tremendous impact on American national resilience. The riot revealed large political rifts between groups in the United States and raised questions about fundamental democratic procedures like the electoral process. The riot also hinted both to the American people and to the agencies themselves that the agencies that are meant to protect American democracy, institutions and people are lacking, as they had insufficient information about the scale and depth of the riots, and they did not manage to provide fast solutions in critical moments. It was hours before the American National Guard came to the aid of local police and Federal forces.[23] Furthermore, the riots hinted to the world, specifically to rival powers like Russia and China, that the United States was indeed vulnerable. It made it clear that sharp power does work and that social and ideological rifts are only on the rise in the United States. My assessment is

---

[20] Jeppesen et al. (2022), Yonker and Topor (2021), Thorbecke (2021).

[21] Cleave (2022), Dilanian (2022), Dilanian (2021).

[22] See the Capitol Breach Cases in the US Attorney's Office of District of Columbia: https://www.justice.gov/usao-dc/capitol-breach-cases

[23] Mazzetti and Broadwater (2021)

that the future holds more of these riots and protests in the United States, at least as long as no legal and regulatory measures are taken against domestic and foreign tech companies.

The United States is not the only country susceptible to such methods of political warfare. In the case of the Brexit referendum in the United Kingdom, the British government issued a report stating that they did not know if Russia had interfered with the referendum; however, the report also states that intelligence agencies and politicians did not attempt to investigate the issue since some of them wanted to promote the departure from the European Union. Since sharp power operations are often based on existing social and political rifts, British agencies and research institutions, such as the Center for Strategic and International Studies, suggest there is no decisive answer regarding the existence of such an operation.[24] However, the United States Senate issued a report in which it is suggested that Russia could have used British finance laws to its advantage to fund non-British companies or others that did not operate in the United Kingdom to promote the "Leave" campaign. As a few hundred thousand fake Twitter accounts posted pro "Leave" posts, it is plausible to assume that Russia, and/or another country, used sharp power to weaken the EU in this way.[25]

Foreign involvement in the Brexit referendum manifested through diverse channels. Reports indicated potential interference from entities linked to Russia and other non-state actors utilizing social media platforms to disseminate misleading information. Again, the utilization of cyber platforms to manipulate public opinion played a pivotal role in the Brexit discourse. Cyber operations, including the spread of false narratives and the amplification of divisive content, exploited vulnerabilities in social media algorithms to target specific demographics, just as in the American case, both in 2016 and the riots in 2021. These tactics not only influenced the referendum outcome but also fueled social unrest post-Brexit. In the aftermath of the Brexit referendum, the United Kingdom saw a surge in protests and riots, partly driven by heightened emotions and disagreements over the decision but nevertheless well organized, meaning that someone had planned and financed them. Foreign and domestic actors capitalized on this volatile situation, employing influence strategies on social media platforms to escalate tensions, disseminate misinformation and coordinate disruptive activities, further complicating the political landscape.[26]

The referendum took place in June 2016, and only in March–April 2017 did the British House of Commons express that their whole approach had been mistaken:

> The US and UK understanding of 'cyber' is predominantly technical and computer-network based, while Russia and China use a cognitive approach based on understanding of

---

[24] Ruy (2020).

[25] Wintour (2018), "Putin's Asymmetric Assault on Democracy in Russia and Europe: Implications for U.S. (2018), Kirkpatrick (2017).

[26] Ibid.

mass psychology and of how to exploit individuals. We commend the Government for promoting cyber security as a major issue for the UK.[27]

Of course, it was not only Russia that stood to benefit from Brexit. Global trade agreements would be revised after Brexit, and even the United States had some share in influencing the Brexit issue. Nevertheless, national resilience was tampered with—before, during and especially after Brexit. The foreign influence over Brexit raises questions about democracy in the United Kingdom. As in the American case, one must ask who voted—citizens or foreign entities that influenced hearts and minds?[28]

Continental Europe is also susceptible to foreign dis/misinformation through the cyber domain. In January 2016, Russian media outlets such as RT News, Sputnik, and the TV channel First Russian, as well as social media groups on Facebook and VK, circulated a story that a 13-year-old girl had been raped by migrants in Germany. The story, first reported by a minor website for Russian expats living in Germany, spread like wildfire across Russian-language social media and media outlets. The narrative was amplified by pro-Kremlin media and official Russian media outlets. Even Russian Foreign Minister Sergey Lavrov made two public statements of concern about the inability of the German police and legal system to take such cases seriously because of political correctness.[29]

One primary goal appears to have been to promote anti-immigrant sentiment in Germany, particularly targeting those of Middle Eastern origin. By portraying Germany as unsafe and hostile to immigrants, the perpetrators aimed to fuel existing prejudices and divisions within German society. Another potential motive was to discredit the German government and its handling of the refugee crisis. By portraying Germany as incapable of protecting its own citizens, the disinformation campaign sought to undermine public trust in the government and its institutions and to boost anti-immigrant sentiments. Additionally, the campaign may have been intended to serve as a warning to other European countries that were considering accepting refugees or providing assistance to Ukraine. By highlighting the alleged dangers of immigration, the perpetrators aimed to dissuade other nations from taking similar actions.[30]

This story also served to weaken Chancellor Angela Merkel. "The refugee crisis and the Lisa case have allowed (Moscow) to exploit more strongly groups like Russian-speaking Germans, and to play with Germans' angst and insecurities," claimed Stefan Meister from the German Council on Foreign Relations. Indeed far-right groups and activists sought to harm Muslim immigrants in particular and called on Merkel's government to resign.[31]

---

[27] UK House of Commons (2017).

[28] Cadwalladr and Graham-Harrison (2018), Cadwalladr (2017), Black et al. (2017).

[29] Janda (2016), Rinke and Carrel (2016), Meister (2016).

[30] Ibid; Sablina (2021).

[31] Ibid.

In this case, Russia used sharp power and the openness of German media to disseminate a fabricated story. Moscow also used the Russian-speaking population within Germany as a vehicle to deliver this disinformation. Official and semi-official media outlets and anonymous accounts on social media promoted the Lisa case. Interestingly, even Russia's Foreign Minister addressed the case, strengthening, legitimizing and giving credibility to the propagated story. Unfortunately, this case cannot be considered illegal under international norms, as it is a reported story. Could Germany retaliate against fake news? Clearly, a news story with no origin cannot be considered a threshold for starting a war or diplomatic crisis. The Lisa case is a type of story propagated in many versions throughout Europe and NATO member states, in Poland, Lithuania, Ukraine and other places. It is believed to be customized for every specific country and disseminated by Russian proxies to cause unrest and destabilize Europe by enhancing social rifts between the right and the left.[32]

Russia attempts to weaken not only the European Union but NATO as well. For instance, in Russia's border region of the Baltic countries, Ukraine and Georgia, it has used political warfare methods such as influence campaigns using mis/disinformation, among other tactics, to either create chaos in target countries or to shift political opinions and processes away from the West and from collaboration with NATO. It also promoted opinions supportive of Russia. For instance, since 2014, Russian media outlets like RT and Sputnik, as well as Russian-speaking Facebook and VK groups, have promoted misleading and false information about possible Swedish collaboration with NATO to influence the Swedish people away from supporting this. Among the ideas and content that have been circulated by alternative media outlets and bots on social media are claims that NATO could store nuclear weapons on Swedish soil, that NATO would attack Russia from Sweden and that NATO soldiers could potentially rape Swedish women without fear of prosecution as they would allegedly be diplomatically immune. The latter is false, and the other examples are very misleading. Nevertheless, Russia has launched similar campaigns across the whole Baltic region, Ukraine, Georgia and other countries of interest to Moscow. In January 2017, the Swedish Institute of International Affairs accused Russia of spreading disinformation as part of a coordinated propaganda campaign in an attempt to influence public opinion and decision-making in Sweden, altering Sweden's national resilience. Anders Thornberg, former head of Sweden's security service, the SÄPO, argued in January 2018 that Russia was attempting to influence Sweden by spreading chaos in the Swedish political arena rather than promoting a particular ideology, political candidate or party.[33]

In another case in Sweden, Swedish authorities accused Russia of spreading misinformation and disinformation about Qur'an burning. Sweden's Psychological

[32] Shuker and Topor (2021).

[33] Ibid.

Defense Agency, part of its Ministry of Defense, said that Russian state-controlled media outlets RT and Sputnik had published a series of articles in Arabic, falsely claiming that the Swedish government supported Qur'an burning. This caused unrest and violence around the Islamic world, with many Swedish embassies facing protests and vandalism. Yet it also caused unrest in Sweden as its Muslim citizens protested the government's alleged decision to allow Qur'an burning as part of the Swedish freedom of expression laws.[34] Sweden could only act as the United States, United Kingdom, Germany and other countries had done—by debunking the fake news.

In conclusion, sharp power is used by non or less-open countries to influence target countries that are more open, mainly in terms of information flow, use of social media and similar matters. The more open a country's mass communications, the more susceptible it is to mis/disinformation from its adversaries, as well as from its allies.

5.3 Fake News in Israel: Trends and Cases

Israel has been surrounded by adversaries for the entirety of its existence. Since its establishment in 1948 (and even before that), such adversaries and others have constantly tried to undermine the Jewish state and influence its decisions.[35] However, it is not only neighboring countries that try to influence its decisions and the opinions of its citizens; as a regional power in the Middle East, Israel is constantly under the influence of other regional powers, like Iran, and global powers, such as the United States, Russia and China. Yet, since Israel is a liberal democracy, American and European influences are not seen as attempts to undermine its stability but as a diplomatic dialogue between countries. Israel enjoys Western support and, at the same time, the West benefits from the fact that a strong democracy is fighting war, genocide and abuse of human rights in the region, as well as providing intelligence and support for Western forces in the region.

Israel is indubitably an American (and Western) proxy in the Middle East, and although it was especially true during the Cold War, ideological similarities are what make Israeli–Western relations strong.[36] The West is not engaged in political warfare toward Israel but rather in propaganda. In contrast, Israel's adversaries are engaged in political warfare and influence campaigns, not simple propaganda—they use mis/disinformation that in many cases includes age-old anti-Semitism.[37]

Influence from powers like Russia, China or Iran is not seen as supportive by many Israelis, particularly because these countries strongly support most of

[34] Bryant (2023), Comerford (2023).

[35] See, generally, Bregman (2016).

[36] Lipson (1996), Koplow (2011).

[37] Topor (2021b)

Israel's adversaries and promote the Palestinian cause, which directly undermines Israel's right to exist as a state.[38] Furthermore, while Western influence is mostly exerted directly, Russian, Chinese and Iranian influence is exerted under the table, using strategies and methods similar to (Soviet) active measures. Such influence campaigns are not aimed at negotiation but at enhancing social and political rifts within Israel and destabilizing it—making it, and thus the West, weaker. The examples presented in this section raise a crucial question—can Israel withstand mis/disinformation campaigns that attempt to destabilize it, and can it maintain or regain its economic, political, strategic and social functions?

One example of influence on Israel is connected to its Russian-speaking population. This example is not necessarily negative, nor does it represent an act of political warfare; however, the over 1.2 million Russian-speaking citizens in Israel are susceptible to Russian influence. Many consume Russian media, read Russian newspapers and outlets, socialize on Russian social media platforms (like Odnoklassniki or VK), engage with Russian-speaking groups on Facebook (or other social media platforms) or with Russian channels on Telegram and WhatsApp, and keep in close contact with Russian-speaking friends and family members in other countries. The fact that the number of Russian-speaking citizens is such a significant percentage of the total population of Israel (approximately 9.6 million citizens in total, of which approximately 7.1 are Jewish) means that they are a sought-after identity group that has tremendous influence on decisions and elections.[39]

The Russian-speaking Israeli population consumes Russian media online and is thus, at times, influenced by narratives other than Western or American ones. The worrying aspect, however, is that Russia tends to initiate influence campaigns that enhance social rifts, which subsequently lead to domestic unrest.[40] For instance, in the case of the 2023 judicial reform in Israel, some Russian narratives ran counter to American narratives, dividing populations and enhancing the rift between the right and the left.[41] In such cases, domestic unrest is enhanced not only by Russian narratives but also by Western narratives. Years before the reform was initiated, in 2019, an Israeli request was sent to Russia, asking Moscow to avoid interfering in the Israeli general elections. This request was also aimed at future elections and public events. The Kremlin replied that it "did not intervene, does not intervene and does not intend to intervene."[42] However, this kind of intervention is not simple propaganda but a tool of political warfare. In another example, in the aftermath of the terrorist massacre on October 7, 2023, Russia, China and Iran have all

[38] Ibid.

[39] Central Bureau of Statistics (2023).

[40] Shuker and Topor (2021).

[41] "What to Know About Israel's Judicial Reforms" (2023).

[42] Landau (2019); this was confirmed in an interview with a former senior figure in the Israeli security sector; Lerman (2023).

promoted mis/disinformation and backed the terrorist organization Hamas online, including with content aimed at Russian-speaking Israelis.[43]

Another example of influence on Israel is connected to its Arab population, which is susceptible to influence from foreign countries like the ones already mentioned but mainly from anti-Israeli and anti-Semitic countries, terror organizations, agents of influence and media outlets. Since Arab Israeli citizens make up around 21% of the total population (approximately 2 million citizens of the total 9.6), and some hold anti-Israeli or anti-Semitic world views, they hold a lot of political and actual power. In May 2021, during a conflict between Israel and the terror organization Hamas, violent riots erupted in Arab and mixed cities (Acre, Haifa, Jaffa, Lod and Ramla, among others). During the riots, Arab Israeli citizens expressed support for Hamas and attacked Jewish citizens and Israeli security forces. The riots were choreographed by Iran, Hezbollah and Hamas using social media (i.e., Facebook, TikTok) and SMAs (i.e., Telegram, WhatsApp), and related content was also promoted by Russia and China. The riots created chaos and personal insecurity for Jewish citizens and deepened the gap between the peaceful Arab and Jewish citizens and between the right and the left.[44]

A recent example of influence on Israel was the Iranian influence on the judicial reform. During the summer of 2023, the Israeli Security Service noted that online groups were inciting violence in the context of the judicial reform. Moreover, the Israeli disinformation watchdog, Fake Reporter, revealed a network of dozens of fake accounts encouraging Israeli citizens to commit illegal acts during anti-reform or pro-reform demonstrations (both from the left and the right). These influence campaigns were part of Iran's arsenal of political warfare tactics to undermine Israel and make it a weaker regional player. Furthermore, Russia is also suspected of conducting such influence campaigns to complement Iran's efforts. The chaos created in the context of the judicial reform did indeed weaken Israeli solidarity and, consequently, overall Israeli security.[45]

As for the October 7, 2023, terrorist attack by Hamas, Russia and Iran have been quick to use it to create civil chaos in Israel. Some use Facebook, some use TikTok, and some use Telegram, but most Russian or Iranian bots and trolls circulate similar mis/disinformation about the terrorist attack, not only to undermine Israeli efforts to fight Hamas but also to create social unrest and chaos.[46] Just as Soviet anti-Zionist campaigns were aimed at discrediting Israel as a humane and democratic country during the Cold War, influence campaigns inciting violence by the left and the right are also aimed at discrediting Israel as a humane and democratic country. Methods similar to those that were used to influence the United States, United Kingdom, European Union and NATO are now being used against

[43] "Russia (2023).

[44] Frenkel (2021); Jerusalem Center for Public Affairs (n.d.).

[45] Peleg et al. (2023), Barel (2023).

[46] "Russian Propagandists Use ToI logo and Brand to Propagate Fake News against Ukraine, Report Shows" (2023), Benjakob (2023).

Israel, and have been for a few years now. Moreover, Shuker and I have shown that Russia utilizes Russian-speaking populations to mediate and promote its influence among the general population; this was and is done in Estonia, Latvia, Lithuania, Finland, Sweden, Ukraine and Georgia, and Israel is not immune to these efforts.[47]

One particularly interesting example, which came to my attention after hearing some of my neighbors speak about it, was the fear and chaos that spread in the days following the October 7 terror attack. Immediately following the attack, a rumor with no apparent origin sprung up: some construction workers, mainly from Gaza or from the West Bank, and who resided in Israel, had taken footage of roads, buildings, kindergartens and more, allegedly gathering information for possible attacks. This rumor spread at a time when Hamas terrorists had infiltrated from the Gaza Strip, and some were hiding within Israel. Even though the whole country was flooded with security, police officers and soldiers, citizens began to panic and patrolled the streets on their own, carrying weapons and barricading their surroundings. Furthermore, some fake images of Arab Israelis celebrating the October 7 terror attack were spread in an attempt to enhance rifts between Arab and Jewish citizens and to encourage Jewish Israelis to attack Arab Israelis. However, as Israeli security services determined, the images were either fake or misleading; they had been taken elsewhere, not in Israel, and the footage was not of Arabs. The rumor about the construction workers was a form of misinformation built on occasions when city workers, construction workers or real-estate agents had taken pictures of buildings or others. The misinformation spread tremendous chaos within Israeli cities, and, as mentioned, I myself learned about it from my panicking neighbors.[48]

Former and present government and security services officials, both in Israel and abroad, have hinted that Russia, China and Iran are behind such influence campaigns. Others, like senior business chiefs, have raised their tone further. For instance, Brad Smith, Microsoft's president and vice chair, noted, "We are getting very good at identifying a Russian campaign, like when they tried to tell people not to get the COVID vaccine." He added, "Or today, when we see Russian disinformation in the Middle East… [but] There is no societal consensus about what companies should do."[49]

Companies are waiting to follow laws and regulations. In the Israeli cases, in the wake of the judicial reform or the post-October 7 panic, what can be done, and how can Israel retaliate? Clearly, such campaigns have enhanced social rifts and weakened Israel, but with no direct attribution possible, retaliation is difficult to justify.

---

[47] Shuker and Topor (2021)

[48] "The Iranians Are Also Involved: The Fakes Spread on Arab Citizens of Israel" (2023).

[49] "Microsoft Chief Says Russia Is Spreading Middle East Disinformation" (2023).

5.4 Conclusion

National resilience refers to a nation's ability to withstand difficult situations and regain internal balance, stability and function after situations such as conflicts, war or disasters. This is especially crucial for democracies, as harming a nation can lead to a loss of power and a decline in democracy and human rights. This chapter focused on the impact of mis/disinformation campaigns, widely known as "fake news," on national resilience, particularly on these trends in the cyber domain. It comes after Chap. 4, which examined cyber warfare in general, and it concludes that the most difficult strategy to fight is the use of sharp power in cyberspace. How can a country remain open and free but also protect itself from fake or unwanted information? And how can a country retaliate over the damage done by a fake story?

In this chapter, I presented the concepts and theory of political warfare, influence campaigns and propaganda, highlighting the use of mis/disinformation in various contexts. I also discussed the concept of sharp power in international affairs, illustrating it with cases from the United States, United Kingdom, Germany, Sweden and NATO. These were compared to the cases of mis/disinformation in Israel in 2023, which were presented in more detail. Russia and/or Iran employed similar strategies and tactics in the United States, Europe and Israel, which included engagement with the Russian-speaking or Arab-speaking populations to promote other narratives and the spread of forged or misleading material, which, in every case, were intended to widen societal rifts and create chaos.

Israel, a regional power in the Middle East, is affected by mis/disinformation campaigns conducted by its adversaries, be they regional powers, terror organizations or global powers. These campaigns influence Israeli citizens' perceptions and decisions, likewise affecting policymakers and politicians. They sow chaos and panic within society. Those who seek to harm Israel or downgrade its regional influence conduct mis/disinformation campaigns using cyberspace—online media and social media. Such influence campaigns create chaos and social stagnation and harm the security of Israel. They can also lead to negative views of Israel, in the context of the judicial reform or, in particular, in the context of the retaliation after October 7.

Israel's adversaries mainly use mis/disinformation campaigns as a tool in their arsenal of political warfare strategies. For instance, Iran or, as sometimes hinted, Russia, have attempted to incite Israeli citizens into acting illegally; this was revealed in the context of the judicial reform of 2023. Furthermore, these international players also incited the Israeli Arab population to riot in violence against Jewish citizens in May 2021. It has also been revealed that these players attempted to interfere in the 2019 general elections. These acts of foreign interference are in addition to more legal and palatable propaganda, like the narratives consumed by the Russian-speaking citizens in Israel (which are not necessarily wrong, even as they sometimes oppose Western/American narratives—though this gap between American and Russian online information leads, at times, to conflict).

"Fake news" campaigns are used by international players to influence and/ or downgrade Israel. However, the important question is as follows: What is the impact of such mis/disinformation campaigns on Israel's national resilience? Unfortunately, such campaigns, conducted using the elusive cyberspace, do harm Israeli national resilience and regional influence. Mis/disinformation and propaganda using cyberspace are very difficult to trace as they often make use of proxy usernames, devices and addresses.

As a note about the particular Israeli case, in early and mid-2023, several issues affecting Israel's solidarity, resilience and military power arose, some of which were exacerbated by the above-mentioned examples of mis/disinformation. First, due to the increased internal debate over judicial reform, Israeli society saw widened rifts, mainly between the left (and center) and the right but also between less observant Jewish citizens and more observant religious citizens. Second, some reserve soldiers, mainly pilots, special operations personnel and technological personnel, declared that they would refuse to serve the country while the judicial reform was promoted. Moreover, even some active military members argued they might refuse to serve the country. While the number of those refusing to serve in the military was very small, the media enhanced their declarations, which affected national morale in general.[50] It is widely suggested that the October 7 terrorist attack by the terror organization Hamas was carried out because it saw a weakness in Israeli society and government. However, the terror attack by Hamas actually brought Israeli citizens together, bridging gaps between religious and non-religious citizens, between Jewish, Arab, Druze and Bedouin people. Apparently, Hamas, Iran and others did not fully consider the solidarity effect of their terror attack.[51]

References

Baker, Peter. 2016. Soviet document suggests Mahmoud Abbas was a K.G.B. spy in the 1980s. *New York Times*, September 7. https://www.nytimes.com/2016/09/08/world/middleeast/mahmoud-abbas-israel-palestine-kgb.html

Barel, Ofir. 2023. Is Iran encouraging illegal acts in Israel over judicial reform?—opinion. *Jerusalem Post*, January 31. https://www.jpost.com/opinion/article-730207

Benjakob, Omer. 2023. Russian op pushes Gaza disinfo with spoofed Fox News site and 'deep-fake' Israeli soldiers. *Haaretz*, November 20. https://www.haaretz.com/israel-news/security-aviation/2023-11-20/ty-article/.premium/deep-faked-soldiers-and-spoofed-websites-russian-campaign-pushes-gaza-disinformation/0000018b-ed5c-d36e-a3cb-fd5fadd90000

Black, James, Alexandra Hall, Kate Cox, Marta Kepe, and Erik Silfversten. 2017. *Defence and security after Brexit: Understanding the possible implications of the UK's decision to leave the EU—Compendium report*. Santa Monica, CA: RAND Corporation.

Bregman, Ahron. 2016. *Israel's wars: A history since 1947*. Routledge.

[50] Kingsley and Bergman (2023).

[51] Chen (2023).

Bryant, Miranda. 2023. Russia spreading false claims about Qur'an burnings to harm Nato bid, says Sweden. *Guardian*, August 6. https://www.theguardian.com/world/2023/aug/06/russia-spreading-false-claims-about-quran-burnings-to-harm-nato-bid-says-sweden

Cadwalladr, Carole. 2017. The great British Brexit robbery: How our democracy was hijacked. *Guardian*, May 7. https://www.theguardian.com/technology/2017/may/07/the-great-british-brexit-robbery-hijacked-democracy

Cadwalladr, Carole and Emma Graham-Harrison. 2018. Revealed: 50 million Facebook profiles harvested for Cambridge Analytica in major data breach. *Guardian*, March 17. https://www.theguardian.com/news/2018/mar/17/cambridge-analytica-facebook-influence-us-election

Canetti, Daphna, Israel Waismel-Manor, Naor Cohen, and Carmit Rapaport. 2014. What does national resilience mean in a democracy? Evidence from the United States and Israel. *Armed Forces & Society* 40 (3): 504–520.

Central Bureau of Statistics. 2023. Population of Israel on the eve of 2023. December 29.

Chen, Hadassah. 2023. Judicial reform split Israel apart, Hamas's attack helped us find God—opinion. *Jerusalem Post*, November 26. https://www.jpost.com/opinion/article-775218

Cleave, Michelle. 2022. I was there Jan. 6: We need to counter foreign influence as well as address domestic division. *The Hill*, January 4. https://thehill.com/opinion/national-security/588079-i-was-there-jan-6-we-need-to-counter-foreign-influence-as-well-as/

Cohen, Zachary. 2021. China and Russia 'weaponized' QAnon conspiracy around time of US Capitol attack, report says. *CNN*, April 19. https://edition.cnn.com/2021/04/19/politics/qanon-russia-china-amplification/index.html

Congressional Research Service. 2023. *What is political warfare?* United States Congress, January 9.

Comerford, Ruth. 2023. Violent protests after Quran burning in Sweden. *BBC*, September 4. https://www.bbc.com/news/world-europe-66706937

Creedon, James. 2021. 'Pallywood': Truth and falsehoods about the Israeli-Palestinian conflict. *France 24*, November 4. https://www.france24.com/en/tv-shows/truth-or-fake/20211104-pallywood-truth-and-falsehoods-amid-political-communications

Dilanian, Ken. 2021. FBI probing if foreign governments, groups funded extremists who helped execute Capitol attack. *NBC News*, January 17. https://www.nbcnews.com/politics/national-security/fbi-probing-if-foreign-governments-groups-funded-extremists-who-helped-n1254525

Dilanian, Ken. 2022. Trump administration has known for weeks that Iran, Russia hacked local governments, officials say. *NBC News*, October 22. https://www.nbcnews.com/politics/2020-election/trump-admin-has-known-weeks-iran-russia-hacked-local-governments-n1244309

Frankel, Jonathan. 1972. The Anti-Zionist press campaigns in the USSR 1969–1971: An internal dialogue? *Soviet Jewish Affairs* 2 (1): 3–26.

Frenkel, Sheera. 2021. Lies on social media inflame Israeli-Palestinian conflict. *New York Times*, May 14. https://www.nytimes.com/2021/05/14/technology/israel-palestine-misinformation-lies-social-media.html

Gambino, Lauren, and Daniel Strauss. 2021. Congress certifies Joe Biden as next president hours after storming of Capitol. *Guardian*, January 7. https://www.theguardian.com/us-news/2021/jan/06/congress-certify-election-biden-republicans-object

Gleefully picking up on Herzog warning, Nasrallah says Israel tearing itself apart. 2023. *Times of Israel*, February 16. https://www.timesofisrael.com/gleefully-picking-up-on-herzog-warning-nasrallah-says-israel-tearing-itself-apart/

Graham, Kirk Robert. 2021. *British subversive propaganda during the Second World War: Germany, national socialism and the political warfare executive*. London: Palgrave Macmillan.

Haber, Eldar and Lev Topor. 2023. Sovereignty, cyberspace, and the emergence of internet bubbles. *Journal of Advanced Military Studies* 14 (1): 144–165.

Janda, Jakub. 2016. The Lisa case: STRATCOM lessons for European states. Security Policy Working Paper No. 11. Federal Academy for Security Policy.

Jeppesen, Sandra, Henry Giroux, Michael Hoechsmann, Chenjerai Kumanyika, David VanDyke, and Miranda McKee. 2022. *The capitol riots: Digital media, disinformation, and democracy under attack*. Routledge.

Jerusalem Center for Public Affairs. n.d. The forces driving the Israeli Arab sector from the Galilee to the Negev. https://jcpa.org/an-in-depth-analysis-of-the-forces-driving-the-israeli-arab-riots-of-may-2021/

Kessler, Glenn. 2023. The truth about Russia, Trump and the 2016 election. *Washington Post*, May 17. https://www.washingtonpost.com/politics/2023/05/17/truth-about-russia-trump-2016-election/

Kingsley, Patrick and Ronen Bergman. 2023. Over 1,000 air reservists threaten to stop serving, as Israel's political crisis grows. *New York Times*, July 21. https://www.nytimes.com/2023/07/21/world/middleeast/israel-judicial-plan-reservists-netanyahu.html

Kirkpatrick, David. 2017. Signs of russian meddling in brexit referendum. *New York Times*, November 15, 2017. https://www.nytimes.com/2017/11/15/world/europe/russia-brexit-twitter-facebook.html

Koplow, Michael J. 2011. Value judgment: Why do Americans support Israel? *Security Studies* 20 (2): 266–302.

Landau, Noa. 2019. 'Russia doesn't interfere': Kremlin shrugs off Israeli warning on election meddling. *Haaretz*, January 9. https://www.haaretz.com/israel-news/elections/2019-01-09/ty-article/.premium/russia-doesnt-interfere-kremlin-denies-it-will-meddle-in-israels-election/0000017f-e938-df5f-a17f-fbfece180000

Larson, Eric V., Richard E. Darilek, Daniel Gibran, Brian Nichiporuk, Amy Richardson, Lowell H. Schwartz, and Cathryn Q. Thurston. 2009. *Foundations of effective influence operations: A framework for enhancing army capabilities*. Santa Monica, C.A: RAND Arroyo Center.

Lerman, Eran. 2023. Unusual American intervention in domestic Israeli issues: A problematic approach which needs calculated responses. *JISS*, July 17. [Hebrew]. https://jiss.org.il/he/lerman-the-unusual-american-intervention/

Lipson, Charles. 1996. American support for Israel: History, sources, limits. *Israel Affairs* 2 (3–4): 128–146.

Mazzetti, Mark, and Luke Broadwater. 2021. The lost hours: How confusion and inaction at the Capitol delayed a troop deployment. *New York Times*, February 21. https://www.nytimes.com/2021/02/21/us/politics/capitol-riot-security-delays.html

Meister, Stefan. 2016. The Lisa case: Germany as a target of Russian disinformation. *NATO Review*, July 25. https://www.nato.int/docu/review/articles/2016/07/25/the-lisa-case-germany-as-a-target-of-russian-disinformation/index.html

Microsoft chief says Russia is spreading Middle East disinformation. 2023. *Radio Free Europe Radio Liberty*, November 11. https://www.rferl.org/a/russia-middle-east-disinformation-microsoft-smith/32680667.html

Nye, Joseph S. 2016. Deterrence and dissuasion in cyberspace. *International Security* 41 (3): 44–71.

Peleg, Bar, Josh Breiner, and Omer Benjakob. 2023. Iran, Russia or both | A foreign influence operation to incite violence in Israel is reemerging. *Haaretz*, July 3. https://www.haaretz.com/israel-news/2023-07-03/ty-article/.premium/an-already-exposed-foreign-influence-operation-to-incite-violence-in-israel-is-reemerging/00000189-17fe-dcb5-a5df-57ffa4120000

Putin's asymmetric assault on democracy in Russia and Europe: Implications for U.S. 2018. National Security Committee on Foreign Relations, United States Senate, January 10. https://www.foreign.senate.gov/imo/media/doc/FinalRR.pdfc

Rinke, Andreas and Paul Carrel. 2016. German-Russian ties feel Cold War-style chill over rape case. *Reuters*, February 1. https://www.reuters.com/article/us-germany-russia-idUSKCN0VA31O

Robinson, Linda, Todd C. Helmus, Raphael S. Cohen, Alireza Nader, Andrew Radin, Madeline Magnuson, and Katya Migacheva. 2018. Modern political warfare: Current practices and possible responses. Rand Corporation.

Russia, China and Iran are backing Hamas online-report. 2023. *Times of Israel*, November 6. https://www.timesofisrael.com/russia-china-and-iran-are-backing-hamas-online-report/

Russian propagandists use ToI logo and brand to propagate fake news against Ukraine, report shows. 2023. *Times of Israel*, November 21. https://www.timesofisrael.com/liveblog_entry/russian-propagandists-use-toi-logo-and-brand-to-propagate-fake-news-against-ukraine-report-shows/

Ruy, Donatienne. 2020. Did Russia influence Brexit? *CSIS*, July 21. https://www.csis.org/blogs/brexit-bits-bobs-and-blogs/did-russia-influence-brexit

Sablina, Liliia. 2021. We should stop the Islamisation of Europe!: Islamophobia and right-wing radicalism of the Russian-speaking Internet users in Germany. *Nationalities Papers* 49 (2): 361–374.

Schmitt, Michael N. ed. 2017. *Tallinn manual 2.0 on the international law applicable to cyber warfare*. Cambridge: Cambridge University Press.

Shalev, A. Russel. 2022. Israel needs to talk about the Arab riots of May 2021. *Fathom*, March. https://fathomjournal.org/israel-needs-to-talk-about-the-arab-riots-of-may-2021/

Shuker, Pnina, and Lev Topor. 2021. Russian influence campaigns against NATO in the Baltic region: Spread of chaos and divide et impera. In *The Russian Federation in global knowledge warfare*, 295–314. Springer, Cham.

Shultz, Richard H. and Roy Godson. 1984. *Dezinformatsia: Active measures in Soviet strategy*. Pergamon-Brassey's International Defense Publishers.

Smith, B. Lannes, "Propaganda," *Encyclopedia Britannica*, October 6, 2022. https://www.britannica.com/topic/propaganda

Sokolski, Henry D., ed. 2004. *Getting MAD: A nuclear mutual assured destruction, its origins and practice*. Strategic Studies Institute, US Army War College.

Solmar, E.L. 1978. Protocols of the anti-Zionists. *Soviet Jewish Affairs* 8 (2): 57–66.

Tabarovsky, Izabella. 2019. *Soviet anti-Zionism and contemporary left antisemitism*. Fathom

Tabarovsky, Izabella. 2023. Mahmoud Abbas' dissertation. *Tablet Magazine*, January 18. https://www.tabletmag.com/sections/arts-letters/articles/mahmoud-abbas-soviet-dissertation

The Iranians are also involved: The fakes spread on Arab citizens of Israel. 2023. *Globes*, October 23. [From Hebrew: גם האיראנים מעורבים: הפייקים שמופצים על ערבים אזרחי ישראל]. https://www.globes.co.il/news/article.aspx?did=1001460687

Thorbecke, Catherine. 2021. Social media companies restricting Trump accounts cite risk for violence. *ABC News*, January 13. https://abcnews.go.com/Technology/social-media-companies-restricting-trump-accounts-cite-risk/story?id=75176327

Topor, Lev. 2021a. Antizionist disinformation: Tips for Hanan Ashrawi. *Times of Israel Blogs*, December 5. https://blogs.timesofisrael.com/antizionist-disinformation-tips-for-hanan-ashrawi/

Topor, Lev. 2021b. The covert war: From BDS to de-legitimization to antisemitism. *Israel Affairs* 27 (1): 166–180.

Topor, Lev. 2022. *Phishing for Nazis: Conspiracies, anonymous communications and white supremacy networks on the Dark Web*. London: Routledge

Topor, Lev, and Alexander Tabachnik. 2021. Russian cyber information warfare: International distribution and domestic control. *Journal of Advanced Military Studies* 12 (1): 112–127.

UK House of Commons. 2017. Lessons learned from the EU Referendum—Twelfth Report of Session 2016–17.

Walker, Christopher. 2018. What is 'sharp power'? *Journal of Democracy* 29 (3): 9–23.

What to know about Israel's judicial reforms. 2023. *AJC*, June 13.

Wintour, Patrick. 2018. Russian bid to influence Brexit vote detailed in new US Senate report. *Guardian*, January 10. https://www.theguardian.com/world/2018/jan/10/russian-influence-brexit-vote-detailed-us-senate-report

Yonker, Carl and Lev Topor. (2021). The United States: Antisemites attack democracy. In *Antisemitism Worldwide—Report 2021*, 24–28. The Center for the Study of Contemporary European Jewry, Tel Aviv University

Zimdars, Melissa. 2022. Mis/Disinformation and social media. In *The social media debate*, 120–136. London: Routledge.

Chapter 6
Secure Cyber Domains (SCD): Mature Models

Throughout this book, and specifically in Chaps. 4 and 5, it has become clear that countries, organizations and, of course, individuals are suffering from increasing numbers of cyberattacks. While some cyberattacks are evident, like DoS, data manipulation and data breaches, other cyberattacks are less evident—attacks such as cyber mis/disinformation influence campaigns. Moreover, since there are no internationally applicable laws, regulations or norms to the use of cyberspace, and since forensic attribution in cyberspace is very difficult, open and unrestricted countries like the United States, the United Kingdom, European countries and Israel cannot directly and overtly retaliate when faced with cyberattacks carried out by proxies. That is, they can, and they have done so, but not under an internationally accepted umbrella. Moreover, they cannot retaliate over "stories" that have been spread online, even if these fake or misleading stories cause civil panic or unrest and harm the very essence of democracy and the democratic process, as demonstrated in Chaps. 4 and 5.

However, as the "Twitter Revolutions" of 2011 showed, not only democracies are vulnerable in the online domain. During these revolutions, the role of social media platforms like Twitter was very significant in facilitating and organizing various uprisings and protests. Some of the key events associated with the Twitter Revolutions of 2011 include the Egyptian Revolution, the 2009 Moldova civil unrest, the 2009–2010 Iranian election protests and the Tunisian Revolution. These movements demonstrated the power of unrestricted use of social media in mobilizing and organizing large-scale protests and dissent.[1]

How can countries respond, and should this lawless situation be accepted as a fact of life? Some countries will enhance platform regulation, making businesses accountable, while others, mainly in non-Western parts of the globe, will simply utilize their sovereignty and close or restrict their cyber domains, raising

[1] Passini (2012).

L. Topor, *Cyber Sovereignty*, Global Power Shift,
https://doi.org/10.1007/978-3-031-58199-1_6

their cyber borders. In this way, they can prevent many cyberattacks, but they can also prevent fake, misleading or simply unwanted information from entering their country and influencing their citizens. It is true that human rights, particularly freedom of speech, are harmed by this, and citizens of authoritarian countries are deprived of more freedoms when the ruler tightens their rule. However, this book is not about human rights, it is about the strategic balance of power between sovereign countries.

This chapter, which discusses these restricted cyber domains in detail, is presented before the chapter on less regulated and less restricted cyber domains to make a clear point, especially in the wake of Chap. 5's discussion of the cyberattacks and influence campaigns in which powerful countries like the United States, United Kingdom and Israel were helpless. The placement of this chapter aims to present an alternative to Western models of cyber domains, which in this and subsequent chapters I refer to as Secure Cyber Domains (SCDs). An SCD is a cyber domain that prioritizes cybersecurity, regime or state resilience, and sovereignty and control. To achieve these ends, an SCD is restricted, inhibiting the constant and free flow of information and communication.

In this chapter, I present several examples of protected, monitored and regulated cyberspaces, such as the North Korean model and the developing models of Russia and China. I also analyze cases like Saudi Arabia and Iran. The cases and analysis are not meant to be exhaustive and present a comprehensive historical, political and legal review of any given cyber domain; rather, they are meant to be indicators of what an SCD looks like and how it develops. In addition, I address several examples from other countries like India and Myanmar. I analyze each example by reviewing its respective cyber domain using a structured method, which I also use in the following chapter—I review each case based on the structure of cyberspace as presented in Chap. 2: by layer. Thus, in each case, I review four layers—the physical, logical, information and user layers—and address the legal and technical regulations that restrict each. The main goal is to get an indication of a country's level of control over its cyber domain. Thus, I ask the following questions about each layer:

- Physical Layer: Does the country regularly restrict or control its physical connections by design? Can it restrict the physical layer on demand? I.e., does the country have no physical connections or can it disconnect itself from the outside world but retain an intranet?
- Logical Layer: Does the country regularly restrict or control its network gateways and routes? I.e., does the country shut down the internet in specific areas or at specific times?
- Information Layer: Does the country regularly restrict or control the content within its borders? I.e., does the country disallow the dissemination of generally diverse and at times critical content, like criticism of the country's officials, regime or actions?

- User Layer: Does the country regularly restrict or control the way its citizens and even visitors use the internet? I.e., does the country put up technological barriers like the mandatory installation of applications or prohibit the use of certain applications or services?

Answers to these four questions will yield an indication of a country's level of control over its cyber domain. A country that regularly restricts and controls cyberspace will be defined as restricted.

Restricted internets like the ones described in this chapter were termed "internet bubbles" by myself and Eldar Haber; each country has a bubble, and some are more restricted than others. Building on Huntington's concept of the Clash of Civilizations, I predict, as noted further on in this book, that such individual bubbles will merge to form cyber blocs (i.e., a North American bloc, a European bloc, a post-Soviet bloc, a Middle Eastern-Gulf bloc and so on). The cases of North Korea, Russia, China, Saudi Arabia and Iran were selected by reviewing information from the non-profit organizations Freedom House (see Table 1.1) and Access Now (see Chap. 1). While there are many countries with restricted internet access, I focus on those that compete against the American and Western control of cyberspace, that is, I focus on global and regional powers because history has taught us that powers set the global scene.

Following this introduction, I review the cyberspaces of North Korea, China, Russia, Iran and Saudi Arabia, and also address, to a limited extent, India and Myanmar. Afterward, I summarize the main points and conclude this chapter. The insights from this chapter and the next (about free cyber domains) are compared in Chap. 8, the final chapter of this book.

6.1 North Korean Cyberspace

Authoritarian regimes face a challenging dilemma regarding telecommunications like the internet (as well as phones and satellites); on the one hand, accessible and available communication methods provide a platform for modernization, development and growth. On the other hand, they can also lead to a loss of control as people may be exposed to information that influences them to criticize and oppose the government. Every country faces this dilemma between freedom, with its opportunities for development, and control.[2]

North Korea's Kwangmyong ("bright star") internet, a heavily restricted domestic network, presents a unique case study in information control and internet access. Unlike the global internet we are all familiar with, Kwangmyong is like an intranet—it operates within a closed system, isolated from the outside world. It is an island or, as Haber and myself previously described, a bubble. As detailed

[2] Noland (2009).

in Chap. 2, this bubble consists of both legal and technical frameworks and has four main layers: infrastructure, logical control, information and users. Since the Kwangmyong intranet is so restricted, it resembles a completely isolated bubble. As shown in Fig. 2.2, North Korea does not have any overt physical connection points with the outside world, at least ones known to the public (apart from satellites). A recent investigation by WIRED and a report by the non-profit PSCORE suggest that North Korea uses Chinese and Russian connection points to connect to the global grid.[3]

However, regarding the issue of connectivity, the question is not only whether a country has physical connections, but whether it allows all users to connect to the outside world. It is important to note that this review of the North Korean bubble is very limited; North Korea shares very little open-source information with the outside world; therefore, this review and analysis will necessarily be somewhat incomplete.

Kwangmyong operates as a closed-loop intranet, physically disconnected from the global internet and relying on its own internal infrastructure. It also relies on outdated technology, meaning that the limited connections are slow and restricted. While details remain scarce, reports by researchers, analysts and journalists suggest that North Korea utilizes a combination of terrestrial and satellite links, with access points primarily concentrated in major cities and government institutions. Universities and select organizations may also have access, while individual citizens face significant barriers. While connections with the outside world are very limited, as demonstrated below, North Korea does allow a few hundred or thousands of individuals to access the global network under restrictions of time and surveillance. Thus, the name Kwangmyong is used in this chapter and onwards to describe both the intranet and North Korea's very limited connection with the outside world.

From a legal perspective, Kwangmyong's existence rests heavily upon North Korean legislation aimed at controlling information and restricting access to external influences. The Socialist Constitution of the Democratic People's Republic of Korea, while guaranteeing freedom of speech and press, also grants the state the power to regulate the dissemination of information considered harmful to the social order. This ambiguity allows for a broad interpretation of the constitution and justifies Kwangmyong's censorship practices. As stated in Article 67 of the Socialist Constitution: "The State shall guarantee the conditions for the free activities of democratic political parties and social organizations."[4] Furthermore, in December 2020, North Korea's Supreme People's Assembly approved the Reactionary Ideology and Culture Rejection Law, which prohibits the possession and consumption of foreign information that is either illegally provided by officials or Kim Jong Un's family members or by citizens and foreigners that bring

[3] PSCORE (2023), Burgess (2023).

[4] See the Socialist constitution of the Democratic People's Republic of Korea (2014, Article 67).

foreign content with them from their travels using storage devices like flash drives. This law did not spring up in a vacuum; rather, it builds on previously existing laws and regulations about foreign content that used to be smuggled in on CDs, DVDs and even VHS tapes. Such laws impose strict limitations on internet usage and content. They empower the authorities to monitor online activity, block websites and punish those who attempt to access unauthorized information.[5]

What can users access? Based on PSCORE's report, some citizens have handheld devices and computers that can access the intranet, but access to the outside grid is limited. Citizens have to undergo an approval process to gain an hour of internet access; the process can take a few days and cannot be frequent. Once approval has been granted, the user sits in front of the computer, usually at a university or a state-owned facility, and surfs the internet. The computer screen freezes every five minutes, and a librarian, or another state official, has to unlock it as they also monitor content. The government employs various gateway filtering techniques, including deep packet inspections (DPI), DNS manipulation and other filtering methods, to ensure tight control over the information landscape. This creates a highly sanitized online environment that reinforces the government's narrative and restricts access to diverse perspectives. Any information deemed critical of the regime or promoting Western values is strictly censored.[6]

Who are the users that have access to the internet? According to PSCORE's report, based on 24 face-to-face interviews with defectors and a survey of 158 others, 63% of the defectors who used the global internet while in North Korea were students, 9% were business retailers, 8% were clerks, 7% were workers, 4% were others, 2% were soldiers and 7% had no occupation. Of those who used the internet, 61% used it in cities, 20% used it in towns, 14% used it in villages and 5% used it in other regions. Based on the survey, the middle class used the internet the most, with 56.3% of users belonging to this class, while 18.4% were in the upper class and 24.1% in the lower class. Older people aged 60 and above used the internet rarely (5%), while 27% of the 18–29 age group used it, 31% of the 30–39 age group, 21% of the 40–49 age group and 16% of the 50–59 age group. In total, 70% of users were women.[7]

Interestingly, the vast majority (74.9%) of users resided in the Northern provinces of Ryanggang and North Hamgyeong, indicating that they possibly accessed the internet using clandestine connections with terrestrial lines, either with Russia's Vladivostok regional node or China's Baishan city lines (specifically, China Telecom's cable between Dunhua and Dandong (see Fig. 6.1, provided by the International Telecommunication Union (ITU)).[8]

[5] Williams (2021).

[6] PSCORE (2023), Chen et al. (2010).

[7] Ibid.

[8] Ibid; maps provided by the International Telecommunication Union (ITU) and updated to early 2023. See an interactive map with more information: https://bbmaps.itu.int/bbmaps/.

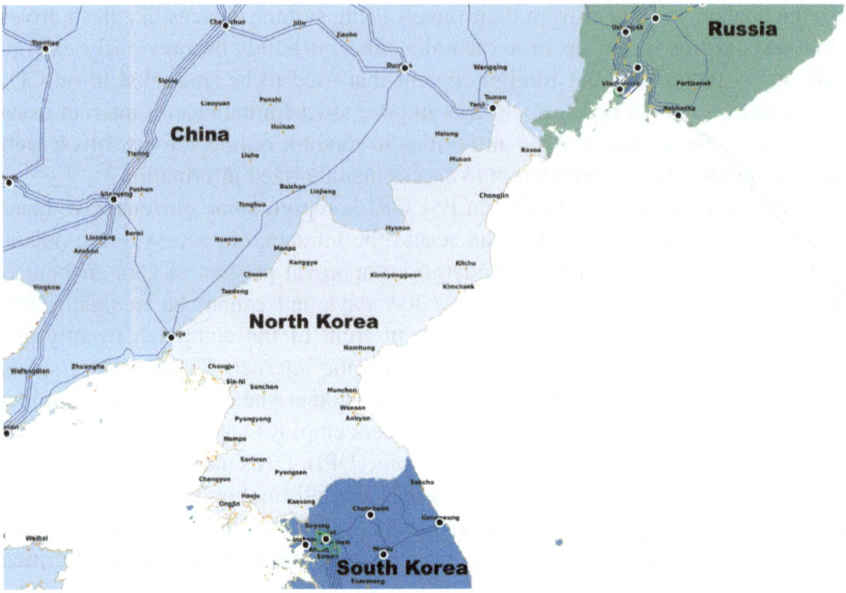

Fig. 6.1 Submarine and terrestrial internet cables around North Korea; *Source* Infrastructure Connectivity Map, International Telecommunication Union. * Blue lines are terrestrial, thin gray lines in seas and oceans are submarine fiber-optic cables, IXPs are in green circles. **Note that the cables and nodes in this figure do not directly connect to North Korea

Despite the restrictions, some users thus manage to circumvent censorship through various means. Flash drives containing unauthorized information are smuggled from abroad and circulated on the black market. Additionally, some users have developed techniques to access external websites through proxy servers and other clandestine methods, and some use radio and satellite television to consume foreign information. All this demonstrates the human desire for information freedom despite significant obstacles.

So, when we look at the four questions about the four layers of cyberspace presented in the introduction, can we conclude that North Korean cyberspace is restricted? Yes, the North Korean network is heavily controlled, limited and restricted, as summarized in Table 6.1.

6.2 Chinese Cyberspace

China has a population of around 1.43 billion people, and, as of 2022, 75.6% of them use the internet. Interestingly, the country has only 3 IXPs according to the ITU but 27 IXPs according to the Packet Clearing House, and it has around 3500 ISPs (although China Telecom, China Mobile, China Education & Research Network, and China Unicom are the main ones), a fact that makes internet control

Table 6.1 Restriction of internet layers in North Korea

Restriction of network layer	Answer
Does the country regularly restrict or control its physical connections by design? Can it restrict the physical layer on demand?	Yes, the country does not have any publicly available connections with the global internet grid
Does the country regularly restrict or control its network gateways and routes?	Yes, even when users use the internet and not the intranet, websites and content are blocked and monitored
Does the country regularly restrict or control the content within its borders?	Yes, websites and content are censored
Does the country regularly restrict or control the way its citizens and even visitors use the internet?	Yes, users can only use the internet and the intranet in a very limited manner

more feasible.[9] China is a global competitor of the United States, alongside Russia. It competes with the United States to exert global influence and power in general, specifically economic influence. The fact that China is much closer to Russia, not just geotropically but ideologically and diplomatically, reduces the power of the United States.[10] China is a fast-growing economy that has a developing military with nuclear capabilities, which makes it more resilient to foreign, mainly Western, pressure. One of the most significant projects of the Chinese Communist Party (CCP) is the Belt and Road Initiative (BRI), a massive China-led infrastructure project that aims to connect Asia with Africa and Europe through a network of railways, roads, ports and other infrastructure. Launched in 2013 by President Xi Jinping, it consists of two main components: the Silk Road Economic Belt and the 21st Century Maritime Silk Road. The initiative has met with both support and opposition. Some, like the United States, see it as a way for China to extend its economic and political influence, while others view it as a means to address the "infrastructure gap" and accelerate economic growth across various regions. The project is considered one of the largest infrastructure and investment projects in history. Interestingly, the BRI has a side project that competes against American and Western digital supremacy—the Digital Silk Road (DSR).[11]

The DSR is a key component of the BRI that aims to advance China's technological reach and influence. Launched in 2015, the DSR covers various areas, including developing and improving telecommunications networks, artificial intelligence capabilities, cloud computing, e-commerce, mobile payment systems, surveillance technology, smart cities and even quantum computers. It also provides support to Chinese exporters, including prominent technology companies

[9] See "China" on ITU's DataHub: https://datahub.itu.int/data/?e=CHN; also see "China" on Packet Clearing House: https://www.pch.net/ixp/dir#!mt-filters=%7B%22ctry%22%3A%5B%22dropdown%22%2C%22%22%2C%22China%22%5D%7D.

[10] See, generally, Attinà (2023), Ali (2022).

[11] Huang (2016), Mobley (2019), Greene and Triolo (2020).

like Huawei. The DSR has been the subject of intense geopolitical and commercial competition, with China positioning itself to reap strategic and commercial rewards, especially in emerging economies. However, China has also exported 5G technologies, alongside other technologies and services, to the United States, the United Kingdom and Europe. Essentially, China is trying to rewire the globe in terms of infrastructure, routing, services and usability and thus compete against American cyberspace supremacy.[12]

In September 2023, the Global Engagement Center (GEC), an American State Department agency tasked with addressing foreign propaganda and disinformation, released a report warning that Beijing's information campaign could eventually sway how decisions are made around the world and undermine American interests. It followed the August 2020 report on Russian disinformation campaigns. Both Russia and China, as suggested by the American reports, are using sharp power to promote chaos and undermine state and social resilience and solidarity. In this regard, one of the main concerns of the United States is that the BRI and the DSR will allow China to take over cyberspace dominance from the United States.[13] China takes advantage of the open and free mass communication systems of the United States and Europe while protecting itself from such incoming dangers.[14]

At home, China controls its cyber domain. It censors content and prefers Chinese technology, both hardware and software, over foreign options. China has created a "Great Firewall" (GFW) which blocks foreign incoming information. The GFW is part of the larger Golden Shield Project (GSP), an initiative that was promoted by Deng Xiaoping, the revolutionary leader of the People's Republic of China (PRC) after Mao Zedong's death in 1976. Deng Xiaoping used to say, "If you open the window for fresh air, you have to expect some flies to blow in." Xiaoping meant that whoever opens their doors to foreign information should expect unwanted information; this unwanted information, whether true, manipulated or false, should be dealt with to protect the Communist regime.[15]

The GFW and the GSP are a combination of legislative actions and technologies enforced by the PRC from the 1990s onwards to regulate the internet domestically. Their primary role is to block access to selected foreign websites and slow down cross-border internet traffic. The GFW operates by checking TCP packets for keywords or sensitive words, and if these are detected, censoring access to the content. It also limits access to foreign information sources like websites by blocking DNS and IPs, blocks foreign internet tools and mobile apps, and requires foreign companies to adapt to domestic regulations, such as the requirement to store data in China. The firewall's goal is to protect the Chinese regime, and, as argued by the CCP, the Chinese population, by preventing access to what they consider to

[12] Ibid; Hillman (2021), Cheney (2019).

[13] Global Engagement Center (2023), Global Engagement Center (2020).

[14] Haber and Topor (2023).

[15] Shullman (2019).

be unwanted, fake or sensitive topics, such as the names of government leaders, political movements or religious movements. These include issues like the Falun Gong cult, issues related to the Uyghur Muslims, and, of course, the three banned Ts: the Tiananmen Square massacre, Tibet and Taiwan.[16] Further, in order to use most services and applications, users cannot use anonymous tools or pseudonyms; rather, they have to register with their real national ID and phone number.[17] In addition to social control, the GFW also acts as a form of trade protectionism, allowing China to grow its own internet giants, such as Tencent, Alibaba and Baidu. The GFW restricts Facebook, Google, Twitter, Tinder, WordPress, Telegram, WhatsApp, YouTube, Netflix, the New York Times, the BBC, Wikipedia and even German DW News.[18]

In November 1990, China registered its *.cn* top-level domain using the China Internet Network Information Center (CNNIC). On April 20, 1994, China gained full internet functionality, by January 1995 the Ministry of Posts and Telecommunications had granted internet services to the public, and by 1996–1997 China had enacted its first laws criminalizing online activities that were believed to undermine the regime. It was in the early 2000s that China began to intensively block and filter cyberspace. In December 2015, at the opening of the country's second internet conference, President Xi Jinping said, "We [China] should respect the right of individual countries to independently choose their own path of cyber-development," while signaling that the internet is a form of mass communication that should be regulated and censored like any other. Jinping followed the path Xiaoping laid out, and since then, information that the regime perceives as unwanted has been censored, and this censorship has been justified with the argument it ensures domestic stability and resilience, territorial integrity and modernization, and protects economic growth.[19]

In December 2016, China released its first National Security Strategy, which states that there is no national security without cybersecurity. It reaffirmed that sovereignty over information is an important part of state sovereignty. China's cybersecurity law from June 2017 acts as the baseline of its cyber regulation, alongside additional laws and policies that have been enacted to ensure complete control over the internet—to ensure the CCP's "cyber sovereignty." The CCP promotes six key issues: it pursues economic development through cyberspace, spreads pro-communist propaganda, engages in domestic censorship, uses cyberattacks to express discontent with acts of foreign powers, develops Chinese cyber infrastructure and capabilities, and promotes domestic surveillance.[20]

Although China is currently connected to the outside world via foreign cables, mainly of American, Japanese and French origin, it plans to replace or add to

[16] Chepenko (2020), Zittrain and Edelman (2003).

[17] Qu (2021).

[18] Haber and Topor (2023), Gibson (2009).

[19] Yang (2012), Economy (2018).

[20] See, generally, Chang (2014), Maranto (2020).

Fig. 6.2 Submarine and terrestrial internet cables and internet exchange points in and around China; *Source* Infrastructure Connectivity Map, International Telecommunication Union. * Blue lines are terrestrial, thin gray lines in seas and oceans are submarine fiber-optic cables, IXPs are in green circles. China is highlighted in gray

existing connections. For instance, China's main telecommunication firms—the China Telecommunications Corporation (China Telecom), China Mobile Limited and the China United Network Communications Group Co Ltd (China Unicom)—are planning to develop a $500 million submarine fiber-optic cable linking Asia, the Middle East and Europe to rival a similar American-backed project.[21] Furthermore, neighboring countries like Vietnam, Mongolia and North Korea rely on connections from China, and others also connect to cables passing through Chinese nodes (see Fig. 6.2). For instance, the SEA-ME-WE 3 and 6 cables pass through Southeast Asia, the Middle East and West Europe.[22] There are nearly 1.4 million kilometers of fiber-optic cables globally, and China is challenging both their quantity and quality; in late 2023 it unveiled that it has built the world's fastest internet network.[23]

On September 28, 2023, the Cyberspace Administration of China (CAC) issued its Provisions on Regulating and Facilitating Cross-Border Data Flow (a draft for comments) for public comment, a part of the Measures for the Security Assessment

[21] Brock (2023), Gross et al. (2023).

[22] See details on the SEA-ME-WE 3 and 6 cables here: https://www.submarinenetworks.com/en/systems/asia-europe-africa/smw3; https://www.submarinenetworks.com/en/systems/asia-europe-africa/smw6.

[23] Kelly (2023).

Table 6.2 Restriction of internet layers in China

Restriction of network layer	Answer
Does the country regularly restrict or control its physical connections by design? Can it restrict the physical layer on demand?	Partially, though China has foreign connections, it is also working to develop an infrastructure that can replace foreign connections
Does the country regularly restrict or control its network gateways and routes?	Yes, China filters packets, DNS and IPs and controls routing in general
Does the country regularly restrict or control the content within its borders?	Yes, websites, services and content are censored
Does the country regularly restrict or control the way its citizens and even visitors use the internet?	Yes, users can mainly use local websites, applications and services

of Data Exports, which were adopted in May 2022 at the 10th office meeting of the CAC for 2022. Unlike previous regulations that restrict incoming information, this one is aimed at data export, restricting the export of private information about Chinese citizens to the outside world and setting rules about when, where and how private information should be exported.[24] Indeed, in the lawless world of cyberspace with its lack of regulations regarding personal privacy, these provisions and assessments might actually benefit Chinese citizens and not just the government, bringing the measures, though not the essence, of cyber privacy in China closer to the European GDPR and further from the American (lack of) regulations.

Lastly, as summarized in Table 6.2, Chinese cyberspace is indeed an SCD as China restricts and regulates all layers of cyberspace and provides Chinese alternatives to American or Western-promoted technologies and services.

China has developed or is currently developing its own physical infrastructure and its own platforms and services, as well as legal and normative guidelines for its citizens and visitors about how to use the Chinese version of the internet. However, foreign services and companies have proliferated in China. For instance, Apple, Samsung and other technology giants have a significant market share in China as their products are (or were?) more developed than Chinese options. Many prefer an iPhone or a Mac over a Huawei; however, this preference is shifting. Alongside significant developments by technology giants like Huawei, the Chinese government itself has begun issuing orders to officials prohibiting the use of foreign technology companies' devices, such as Apple or Samsung phones or computers. This move might be intended to counter the American ban on Chinese hardware, on Huawei and ZTE; nevertheless, with perseverance and in due time, it will lead to the replacement of Western devices (and services) in China, making the Chinese internet even more independent.[25]

[24] "Provisions on Regulating and Promoting Cross-border Data Flows (draft for comments)" (2023).

[25] "China's iPhone Ban Accelerates Across Government and State Firms" (2023), Bartz and Alper (2022).

6.3 Russian Cyberspace

The Russian internet, often referred to as RuNet, presents an interesting picture of a cyber domain shaped by unique legal, technical, and political dynamics. Although Russia is a key rival of the US and Europe, it is highly connected to the "Western" internet with over 20 IXPs in Moscow alone and dozens of others around the country (a total of 43 IXPs). The Russian population is overwhelmingly connected; of the approximately 146 million Russian citizens, 90.4% are connected to the internet (true to 2022) and there are around 7000 ISPs operating in Russia. Moreover, of these 146 million Russians, approximately 86.6% have internet access at home. Russia's internet use is comparable to the United States, where 91.8% of the around 338 million citizens are connected, 88.1% of which have access at home. China's 1.43 billion citizens are less connected: only 75.6% of them use the internet.[26] Russia's overall connectivity rates are much higher than the global average, which stands at 66.3% of individuals.[27]

In March 2000, the largest ISP in Russia was the government-owned RELCOM (Reliable Communications). Established in 1990–1991, the company signaled the beginning of a massive wave of internet adoption in Russia (although international networking had been available since the 1980s, and domestic networking had been developed before that, see Chap. 2). The companies Demos and Russia On-line sprung up soon after. RELCOM once enjoyed a near-monopoly in the market, but by 2003, the ISP market was dominated by five operators, who controlled approximately 84% of services; in turn, however, they were controlled by the government.[28]

Russia's internet regulator is a government agency known as Roskomnadzor, the Federal Service for Supervision of Communications, Information Technology and Mass Media. It began to emerge in 2007–2008 with various federal decisions like Federal Decree number 419 of June 2, 2008, on "the Federal Service for Supervision in the Sphere of Communications and Mass Communications." Later, the Russian Federation officially enacted mass communication regulations, such as Decision number 228 of March 16, 2009, effectively creating present-day Roskomnadzor, which generally deals with the regulation of information on mass communication platforms like television, radio, the internet and more.[29]

Tabachnik and I argued that Russian authorities perceive cyberspace as a political tool that allows them to conduct cyber information warfare against their adversaries while simultaneously resisting any similar threats through laws and

[26] See "Russia" on ITU's DataHub: https://datahub.itu.int/data/?e=RUS; also see "Russia" on Packet Clearing House: https://www.pch.net/ixp/dir#!mt-filters=%7B%22ctry%22%3A%5B%22dropdown%22%2C%22%22%2C%22Russia%22%5D%7D.

[27] Ibid.

[28] Marcus (2004), Bulashova et al. (n.d.).

[29] See "Statute on Roskomnadzor." The Federal Service for Supervision of Communications, Information Technology and Mass Media, Russian Federation. https://eng.rkn.gov.ru/legal_information/.

regulations that control the information entering Russia. This, of course, comes in the wake of the successful restriction and censorship of television, radio and newspapers in the 2000s and the earlier Soviet "Iron Curtain," and it resembles Chinese efforts to block foreign influence. Tabachnik and I noted that Russian internet regulations can be divided into legal–technological restrictions and legal–psychological restrictions.[30] In this way, Russian authorities control all layers of cyberspace: the physical and logical layers as well as the layers of information and users. That is, they control both the car and the driver.

The legal–technical restrictions include several laws. For instance, on April 13, 2005, the Russian Federation issued Decree number 214 "On approval of the Rules for the organization and conduct of work on mandatory confirmation of compliance of communication means" (changes were made to this Decree on October 13, 2008), requiring the mandatory installation of a system of operational-investigatory measures (SORM) by telecommunication service providers, including ISPs. The SORM was provided by the Federal Security Service of the Russian Federation and allowed it, and other security entities, to monitor users' communications metadata (such as traffic) and content, including their web browsing activity, emails, phone calls, messages, social media platforms and more. Moreover, SORM has DPI capability, a filtering inspection mechanism that filters transmitted data and blocks non-compliant or unwanted material like spam, viruses or unwanted content such as foreign websites, much like China's GFW. This system, SORM, is one of the major technological tools in the implementation and regulation of the Yarovaya law.[31]

In 2012, the Russian Parliament unanimously adopted a law that boosts governmental control over the internet. The law was introduced as a means to battle child pornography and illegal content, but it granted the power to create a blacklist of websites and services that were—or could be—censored. Yandex, LiveJournal, Russian Wikipedia and other websites criticized the law, and some were immediately shut down.[32] In 2014, Pavel Durov, the founder of the Russian social media platform VKontakte (VK) fled Russia over a severe dispute with Moscow as it sought to restrict, control and monitor the social media company in response to anti-governmental protests that were organized on VK in early 2012.[33]

Further, the Yarovaya law (Russian: Закон Яровой), named after the Deputy Chairwoman of the Russian State Duma, is a set of two Russian Federal Bills (374-FZ and 375-FZ) that were passed on May 13, 2016, and signed by Russian

---

[30] Topor and Tabachnik (2021).

[31] "Decree of the Government of the Russian Federation of April 13, 2005 Number 214." Ministry of Digital Development, Russian Federation [In Russian: Постановление Правительства РФ от 13 апреля 2005 г. N 214 «Об утверждении Правил организации и проведения работ по обязательному подтверждению соответствия средств связи» (с изменениями от 13 октября 2008 г.). https://digital.gov.ru/ru/documents/3034/?utm_referrer=https%3a%2f%2fwww.google.com%2f#tdocumentcontent.

[32] Elder (2012).

[33] Walker (2014).

President Vladimir Putin in early July 2016. The Yarovaya law aims to combat terrorism and extremism, but it has been highly controversial due to its implications for privacy, freedom of expression and internet access. Among other things, it requires ISPs or content providers to store content like voice calls, images, text and more, and it has forced secure platforms (like SMAs) to provide decryption keys to the authorities.[34] Effectively, this law has made political criticism and opposition of the Federal government much riskier.

One of the most significant changes Russia has made to its "relationship" with the global internet is the "sovereign internet" law. Federal law number 90-FZ (90-ФЗ) came into force on November 1, 2019, and aimed to develop an internal internet traffic system. According to the Russian State Duma, it was designed to "protect the domestic segment of the internet from possible external threats" [from Russian: акон призван обезопасить отечественный сегмент интернета от возможных внешних угроз].[35] The "sovereign internet" law essentially created RuNet, as it allowed Russia to develop its own routing system, physical and logical, its own IXPs, and even its own DNS system. In practice, it allows Russia to disconnect from the global grid while maintaining an operational intranet. It also made foreign companies store Russian-user-related data on Russian soil. Unlike China's GFW, which was developed early on during the expansion of the internet in China, the Russian law is an attempt to regulate the already extensive and free internet use within Russia.

Additionally, further regulations that formed part of the "sovereign internet" law-making process were approved in mid-2019, adopted by the Kremlin on December 2, 2019, and came into force on July 1, 2020. Law number 425-FZ (425-ФЗ) of December 2, 2019, makes Russian applications mandatory on smartphones, computers, tablets and so on. This law, nicknamed the "anti-Apple" law, requires technology companies to sell their devices with applications from Yandex and Mail.ru pre-installed. Apple did agree to install these applications in an attempt to remain in the Russian market.[36]

Legal–psychological measures that control internet use in Russia, published between 2019 and 2022, include three major measures: the "disrespect laws" and

[34] "Federal Law of July 6, 2016 No. 374-FZ." President of Russia, Russian Federation [In Russian: Федеральный закон от 06.07.2016 г. № 374-ФЗ. О внесении изменений в Федеральный закон «О противодействии терроризму» и отдельные законодательные акты Российской Федерации в части установления дополнительных мер противодействия терроризму и обеспечения общественной безопасности]. http://kremlin.ru/acts/bank/41108.

[35] "The law on "Sovereign RuNet": Answers to the Main Questions." State Duma, Federal Assembly of the Russian Federation (April 8, 2021), [In Russian: Закон о «суверенном Рунете»: ответы на главные вопросы]. http://duma.gov.ru/news/51194/.

[36] "Federal Law of December 2, 2019 N 425-FZ "On Amendments to Article 4 of the Law of the Russian Federation "On the Protection of Consumer Rights." [In Russian: Федеральный закон от 02.12.2019 N 425-ФЗ "О внесении изменения в статью 4 Закона Российской Федерации "О защите прав потребителей"]. https://wilmap.stanford.edu/sites/default/files/2020-05/Law%20on%20pre%20installation%20with%20Russian%20software.pdf; "Apple Reportedly Agrees to Preinstall Russian Software on Gadgets," *Radio Free Europe Radio Liberty*, March 16, 2021, https://www.rferl.org/a/apple-russia-iphone-software/31153385.html.

the “fake news” law (March 18, 2019) (Laws 31-ФЗ [FZ], 30-ФЗ and 28-ФЗ), and the “foreign agent” law (426-ФЗ). These laws allow authorities to fine or imprison people in cases where their online actions have harmed human dignity or public morality or have disrespected the Russian government, as well as in cases where the user is funded by foreign sources, even seemingly independent sources like YouTube (in case a user receives revenue from an online channel/publication). These laws are very obscure, allowing the authorities to interpret them as Moscow wishes, and they are designed to prevent the dissemination of information through mass telecommunication networks, including the internet. Moreover, the “fake news” law allows the authorities to decide whether information might be misleading or undesirable and simply block such unwanted information. Roskomnadzor is responsible for notifying the editorial entities (of a social media platform, a website, etc.) of the unwanted publication and can demand its removal.[37]

Russia, by discouraging foreign companies, services and websites, also promotes native Russian ones—alternatives to Western social media platforms, search engines, websites and more. For instance, VK is the dominant social media platform in Russia, offering features similar to Facebook, such as news feeds, profiles, groups and messaging. Odnoklassniki (“classmates” in Russian) is another popular platform, focusing on reconnecting with old friends and family. Instead of

[37] “Federal Law “On Amendments to the Code of the Russian Federation on Administrative Offenses” dated March 18, 2019 N 28-FZ (latest edition).” (March 18, 2019), [In Russian: Федеральный закон “О внесении изменений в Кодекс Российской Федерации об административных правонарушениях” от 18.03.2019 N 28-ФЗ (последняя редакция)]. https://www.consultant.ru/document/cons_doc_LAW_320403/.

“Federal Law “On Amendments to the Federal Law “On Measures of Influence on Persons Involved in Violations of Fundamental Human Rights and Freedoms, the Rights and Freedoms of Citizens of the Russian Federation” and Article 27 of the Federal Law “On the Procedure for Exiting and Entering the Russian Federation” dated 03/04/2022 N 30-FZ (latest edition).” (March 4, 2022), [In Russian: Федеральный закон “О внесении изменений в Федеральный закон “О мерах воздействия на лиц, причастных к нарушениям основополагающих прав и свобод человека, прав и свобод граждан Российской Федерации” и статью 27 Федерального закона “О порядке выезда из Российской Федерации и въезда в Российскую Федерацию” от 04.03.2022 N 30-ФЗ (последняя редакция)]. https://www.consultant.ru/document/cons_doc_LAW_410885/; “Federal Law of March 18, 2019 No. 31-FZ “On Amendments to Article 15–3 of the Federal Law “On Information, Information Technologies and Information Protection.“(March 18, 2019), [In Russian: Федеральный закон от 18.03.2019 № 31-ФЗ “О внесении изменений в статью 15–3 Федерального закона “Об информации, информационных технологиях и о защите информации”. http://publication.pravo.gov.ru/Document/View/0001201903180031; “Federal Law of December 2, 2019 N 426-FZ “On Amendments to the Law of the Russian Federation “On the Mass Media” and the Federal Law “On Information, Information Technologies and Information Protection.” (December 2, 2019), [In Russian: Федеральный закон от 2 декабря 2019 г. N 426-ФЗ “О внесении изменений в Закон Российской Федерации “О средствах массовой информации” и Федеральный закон “Об информации, информационных технологиях и о защите информации”.]

Fig. 6.3 Submarine cables connected to Russia; *Source* Telegeography

Google, Russia offers Yandex. The leading search engine in Russia, it offers similar functionalities to Google with a focus on Russian-language content and local results. Yandex also offers Yandex.Disk (cloud), Yandex maps and more. YouTube has been replaced by Rutube, an alternative video-sharing platform. In the messenger arena, Russia has TamTam, which, though it has not replaced applications like Telegram, is another example of a non-Western application or service.[38] The above-mentioned platforms are also available outside Russia and are attractive alternatives for Russian-speaking people worldwide.

Russia is the largest country in the world, which makes it very difficult to develop wide network coverage while simultaneously keeping control over the physical layer—mainly the submarine and terrestrial cables connecting Russia to the rest of the world (see Figs. 6.3 and 6.4).[39] However, the technical and psychological laws introduced by Russian authorities in recent years serve

[38] See examples of Russian technologies, services and social media here: VKontakte: https://vk.com; Odnoklassniki: https://ok.ru; Yandex search and other services: https://ya.ru; Rutube: https://rutube.ru; TamTam: https://tamtam.chat.

[39] Maps provided by the International Telecommunication Union (ITU) and updated to early 2023. See an interactive map with more information: https://bbmaps.itu.int/bbmaps/; Also see maps provided by TeleGeography, an interactive map is available: https://www.submarinecablemap.com/.

Fig. 6.4 Russian terrestrial cables and IXPs (around Western Russia and Moscow); *Source* Infrastructure Connectivity Map, International Telecommunication Union. * Blue lines are terrestrial, thin gray lines in seas and oceans are submarine fiber-optic cables, IXPs are in green circles. Russia is highlighted in gray

to tighten control over cyberspace, making it more secure against cyberattacks and cyber-influence campaigns. With its native Russian alternatives to Western, mainly American, technologies and services, Russia offers a wholistic alternative to Western cyberspace. As summarized in Table 6.3, Russia is currently a partial bubble, allowing connections and information flow while preserving its ability to restrict, control and even close cyberspace.

Table 6.3 Restriction of internet layers in Russia

Restriction of network layer	Answer
Does the country regularly restrict or control its physical connections by design? Can it restrict the physical layer on demand?	Partially. Russia has foreign connections, but it is working to develop an infrastructure that can replace foreign connections and is working on an option that will allow it to decouple from the global grid (the RuNet project)
Does the country regularly restrict or control its network gateways and routes?	Yes, Russia filters packets, DNS and IPs and controls routing in general
Does the country regularly restrict or control the content within its borders?	Yes, websites, services and content are censored
Does the country regularly restrict or control the way its citizens and even visitors use the internet?	Yes, although users can use most local or foreign devices, platforms and services, they are held accountable for any violation of information-related laws (like the "fake news" law or the foreign agent law)

6.4 Iranian Cyberspace

The Islamic Republic of Iran has a population of approximately 88.6 million citizens, 78.6% of whom use the internet. As of 2022, Iran had 9 IXPs and 97 ISPs (information may vary—see footnote).[40] Iran embraced the internet in January 1993 and was the second country in the Persian Gulf and Middle East to connect to the global grid, while the first country was Israel. At first, internet connections were very limited, and only universities joined the network. By the early 2000s, as Emerson T. Brooking and Suzanne Kianpour note, the internet had begun to reshape Iranian society, long after the Islamic Revolution of 1979, which changed Iranian politics and power dynamics. The internet offered a new and far-reaching platform for spreading Islam, which seemed beneficial to the Iranian regime; however, at the same time, it offered a refuge where forbidden ideas could be discussed freely. Many young Iranians were quick to adopt the web as it offered a refuge from the strict Islamic regime. By 2001, there were 1,500 internet cafes in Tehran alone, and blogging had become a popular trend—the first Farsi-language blog was launched in 2001.[41]

The internet offered a political alternative and was adopted as a tool for political reform that people—politicians, clerics and others—could use to push back against the Islamic regime. Thus, in 2001, Iranian courts quickly asserted control over ISPs and obliged them to monitor and censor content. On November 7, 2001, the Supreme Court for Cultural Revolution declared that ISPs must remove anti-government and "anti-Islamic" websites from their servers and that all ISPs would be placed under state control, just as television and other means of information dissemination were controlled. In January 2002, a list of banned and illegal websites was created.[42] Currently, Iranian ISPs include 97 service providers, which work as public switched telephone networks or public data networks, including major ones like the Iran Telecommunication Company (ITC), the Mobile Communications Company of Iran (MCI), and the Telecommunications

[40] See "Iran (Islamic Republic of)" on ITU's DataHub: https://datahub.itu.int/data/?e=IRN.
*Please note that information regarding Iranian cyberspace may vary as the ITU states there are 9 IXPs in Iran, but ITU maps and other maps show only 4–5 IXPs in Teheran, Mashhad, Tahriz, Khuzestan and Shiraz. See ITU map: https://bbmaps.itu.int/bbmaps/ and also see the Internet Exchange Map: https://www.internetexchangemap.com/ and the Packet Clearing House map: https://www.pch.net/ixp/.
Also see "Iran Launches 6th Internet Hub in Khuzestan Province," *Financial Tribune*, May 28, 2017, https://financialtribune.com/articles/economy-sci-tech/65386/iran-launches-6th-internet-hub-in-khuzestan-province#:~:text=Company%20of%20Iran."-,Internet%20Exchange%20Point,%2C%20Tabriz%2C%20Shiraz%20and%20Qom.

[41] Brooking and Kianpour (2020).

[42] Rahimi (2003, 2007).

Infrastructure Company (TIC), which is a governmental agency that owns IXPs and is governed by the Iran's Ministry of ICT.[43]

In 2021, Iran established the Supreme Council of Cyberspace (SCC), a powerful Iranian government body established by decree of Supreme Leader Ayatollah Ali Khamenei. This move placed control of the internet in the hands of more religious authorities. The SCC sets the strategic direction for cyberspace in Iran, including content regulation, internet infrastructure development and international cooperation. It also oversees the national filtering system, blocking access to websites deemed politically sensitive, illegal or "contrary to Islamic values." Of course, it also deals with cyber defense as in 2010 the Iranian regime received a blow to its nuclear development program by the alleged Israeli–American Stuxnet computer worm (see the Stuxnet case in Chap. 4).[44]

In November 2019, widespread protests erupted across Iran in response to a sudden increase in fuel prices. The government responded by deploying security forces and imposing severe internet restrictions. Authorities throttled internet speeds and eventually shut down access to the global internet for several days. This blackout severely limited communication among protesters and obstructed the dissemination of information to the outside world. The blackout made it challenging for activists and protesters to organize or share information about the scale of the unrest. Such internet shutdowns continued sporadically into 2020.[45] On September 16, 2022, the death of Mahsa Amini, a young woman who died under suspicious circumstances in police custody, sparked protests against the Ayatollah regime across Iran. The Iranian regime responded by heavily censoring social media platforms and messaging applications to prevent the spread of information and the organization of protests; it also shut down mobile internet services as people used mobile phones in the protests. Access to Instagram, Telegram and other platforms was disrupted, hindering the ability of protesters to coordinate and share information about the demonstrations and the circumstances surrounding Mahsa Amini's death.[46]

Iran follows in the footsteps of North Korea, China and Russia. From 2016 onwards it has developed the National Information Network (NIN) (Farsi: شبکهٔ ملی اطلاعات, Shabake-ye Melli-ye Ettelā'āt). The NIN is a project that aims to create a separate and state-controlled cyberspace within Iran. Since Iranian President Ebrahim Raisi came to power in 2021, the Ministry of ICT has made the development of the NIN a top priority. In February 2023, the National Center for Cyberspace (NCC) announced that 86% of the NIN's operational goals had been met and that investments in fiber-optic infrastructure and long-term evolution

[43] See the Telecommunications Infrastructure Company (TIC) of the Ministry of ICT in Iran: https://www.tic.ir.

[44] See "Iran." Freedom on the Net, Freedom House (2023). https://freedomhouse.org/country/iran/freedom-net/2023.

[45] Esfandiari (2019).

[46] Strzyżyńska (2022).

(LTE) mobile networks would continue. Iran aims to control satellite internet as well, although it comprises only a fraction of the global or even domestic use. In February 2021, the NCC announced that it would establish a dedicated satellite-based internet service as a countermeasure to services like Starlink, which also deploys internet in Iran and might be the global service used by those denied internet access in authoritarian regimes.[47]

Furthermore, on September 6, 2022, the SCC announced its plans to develop and implement the Internet User Protection Bill, which will put more control over internet gateways under the supervision and operation of governmental offices, the armed forces and the Intelligence Organization of the Islamic Revolutionary Guard Corps. Under this bill, foreign technology companies operating in Iran will need to place representatives in Iran, collaborate with the Islamic Republic of Iran on surveillance and censorship efforts, and pay taxes. Big data and critical information like information on citizens will be required to be stored locally in Iran. This bill will also criminalize the use of virtual private networks (VPNs) and other proxy means like the use of encrypted messengers and the American intelligence project, the TOR Dark Web.[48]

As seen in Fig. 6.5, Iran is connected to the global grid through land cables to neighboring countries and via submarine fiber-optic cables like the Falcon submarine cable, which connects Iran, Kuwait, Bahrain, Qatar, the United Arab Emirates, India, Sri Lanka, Yemen, Iraq, Egypt, Sudan, Saudi Arabia, the Maldives and Oman. All the submarine cables are placed in the Persian Gulf, making this an area of crucial importance to Iran, not only in the context of trade but also in the context of communications.

Like Russia and China, Iran is also encouraging the development of alternative technologies, services and social media. For instance, Café Bazaar is an Iranian application store like Google Play; Soroush is a messenger that aims to be an alternative to Telegram and WhatsApp; Snapp! is an Iranian alternative to Uber; Bamilo was an Iranian e-commerce platform that ran for approximately four years and was disbanded in mid-2019, and Mozado is another e-commerce platform, an alternative to Amazon and eBay. The Iranian regime has blocked access to Facebook, Twitter and other social media platforms. Video streaming platforms like Netflix are also blocked.[49] Thus, as shown in Table 6.4, the Iranian regime is moving toward a Russo-Chinese model of the internet, a blocked internet with very limited access to the global grid. The SCC controls Iranian cyberspace, and the NIN project aims to create a working "on-demand" intranet, just like Russia's RuNet project.

[47] "Iran," Freedom on the Net.

[48] "Iran: Human Rights Groups Sound Alarm against Draconian Internet Bill (2022), Esfandiari (2022).

[49] "Iran's Comms Minister Says a Third of Blocked Sites 'Obscene'" (2023).

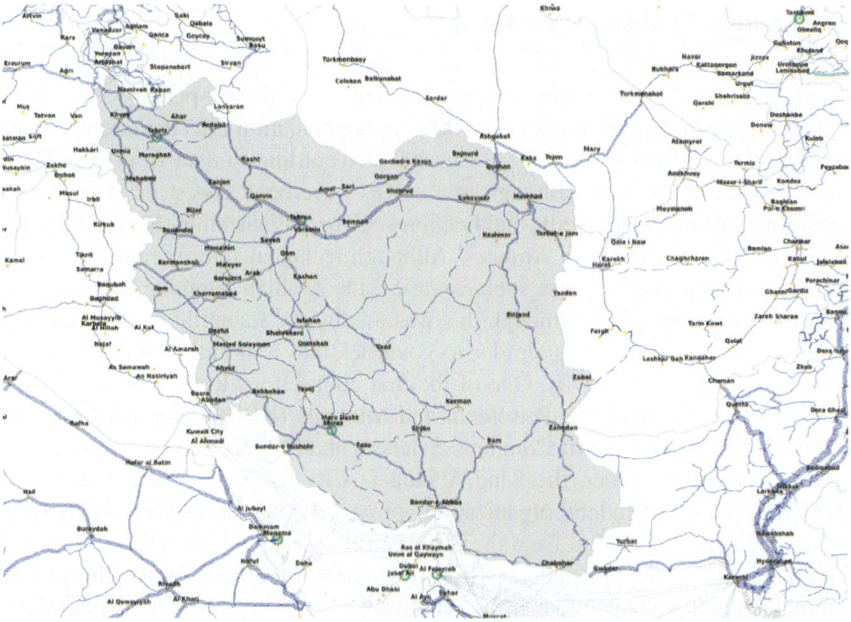

Fig. 6.5 Submarine and terrestrial internet cables and internet exchange points in and around Iran; *Source* Infrastructure Connectivity Map, International Telecommunication Union. * Blue lines are terrestrial, thin gray lines in seas and oceans are submarine fiber-optic cables, IXPs are in green circles. Iran is highlighted in gray

Table 6.4 Restriction of internet layers in Iran

Restriction of network layer	Answer
Does the country regularly restrict or control its physical connections by design? Can it restrict the physical layer on demand?	Partially, Iran has foreign connections, but it is also working to develop an infrastructure that can replace foreign connections via its NIN project
Does the country regularly restrict or control its network gateways and routes?	Yes, Iran filters packets, DNS and IPs and controls routing in general. It blocks websites and services it perceives as unwanted
Does the country regularly restrict or control the content within its borders?	Yes, websites, services and content are censored
Does the country regularly restrict or control the way its citizens and even visitors use the internet?	Yes, users can use only approved services and websites and they are also held accountable for proxy browsing that might bypass censorship; there is a disincentive to use VPNs or browsers like TOR

6.5 Saudi Arabian Cyberspace

Saudi Arabia has a population of approximately 36.4 million people, as of 2022, and according to data from the ITU, 100% of its population uses the internet, compared to 0.011% in 1995 and 12.7% in 2005. According to data from the ITU, it has 2 IXPs and 75 ISPs, although more IXPs have been added in recent years, according to news and media publications.[50] The organization Packet Clearing House lists 6 IXPs in Saudi Arabia.[51] Although technical information from international, official and business sources varies, the Arabian Kingdom has used the internet since early 1993, although this was mainly for scientific or governmental purposes. In this sense, it is similar to countries like Iran and Israel, which also connected in the early 1990s. One of the first connections to the global grid was at King Fahd University of Petroleum and Minerals (KFUPM) in Dhahran. The connection in the College of Computer Sciences and Engineering was used to send and receive emails. Later, the King Abdulaziz City for Science and Technology (KACST), an independent organization, provided internet service to KFUPM using a 64 kbps connection from the King Faisal Specialist Hospital and Research Center. In 1995, KACST made an effort to connect more Saudi universities to the internet, including connections using satellites.[52]

Universities, hospitals, and military and governmental organizations used the internet for a few years before introducing it to the wider public. In March 1997, the Council of Ministers issued Decree number 163 which gave KACST the responsibility of introducing internet services for the public. The required qualifications for ISPs were announced by KACST in December 1998, and KACST worked with the Saudi Telecommunications Company (STC) to provide the necessary communication lines. The company was established in April 1998 for that very purpose.[53] At first, STC was the only ISP in Saudi Arabia, and it also routed Saudi Arabian internet traffic. In May 2005, Mobily, a new company, launched the Saudi Arabian mobile market, and in August 2008, the company Zain joined the Saudi Arabian mobile market as another ISP and also began providing 4G LTE services. In that same year, Saudi Telecom started the 3G deployment process. Thus, Saudi Arabia did not adopt the internet at scale until many other countries were already deeply entangled in emails, websites and the beginnings of social media (Facebook was launched in 2004).[54]

---

[50] See "Saudi Arabia" on ITU's DataHub: https://datahub.itu.int/data/?e=SAU; Bannerman (2022).

[51] See "Saudi Arabia" on Packet Clearing House: https://www.pch.net/ixp/dir#!mt-filters=%7B%22ctry%22%3A%5B%22dropdown%22%2C%22%22%2C%22Saudi%20Arabia%22%5D%7D.

[52] Al-Tawil (2001).

[53] Al-Hajery (2004).

[54] Alshahrani (2016).

As soon as the internet was open for public use, the Kingdom began restricting the information flow to prevent its citizens from being exposed to illegal information and, of course, to block any unwanted information. The Open Net Initiative (ONI) tested roughly 60,000 websites in 2002–2004 and found substantial blocking of provocative attire, the Bahai faith, topics related to the Holocaust, free Web hosting, opposition political groups and Islamic extremist sites. The initiative found that Saudi Arabia blocks pages on gay/lesbian/bisexual issues, sexuality, women's rights, Israel, politics and other topics. The Kingdom blocks few websites related to alcohol, most religions or media. This pattern suggests that a limited filtering regime is more effective, as ONI concluded.[55]

As Saudi Arabia has no modern constitution, it relies on the Qur'an to provide it with laws and guidance. In 2007, Saudi Arabia introduced the Anti-Cyber Crimes Law by Royal Decree number M/17. The law prohibits content harming public order, religious values, public morals and privacy, including drug use, pornography, gambling and terrorism. Offenders face imprisonment for up to 10 years and fines of up to 5,000,000 Saudi Riyals (Article 7). The law is enforced by the Communications, Space and Information Technology Commission (CST) and the National Cybersecurity Authority (NCA), which also oversees international cooperation and awareness campaigns related to cybercrime.[56] In 2010 and 2011, Saudi Arabia published new amendments relating to publications and media that prohibit the dissemination of news or other information without a proper license and also prohibit damaging the reputation of the King and religious scholars.[57]

Saudi Arabia's NCA was established by a Royal Order in October 2017. It serves as the government entity in charge of cybersecurity and has both regulatory and operational functions. The NCA's primary mandate is to ensure the security and resilience of Saudi Arabia's cyberspace; it works closely with national security, critical infrastructures, high-priority sectors, and government services and activities. As stated on the NCA's website, the Saudi definition of cybersecurity is "the protection of information technology systems and networks as well as systems and components of operating technologies, including hardware and software, together with services provided thereby and data included therein, against unlawful hacking, obstruction, modification, access, use or exploitation."[58]

In September 2021, the Saudi government published the Personal Data Protection Law by Royal Decree M/19, and it was later amended in March 2023. The law regulates the collection, processing, storing and transfer of data. However, it also includes a clause stating that the illegal transfer of personal data to foreign

[55] Open Net Initiative (2004)

[56] See "Anti-Cyber Crime Law." Ministry of Communications and Information Technologies, Saudi Arabia. https://www.mcit.gov.sa/sites/default/files/2021-06/la_004_e_anti-cyber_crime_law%20%281%29.pdf.

[57] See "Media policy in the Kingdom of Saudi Arabia." Ministry of Media [in Arabic: "السياسة الإعلامية في المملكة العربية السعودية"]. https://media.gov.sa/en/document-library.

[58] "About," National Cybersecurity Authority, https://nca.gov.sa/en/about.

parties can result in criminal conviction and imprisonment. Moreover, encrypted communications are banned in Saudi Arabia, making E2EE messaging applications like WhatsApp and Telegram, or the TOR Dark Web, illegal.[59]

The Specialized Criminal Court in Saudi Arabia is often in charge of trying cyber-related crimes or acts that the Saudis interpret as illegal. For instance, in January 2021, Salma al-Shehab, a Saudi woman who was studying in the United Kingdom, returned to Saudi Arabia for the holidays and was arrested for supporting online posts calling for reforms in Saudi Arabia. She was sentenced to 34 years.[60] In another case, the Specialized Criminal Court in Saudi Arabia sentenced Nourah bint Saeed al-Qahtani, a Saudi woman, to 45 years in prison for using the internet "to tear the social fabric" and for harming public order by using the internet, although the full details of her arrest are still unclear, as reported by the Guardian.[61]

Saudi Arabia is well connected to the outside world; submarine fiber-optic cables like SeaMeWe4 and the Middle East North Africa (MENA) Cable System/Gulf Bridge International cables connect the Kingdom to Europe, the Middle East and Africa.[62] As can be seen in Fig. 6.6, Saudi Arabia is connected by over a dozen submarine cables and dozens of terrestrial cables within the country. Unlike Iran, which strives for a more restricted model, Saudi Arabia focuses on filtering and, as Tabachnik and I previously noted, on legal–psychological measures that nudge citizens into compliance, as summarized in Table 6.5.[63] All major services and platforms are accessible in Saudi Arabia, including Facebook, Twitter, Telegram and more; however, users often cannot express criticism against the regime. Saudi Arabia is thus partially restricted.

6.6 Shutdowns: Internet Restrictions in India and Myanmar

Other countries also utilize internet restrictions, though of a lesser magnitude. In fact, as mentioned in the introductory chapter of this book, according to Access Now, the organization for digital rights, the internet was shut down 182 times in 2021, 129 times in 2020, 213 times in 2019 and 196 times in 2018. In the cases of India and Myanmar, cyberspace is not as regulated and restricted as it is in Russia, China and Iran, and definitely not as regulated and restricted as in North Korea. However, authorities in India and Myanmar do shut down connections whenever they perceive that the flow of communication and information may harm national

[59] Freedom House (2023).

[60] Kirchgaessner (2022).

[61] Kirchgaessner (2022).

[62] See the ITU interactive map: https://bbmaps.itu.int/bbmaps/.

[63] Topor and Tabachnik (2021).

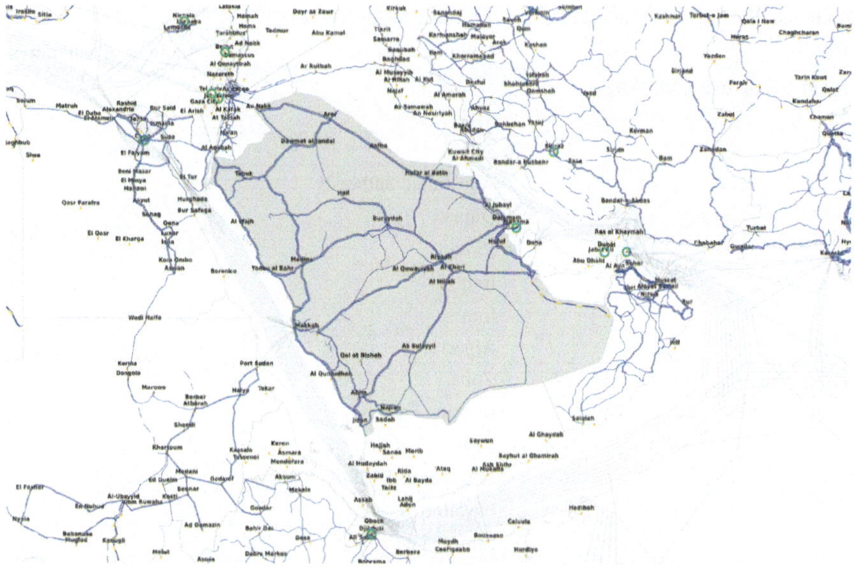

Fig. 6.6 Submarine and terrestrial internet cables and internet exchange points in and around Saudi Arabia; *Source* Infrastructure Connectivity Map, International Telecommunication Union. * Blue lines are terrestrial, thin gray lines in seas and oceans are submarine fiber-optic cables, IXPs are in green circles. Saudi Arabia is highlighted in gray

Table 6.5 Restriction of internet layers in Saudi Arabia

Restriction of network layer	Answer
Does the country regularly restrict or control its physical connections by design? Can it restrict the physical layer on demand?	According to the evidence, it does not heavily restrict the physical domain
Does the country regularly restrict or control its network gateways and routes?	Partially, Saudi filters packets, DNS and IPs and controls routing in general. It blocks websites and services it perceives as unwanted. However, there is no recorded evidence of any internet shutdowns
Does the country regularly restrict or control the content within its borders?	Partially, some websites are restricted, although these mainly include pornographic websites, drug-related websites and LGBTQ+ websites
Does the country regularly restrict or control the way its citizens and even visitors use the internet?	Partially, most mainstream websites are accessible, and only fringe websites are banned

resilience and domestic peace, even though such shutdowns harm human rights. Access Now documented 106 Indian shutdowns in 2021, whereas Myanmar shut down the internet 15 times, and Iran and Sudan shut down the internet 5 times each. The shutdowns are not always general but are sometimes local, affecting

Table 6.6 Internet Shutdowns in 2021, according to Access Now

Region	Country	Number of Shutdowns
Middle East and North Africa	Yemen	2
	Syria	2
	Sudan	5
	Palestinian authority	1
	Oman	1
	Jordan	4
	Iraq	2
	Iran	5
	Algeria	1
Latin America and the Caribbean	Cuba	4
Africa	Burkina Faso	1
	Chad	2
	The Republic of the Congo	1
	Eswatini	2
	Ethiopia	3
	Gabon	1
	Niger	1
	Nigeria	2
	Senegal	1
	South Sudan	1
	Uganda	3
	Zambia	1
Eastern Europe and Central Asia	Russia	1
	Turkmenistan	2
	Uzbekistan	1
	Tajikistan	1
	Kazakhstan	2
Asia Pacific	Afghanistan	1
	Bangladesh	2
	China	1
	India	106
	Indonesia	2
	Myanmar	15
	Pakistan	2

only one city or province. The number of internet shutdowns per country is shown in Table 6.6.[64]

Internet shutdowns have been a recurring issue in countries like India and Myanmar. In India, the government has imposed numerous internet shutdowns,

[64] Access Now (2022).

with the state of Jammu and Kashmir experiencing 85 shutdowns in 2021 and one of the longest shutdowns in history, which began on August 5, 2019, and ended on February 5, 2021, when Article 370 of the Constitution was abrogated and the Indian Constitution itself was applied to Jammu and Kashmir. The people who were demanding independence rioted. In addition, other locations, like the state of Manipur, have faced internet shutdowns following communal clashes and anti-governmental protests. These shutdowns were implemented in response to unrest and public protests in order to prevent violence.[65]

In Myanmar, the military junta has used internet shutdowns as a tool to suppress resistance and facilitate human rights violations. The junta shut down the internet several times to quell resistance and cover up acts of violence. By limiting access to independent media and information, the junta creates an information vacuum where it can control the narrative and manipulate public opinion. Areas experiencing armed conflict or resistance are often subjected to more frequent and prolonged shutdowns to weaken and isolate opposition groups.[66]

The reasons for internet shutdowns in the two countries vary, but they are often linked to political unrest, communal clashes, and the government's efforts to control the flow of information and suppress opposition. According to organizations like Access Now, the shutdowns have had significant implications for the affected populations, including hindering access to vital information, communication and economic activities. The frequent and prolonged nature of these shutdowns has raised concerns about their impact on human rights and the freedom of expression in both countries.[67] As can be seen in Table 6.6, no liberal democratic countries imposed internet shutdowns. Even after massive events like the January 6 Capitol riots in the United States, which were largely organized online, Uncle Sam did not shut down the internet.

6.7 Conclusion

This chapter has provided an overview of several prominent global and regional powers and their SCDs. Interestingly, some of the conclusions of this chapter run counter to the information presented in the ITU's Global Cybersecurity Index (CGI) of 2020, which placed 193 countries and 1 entity on a scale of cybersecurity. In particular, while the index grants the United States a perfect score of 100 (on a scale of 0–100), it grants Russia a cybersecurity score of 98.06, while

65 "Restoration of Internet Services in Jammu and Kashmir: A Timeline," (2021).

66 "Open Call to All International Actors: Do More to Stop Internet Shutdowns Shrouding Torchings and Killings in Myanmar" (2022).

67 Ibid; Rajvanshi (2023).

China's score is 92.53, Iran's is 81.07, and Saudi Arabia's is 99.54—the third highest score, after the United States and the United Kingdom.[68]

How then, could the highest-ranking countries suffer from foreign influence that undermines their very democratic nature, as in the case of foreign intervention in the 2016 American presidential elections or Brexit? One example of the data gathered by the ITU's CGI concerns legal measures; they ask: "Do you have substantive law on illegal online behavior?" And they note, "Substantive law refers to all categories of public and private law, including the law of contracts, real property, torts, wills, and criminal law that essentially creates, defines, and regulates rights." Indeed, this cardinal measure raises the question of why the United States, with its section 230(c)(1) of Title 47 of the United States Code, which grants immunity from liability to providers, scored as more secure than Russia, China, Iran or Saudi Arabia, all of which have a number of laws holding companies and individuals accountable for fake or unwanted information.[69] Cybersecurity is the protection of computer systems and networks, not the expression of free speech, which is, of course, a cardinal aspect of humanity, regardless of cybersecurity measures or regime types.

China, Russia, Iran, Saudi Arabia and North Korea, while not as democratic and free as the United States, the United Kingdom or Israel, are factually more cyber-secure. They restrict, either entirely or partially, all layers of the cyber domain, as has been presented throughout this chapter. The physical layer, the logic layer, the information layer and the user layer are all restricted to ensure that the internet is used in a way that will not harm the regime. Thus, such domains can be described as Secure Cyber Domains (SCDs) or, using a term I previously coined with Haber, as "internet bubbles."

References

Ali, S. Mahmud. 2022. *The US-China-Russia triangle: An evolving historiography*. Berlin: Springer Nature.

Alshahrani, Hamed A. 2016. A brief history of the internet in Saudi Arabia. *TechTrends* 60 (1): 19–20.

Al-Hajery, E. 2004. *History of the internet in the Kingdom of Saudi Arabia* (In the Arabic). Riyadh: Al Obeikan.

Al-Tawil, Khalid M. 2001. The internet in Saudi Arabia. *Telecommunications Policy* 25 (8–9): 625–632.

Attinà, Fulvio. 2023. *China and world politics in transition: How China transforms the world political order*. Berlin: Springer Nature.

Bannerman, Natalie. 2022. LINX and stc Launch Two New IXPs in Saudi Arabia. *Capacity*, April 1, 2022. https://www.capacitymedia.com/article/29ws53zp0s648h8t1nxts/news/linx-and-stc-launch-two-new-ixps-in-saudi-arabia.

[68] See "Global Cybersecurity Index 2020," *ITU* (Geneva, 2023), https://www.itu.int/epublications/publication/D-STR-GCI.01-2021-HTM-E.

[69] Ibid.

Bartz, Diane, and Alexandra Alper. 2022. U.S. Bans New Huawei, ZTE equipment sales, citing national security risk. *Reuters*, December 1, 2022. https://www.reuters.com/business/media-telecom/us-fcc-bans-equipment-sales-imports-zte-huawei-over-national-security-risk-2022-11-25/.

Brock, Joe. 2023. Exclusive: China plans $500 million subsea internet cable to rival US-backed project. *Reuters*, April 6, 2023. https://www.reuters.com/world/china/china-plans-500-mln-subsea-internet-cable-rival-us-backed-project-2023-04-06/.

Brooking, Emerson T., and Suzanne Kianpour. 2020. Iranian digital influence efforts: Guerrilla broadcasting for the twenty-first century. *Iran and the Internet* (Atlantic Council, 2020), 11–14.

Bulashova, Natlia, Dmitry Burkov, Alexey Platonov, and Alexey Soldatov. n.d. An internet history of Russia in 1990s. *Asia Internet History Projects*. https://sites.google.com/site/internethistoryasia/book1/an-internet-history-of-russia-in-1990s.

Burgess, Mat. The Bizarre Reality of Getting Online in North Korea. *WIRED*, June 8, 2023. https://www.wired.co.uk/article/internet-reality-north-korea.

Chang, Amy. 2014. Warring state: China's cybersecurity strategy. *Center for New American Studies*, December 2014.

Chen, Cheng, Kyungmin Ko, and Ji-Yong Lee. 2010. North Korea's internet strategy and its political implications. *The Pacific Review* 23 (5): 649–670.

Cheney, Clayton. 2019. China's Digital Silk Road: Strategic technological competition and exporting political illiberalism. *Issues & Insights* 19.

Chepenko, Daniel. 2020. Demystifying the Great Firewall of China. *Medium*, July 21, 2020. https://medium.com/mobile-asia/demystifying-the-great-firewall-of-china-22f4a97550cc.

China's iPhone Ban Accelerates Across Government and State Firms. *Bloomberg*, December 15, 2023. https://www.bloomberg.com/news/articles/2023-12-15/china-s-apple-iphone-ban-accelerates-across-state-firms-government?embedded-checkout=true.

Economy, Elizabeth C. 2018. The Great Firewall of China: Xi Jinping's internet shutdown. *Guardian*, June 29, 2018. https://www.theguardian.com/news/2018/jun/29/the-great-firewall-of-china-xi-jinpings-internet-shutdown.

Elder, Miriam. 2012. Russia adopts stringent internet control amid censorship concerns. *Guardian*, July 11, 2012. https://www.theguardian.com/world/2012/jul/11/russia-internet-censorship.

Esfandiari, Golnaz. 2019. Iran shuts down internet amid violent protests over gas-price hikes. *Radio Free Europe Radio Liberty*, November 18, 2019. https://www.rferl.org/a/iran-shuts-down-internet-amid-violent-protests-over-gas-price-hikes/30278936.html.

Esfandiari, Golnaz. 2022. Iran accused of secretly implementing controversial draft internet bill. *Radio Free Europe Radio Liberty*, September 9, 2022. https://www.rferl.org/a/iran-internet-bill-controversy-secretly-implementing/32026313.html.

Freedom House. 2023. Saudi Arabia: Freedom on the net. https://freedomhouse.org/country/saudi-arabia/freedom-net/2023.

Gibson, Charles. 2009. China's Facebook status: Blocked. *ABC News*, July 8, 2009. https://abcnews.go.com/theworldnewser/2009/07/chinas-facebook-status-blocked.html.

Global Engagement Center. 2020. *GEC special report: Russia's pillars of disinformation and propaganda*. US Department of State, August 2020. https://www.state.gov/russias-pillars-of-disinformation-and-propaganda-report/.

Global Engagement Center. 2023. *How the People's Republic of China seeks to reshape the global information environment*. US Department of State, September 28, 2023. https://www.state.gov/gec-special-report-how-the-peoples-republic-of-china-seeks-to-reshape-the-global-information-environment/.

Greene, Robert and Paul Triolo. 2020. Will China control the global internet via its Digital Silk Road? *The China Project*, May 8, 2020. https://thechinaproject.com/2020/05/08/will-china-control-the-global-internet-via-its-digital-silk-road/.

Gross, Anna, Alexandra Heal, Chris Campbell, Dan Clark, Ian Bott, and Irene de la Torre Arenas. 2023. How the US is pushing China out of the internet's plumbing. *Financial Times*, June 13. https://ig.ft.com/subsea-cables/.

Haber, Eldar, and Lev Topor. 2023. Sovereignty, cyberspace, and the emergence of internet bubbles. *Journal of Advanced Military Studies* 14 (1): 144–165.

Hillman, Jonathan E. 2021. *The Digital Silk Road: China's quest to wire the world and win the future*. Profile Books.

Huang, Yiping. 2016. Understanding China's belt & road initiative: Motivation, framework and assessment. *China Economic Review* 40: 314–321.

Iran: Human Rights Groups Sound Alarm against Draconian Internet Bill, Article 19 (March 17, 2022). https://www.article19.org/resources/iran-human-rights-groups-sound-alarm-against-draconian-internet-bill/.

Iran's Comms Minister Says a Third of Blocked Sites 'Obscene'. 2023. *Iran International*, July 28, 2023. https://www.iranintl.com/en/202307289603.

Kelly, Samantha M. 2023. China says it's built the world's fastest internet network. *CNN*, November 15, 2023. https://edition.cnn.com/2023/11/15/tech/china-launches-worlds-fastest-internet-network/index.html.

Kirchgaessner, Stephanie. 2022. Saudi woman Given 34-year prison sentence for using Twitter. *Guardian*, August 16, 2022. https://www.theguardian.com/world/2022/aug/16/saudi-woman-given-34-year-prison-sentence-for-using-twitter.

Kirchgaessner, Stephanie. 2022. Saudi woman jailed for 45 years over social media use, Says Group. *Guardian*, August 30, 2022. https://www.theguardian.com/world/2022/aug/30/saudi-woman-given-jail-sentence-for-social-media-use-says-human-rights-group.

Marcus, Alexander. 2004. The internet and democratization: the development of Russian internet policy. *Demokratizatsiya* 12 (4).

Maranto, Lauren. 2020. Who benefits from China's cybersecurity laws? *CSIS*, June 25, 2020. https://www.csis.org/blogs/new-perspectives-asia/who-benefits-chinas-cybersecurity-laws.

Mobley, Terry. 2019. The belt and road initiative. *Strategic Studies Quarterly* 13 (3): 52–72.

National Cybersecurity Authority. n.d. About. https://nca.gov.sa/en/about.

Noland, Marcus. 2009. Telecommunications in North Korea: Has Orascom made the connection? *North Korean Review* 62–74.

Open Call to All International Actors: Do More to Stop Internet Shutdowns Shrouding Torchings and Killings in Myanmar. *Access Now*, June 23, 2022. https://www.accessnow.org/press-release/statement-against-myanmar-shutdowns/.

Open Net Initiative. 2004. Internet filtering in Saudi Arabia in 2004. https://opennet.net/studies/saudi.

Passini, Stefano. 2012. The Facebook and Twitter revolutions: Active participation in the 21st century. *Human Affairs* 22 (3): 301–312.

Provisions on Regulating and Promoting Cross-border Data Flows (draft for comments). *China Law Translate*, September 28, 2023. https://www.chinalawtranslate.com/en/draft-data-export-rule-revisions/.

PSCORE. 2023. *Digital hostages—Internet freedom in North Korea*. http://pscore.org/internet-freedom/.

Qu, Tracy. 2021. China updates rules on real-name registration online in crackdown on schemes to revive banned user accounts. *South China Morning Post*, October 27, 2021. https://www.scmp.com/tech/policy/article/3153887/china-updates-rules-real-name-registration-online-crackdown-schemes.

Rahimi, Babak. 2003. Cyberdissent: The internet in revolutionary Iran. *Middle East* 7 (3): 102.

Rahimi, Babak. 2007. The politics of the internet in Iran. In *Media, Culture and Society in Iran*, 53–72. London: Routledge.

Rajvanshi, Astha. 2023. How internet shutdowns wreak havoc in India. *TIME*, August 15, 2023. https://time.com/6304719/india-internet-shutdowns-manipur/.

Restoration of Internet Services in Jammu and Kashmir: A Timeline. 2021. *India Express*, February 5, 2021. https://indianexpress.com/article/india/jk-4g-internet-mobile-timeline-7176408/.

Shullman, David O. 2019. Protect the party: China's growing influence in the developing world. *Brookings Institute*, January 22, 2019. https://www.brookings.edu/articles/protect-the-party-chinas-growing-influence-in-the-developing-world/.

Socialist constitution of the Democratic People's Republic of Korea. 2014. Foreign languages Publishing House, Pyongyang, [North] Korea, Juche 103.

Strzyżyńska, Weronika. 2022. Iran blocks capital's internet access as Amini Protests Grow. *Guardian*, September 22, 2022. https://www.theguardian.com/world/2022/sep/22/iran-blocks-capitals-internet-access-as-amini-protests-grow.

The Return of Digital Authoritarianism—Internet Shutdowns in 2021. 2022. *Access Now* (April 2022). https://www.accessnow.org/wp-content/uploads/2022/05/2021-KIO-Report-May-24-2022.pdf.

Topor, Lev, and Alexander Tabachnik. 2021. Russian cyber information warfare: International distribution and domestic control. *Journal of Advanced Military Studies* 12 (1): 112–127.

Walker, Shaun. 2014. Founder of Vkontakte Leaves after dispute with Kremlin-linked owners. *Guardian*, April 2, 2014. https://www.theguardian.com/media/2014/apr/02/founder-pavel-durov-leaves-russian-social-network-site-vkontakte.

Williams, Martyn. 2021. North Korea intensifies war against foreign influence. *38 North*, November 10, 2021. https://www.38north.org/2021/11/north-korea-intensifies-war-against-foreign-influence/.

Yang, Guobin. 2012. A Chinese internet? History, practice, and globalization. *Chinese Journal of Communication* 5 (1): 49–54.

Zittrain, Jonathan, and Benjamin Edelman. 2003. Internet filtering in China. *IEEE Internet Computing* 7 (2): 70–77.

Chapter 7
Vulnerable Models of Cyber Domains

As demonstrated in Chaps. 4 and 5, countries are vulnerable both to cyberattacks that cause physical or financial damage as well as to seemingly softer cyberattacks, which usually cannot be regarded as offensive or illegal. Such attacks include mis/disinformation and influence campaigns by foreign actors. Fake stories and the promotion of anti-establishment sentiments can cause liberal and democratic values, institutions and structures to crumble. The United States has suffered from such foreign incitement during and after recent election campaigns, such as during the 2016 presidential election campaign and after President Joe Biden won the 2020 election and extremists raided the Capitol. The United Kingdom has suffered from foreign manipulation of public opinion on the topic of Brexit. In Israel, chaos, fear and public disorder were promoted in the wake of the October 7 terrorist attack. In Germany, "fake news" served to deepen the rift between the right and the left on the subject of immigration. In Sweden, fake stories were used to sway public opinion against NATO membership. In France, the Yellow Vests rioted against rising taxes, but radical ideas were disseminated by foreign entities, allegedly Russia, and the riots led to vandalism on an enormous scale. If Russia, China, Iran or others want to compete with Western dominance, they need not fire a single bullet, they just have to spread lies.

Authoritarian or less-democratic countries often restrict the flow of information to their citizens by restricting the main mass communication medium in our contemporary world—the internet. As described in Chap. 6, they do this by creating Secure Cyber Domains (SCDs). Restricting information flow and creating disincentives for users to criticize the regime gives such countries a strategic advantage: they can use sharp power to influence others without being vulnerable to similar influences. But what defines a Vulnerable Cyber Domain (VCD)? A VCD is a cyber domain that prioritizes free information flow, comfort and usability (i.e., access, speed, etc.) while compromising cybersecurity, national resilience,

L. Topor, *Cyber Sovereignty*, Global Power Shift,
https://doi.org/10.1007/978-3-031-58199-1_7

sovereignty and public order. Freedom of information and freedom of speech are important values, but they can also lead to the rise of dark forces and dark times—Nazi Germany is one prominent example.

In this chapter, I present several models of VCDs. Many countries have vulnerable cyber domains; however, I focus on those countries that either lead the cyber and technological domains globally or have significant indirect power and influence, whether globally or regionally. The chosen cases include the United States, which developed the internet as we know it today and controls the majority of aspects related to it, and the United Kingdom, as it is an ally of Uncle Sam, collaborates strategically with the United States and shares both language and values. Israel is another interesting case, as it is the sole liberal democratic country in the Middle East and the sole proxy of the United States in that region that shares both strategic and cultural values. Israel is also surrounded by authoritarian regimes that have very restricted cyber domains, and which are, or have been, in conflict with it—this makes Israel a particularly interesting case as it must retain high levels of national resilience in the face of conflicts and wars.

In addition to these three cases, the European Union as a whole is reviewed. The European Union makes for a particularly interesting case as it is not a sovereign entity with a sovereign cyber domain but rather a coalition of countries that share similar values and strategic goals; at present, they can be referred to as the European cyber bloc. The European Union has developed mutual regulations regarding cyberspace and its countries' citizens: the Cybersecurity Act, the GDPR, the DSA and the DMA, among others. This, alongside the fact that European citizens can move freely within the European Union and reside and work where they wish to, makes a sort of a cyber bloc. The strength of the European Union lies in its unity; it must protect its cyber domain as a whole since an attack on a single member can affect others. For instance, issues related to immigration, and particularly mis/disinformation about such, have already caused strategic and domestic damage.

Methodologically, as in Chap. 6, I use a structured review based on the structure of cyberspace to analyze the cyber domains of the above-mentioned countries—I analyze the physical layer of cyberspace, the logical layer, the information layer, and the user layer. Subsequently, the cases are compared to one another. In Chap. 8, I present the conclusions of this study and elaborate on the emergence of cyber blocs within global affairs, be those geographical cyber blocs or economic and political cyber blocs, following a comparison and analysis of the cases in this chapter and Chap. 6.

The main goal of this chapter is to uncover indications of a country's level of control and sovereignty regarding its cyber domain, particularly in the context of influence and information flow. The case reviews are not exhaustive but rather aim to find such indications. Thus, the same questions about cyberspace regulation are asked as in the previous chapter:

- Physical Layer: Does the country regularly restrict or control its physical connections by design? Can it restrict the physical layer on demand? I.e., does the country have no physical connections or can it disconnect itself from the outside world but retain an intranet?

- Logical Layer: Does the country regularly restrict or control its network gateways and routes? I.e., does the country shut down the internet in specific areas or at specific times?
- Information Layer: Does the country regularly restrict or control the content within its borders? I.e., does the country disallow the dissemination of generally diverse and at times critical content, like criticism of the country's officials, regime or actions?
- User Layer: Does the country regularly restrict or control the way its citizens and even visitors use the internet? I.e., does the country put up technological barriers like the mandatory installation of applications or prohibit the use of certain applications or services?

Answers to these four questions will yield an indication of a country's level of control over its cyber domain. A country that does not restrict and/or control cyberspace will be defined as strategically vulnerable.

The structure of this chapter is similar to that of the previous; the introduction is followed by a review of the cyber domains of the United States, the United Kingdom, Israel and the European Union. Afterward, I summarize the main points and conclude this chapter.

7.1 The American Cyberspace

The history of the development of ARPANET, a largely American project, which eventually evolved into the global internet we are all familiar with today, was described in Chap. 2. This review of the American cyberspace aims to present the current state of the main regulatory aspects, particularly issues related to information flow, and will review all four layers of cyberspace—as in all cases in this chapter and the previous. According to the ITU, and true to 2022, there are approximately 338 million American citizens, of whom 91.8% are connected to the internet. About 88% of American households are connected to the internet, compared to 65.7% globally.[1] There is no information available on ITU's Datahub website regarding the United States' ISPs and IXPs; however, alternative sources like the IXP Database (IXPDB) and Packet Clearing House do provide further information: There are 221 IXPs in the United States, most of which are located in urban areas, whereas rural areas are far less connected, as is the case in Russia.[2]

The American internet project, which was led by DARPA and researchers like Joseph Carl Robnett Licklider in the 1960s, has evolved into a large and global

[1] See "United States" on ITU's DataHub: https://datahub.itu.int/data/?e=USA.

[2] See the IXP Database: https://ixpdb.euro-ix.net/en/; also see "United States" on Packet Clearing House: https://www.pch.net/ixp/dir#!mt-filters=%7B%22ctry%22%3A%5B%22dropdown%22%2C%22%22%2C%22United%20States%22%5D%7D.

web. In October 1969, the first successful transmission of a message over the ARPANET occurred between the University of California, Los Angeles, and the Stanford Research Institute.[3] The ARPANET was a decentralized network that aimed to ensure communication resilience; it was further developed by research centers and universities in the 1980s and 1990s, which were prompted and funded to do so by the National Science Foundation Network. In the 1990s, the general American public was introduced to the internet, specifically with the first web browser, the World Wide Web, which was launched in 1990 by Tim Berners-Lee, a researcher of computer science.[4] Web browsers made the internet much more user-friendly than early versions of emails or USENET (see Chap. 2).

In terms of work "on the ground," private companies were those that contributed most to developing the internet. A major example is the American Telephone and Telegraph Company (AT&T), which played a significant role in the development of the backbone of the American internet. AT&T's pre-internet influence stemmed from its dominance in the telephone industry via Bell Labs, which, as early as the 1960s and 1970s, allowed the company to provide phone systems and early dial-up internet to other companies. Other companies that laid the internet backbone in the United States include examples like Verizon, Lumen Technologies (CenturyLink), Level 3 Communications (now part of Lumen), Cogent Communications and others. In recent decades, Meta (Facebook) and Google, among others, have also entered the backbone business. As of the twenty-first century, the United States is extensively connected, particularly in urban areas, although it is less so in rural areas (see Figs. 7.1 and 7.2).[5]

Commercial companies providing services began to emerge in the United States in the 1980s and 1990s, particularly companies like America Online (AOL), Netscape, Yahoo!, Amazon and eBay. Later, more companies started to invest not only in standalone hardware and software but also in cyber-related services and products. In the 2000s, Google rose to prominence as an innovative search engine that redefined online information access and quickly became the world's most popular website. The explosive growth of internet companies in the late 1990s, fueled by venture capital and public investment, further democratized internet access and brought it into mainstream American households. As private American ventures invested more in the online domain, the internet became a more dominant aspect of American citizens' daily lives, especially with the rise of social media from 2004/5 onward.[6] According to the Pew Research Center, approximately 7% of Americans aged 18–29 used social media in 2005, and 84% of this age group used social media in 2021, regardless (almost) of race, gender, income, education or community. Indeed, as of 2023, the internet is a tremendously significant part

[3] Kleinrock (2019).

[4] W3 (n.d.).

[5] Hecht (2021) and Ball (2021).

[6] Ortiz-Ospina (2019).

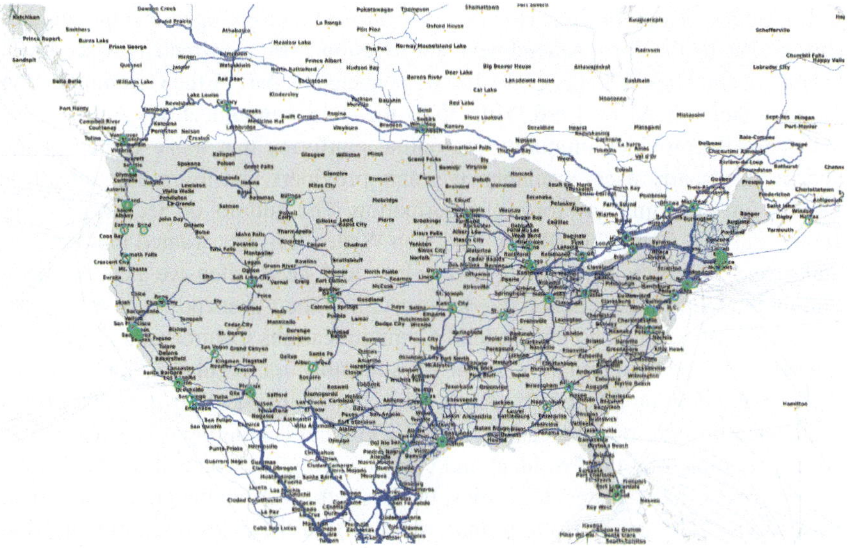

Fig. 7.1 Submarine and terrestrial internet cables and internet exchange points in and around the United States (excluding Alaska). *Source* Infrastructure Connectivity Map, International Telecommunication Union. * Blue lines are terrestrial, thin gray lines in seas and oceans are submarine fiber-optic cables, IXPs are in green circles. The United States is highlighted in gray

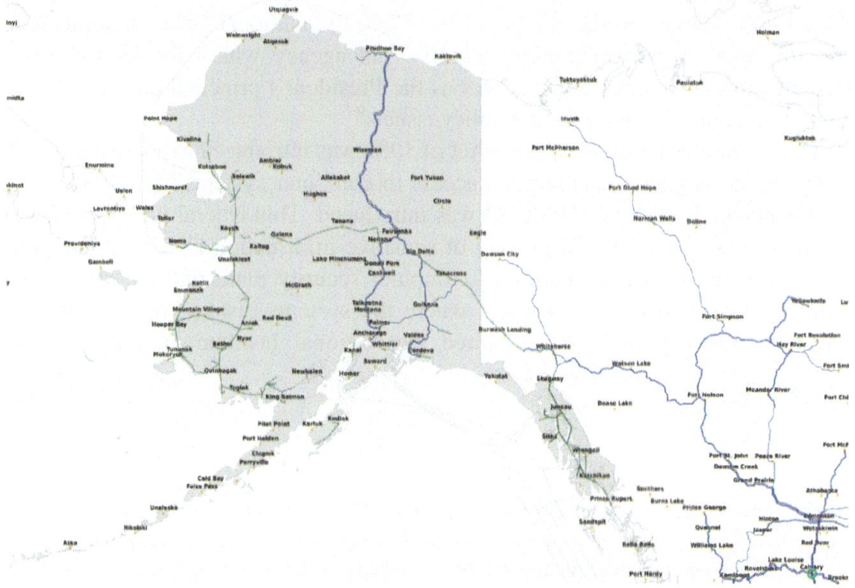

Fig. 7.2 Submarine and terrestrial internet cables and internet exchange points in and around Alaska. *Source* Infrastructure Connectivity Map, International Telecommunication Union. * Blue lines are terrestrial, thin gray lines in seas and oceans are submarine fiber-optic cables, IXPs are in green circles. Alaska is highlighted in gray

of the American way of life.[7] However, it is almost entirely open and unregulated. This is due to the First Amendment and Section 230I(1), which is a section of Title 47 of the United States Code that was enacted as part of the Communications Decency Act (CDA) of 1996, Title V of the Telecommunications Act of 1996, and generally provides immunity for online platforms that make content generated by third-party users available. It grants providers and users immunity from liability for spreading any form of information. The authors of Section 230, then Representatives Chris Cox (R-CA) and Ron Wyden (D-OR), wanted internet companies and platforms to regulate themselves and keep offensive material away, without the fear of being held liable for everything their users post.[8]

In terms of regulations, the Federal Communications Commission (FCC) is an independent Federal regulatory agency responsible for regulating interstate and international communications by radio, television, wire, satellite and cable. It was established by the Communications Act of 1934 and is composed of five commissioners appointed by the President and confirmed by the Senate. The FCC's jurisdiction covers the 50 states, territories, the District of Columbia and United States possessions. The agency is the primary authority in the areas of communications law, regulation and technological innovation in the United States. Its responsibilities include developing and implementing regulatory programs, processing applications for licenses, encouraging the development of innovative services, conducting investigations and analyzing complaints. The FCC's mission is to promote connectivity and ensure a competitive market in the communications industry. The FCC is responsible for regulating the internet backbone as well, and it oversees radio spectrum allocation, infrastructure deployment and competition in the telecom market. In the context of the FCC, the National Telecommunications and Information Administration (NTIA) is an agency within the United States Department of Commerce that serves as the President's principal advisor on telecommunications and information policy issues.[9]

The Computer Fraud and Abuse Act of 1986 was introduced to address computer-related crimes and unauthorized access to computer systems.[10] In 1987–1988, the Computer Security Act of 1987 was introduced. This federal law was enacted to improve the security and privacy of sensitive information in federal computer systems. It required the creation of computer security plans and the appropriate training of system users or owners where the systems display, process or store sensitive information. It also required the National Institute of Standards and

[7] Pew Research Center (2021a); also see Pew Research Center (2021b).

[8] See "Telecommunications Act of 1996," Federal Communications Commission. https://www.fcc.gov/general/telecommunications-act-1996; Siripurapu (2020).

[9] National Telecommunications and Information Administration (n.d.).

[10] See H.R.4718—Computer Fraud and Abuse Act of 1986, 99th Congress (1985–1986). https://www.congress.gov/bill/99th-congress/house-bill/4718.

Technology (NIST) to develop standards of minimum acceptable practices and mandated security awareness training for federal employees using those systems.[11]

Following the CDA of 1996, the Digital Millennium Copyright Act, which criminalizes the dissemination of copyrighted material, was enacted in 1998 as an answer to digital and online piracy. However, information could still flow freely, and it was not until 2015 that the Cybersecurity Information Sharing Act (CISA) was introduced. CISA is a federal law that is aimed at enhancing cybersecurity measures and promoting the sharing of cyber threat indicators between federal, local and private entities. Also in 2015, the FCC adopted the Open Internet Order, known as Net Neutrality,[12] which reclassified broadband internet access as a telecommunications service under Title II of the Communications Act of 1934. This reclassification allowed the FCC to enforce net neutrality rules, prohibiting internet service providers from blocking, throttling or prioritizing online content. However, in 2017, the FCC, under the leadership of former Chairman Ajit Pai, voted to repeal the Open Internet Order, effectively ending the federal government's enforcement of net neutrality in the United States, which lifted federal pressure and observance from private companies. The FCC's former Chairman, Ajit Pai, noted that it was not the FCC's role to determine net neutrality.[13]

Another significant point is the President's Commission on Critical Infrastructure Protection (PCCIP) from 1996, which was released in October 1997 and signed as Executive Order 13010. It was the first national effort to address the novel vulnerabilities of the information age. The commission was responsible for formulating a comprehensive national policy and implementation strategy to protect critical infrastructures from physical and cyber threats. The PCCIP thoroughly reviewed the vulnerabilities and threats facing the nation's infrastructures, assessed the risks and deliberated on how best to protect the nation's critical foundations. Its work led to the report "Critical Foundations: Protecting America's Infrastructures," which focused on the protection of critical infrastructures, including energy, banking, finance and more.[14] Presidential Decision Directive 63 also requires federal departments and agencies to make plans to protect their critical infrastructures.[15]

---

[11] See H.R.145—Computer Security Act of 1987, 100th Congress (1987–1988). https://www.congress.gov/bill/100th-congress/house-bill/145#:~:text=Computer%20Security%20Act%20of%201987%20%2D%20Directs%20the%20National%20Bureau%20of,Bureau%20in%20implementing%20such%20standards.

[12] Net neutrality is the principle that all internet traffic should be treated equally (particularly by ISPs but not only), without discrimination or preference given to any particular content, service or website.

[13] Pai (2014).

[14] See "Critical Foundations: Protecting America's Infrastructures," The Report of the President's Commission on Critical Infrastructure Protection, White House, United States of America (October 1997).

[15] See "U.S. Department of Justice, Critical Infrastructure Protection," Report No. 01-01 (November 2000), U.S. Department of Justice. https://oig.justice.gov/reports/OBD/a0101.htm#:~:text=Presidential%20Decision%20Directive%20(PDD)%2063,for%20protecting%20their%20critical%20infrastructure.

In 2013, Edward Snowden revealed American (and Western) internet surveillance to the world. Snowden revealed the existence of the PRISM program, a tool used by the United States National Security Agency (NSA) to collect private electronic data from users of major internet services such as Facebook, Google and Microsoft. The program was enabled under the 1978 Foreign Intelligence Surveillance Act (FISA) and operated under the supervision of the United States Foreign Intelligence Surveillance Court, which was established in the same year (under Section 702 of FISA).[16] The leaked documents disclosed that PRISM, the code name of a clandestine NSA program, allowed the NSA to collect a vast amount of internet communications, not only from foreign entities but also from American citizens, raising concerns about the extent of the program and its potential violation of constitutional rights.[17]

The revelations about PRISM sparked a significant public debate about government surveillance and privacy rights, but it also raised concerns about the implications in other countries where American tech giants operate. The largest technology companies worldwide have a tremendous footprint in other countries, and many American allies like Germany, France and Brazil expressed criticism over the extent of American surveillance revealed by Snowden. German Chancellor Angela Merkel, for instance, famously declared that "spying on friends is unacceptable."[18] Microsoft had cooperated with the United States under Section 702 of the FISA Act since as early as 2007. Yahoo joined in 2008, Google, Facebook and PalTalk joined in 2009, YouTube came in 2010, Skype and AOL came in 2011, and Apple joined in 2012.[19]

Other internet-related regulations in the United States include state (i.e., not federal) regulations like the California Consumer Privacy Act (CCPA), which was signed into law in 2018 and came into effect on January 1, 2020 (see Chap. 3). The CCPA grants California residents the right to know what is/was collected about them, the right to delete such information and more.[20] The Electronic Communications Privacy Act of 1986 (ECPA, which includes the Electronic Communications Privacy Act and the Stored Wire Electronic Communications Act) "protects wire, oral and electronic communications while those communications are being made, are in transit, and when they are stored on computers. The Act applies to email, telephone conversations, and data stored electronically." It

[16] See Section 702 in S.Amdt.5066 to H.R.6304, 110th Congress (2007–2008), FISA Amendments Act of 2008. https://www.congress.gov/bill/110th-congress/house-bill/6304.

[17] Shubber (2013) and Geiger (2018).

[18] Waterfield (2013).

[19] Shubber (2013), Chen (2017) and Weinstein (2014).

[20] See California Consumer Privacy Act (CCPA), Office of the Attorney General, State of California Department of Justice (2018). https://oag.ca.gov/privacy/ccpa#:~:text=This%20landmark%20law%20secures%20new,them%20(with%20some%20exceptions)%3B.

was enacted to prevent unauthorized government access to private electronic communications.[21]

Moreover, the Children's Online Privacy Protection Act, which was enacted in October 1998 and came into effect in April 2000, regulates the online collection and use of the personal information of children under the age of 13. It applies to commercial websites and online services that are either targeted at children under 13 or have actual knowledge that they are collecting personal information from children under 13.[22] Other regulatory entities involved in internet regulation include the Federal Trade Commission, the uniformly adopted state laws known as the Uniform Commercial Code, the Lanham Act (which counters internet piracy) and, of course, the United States Code, in cases where the Code is relevant to internet use.

A significant development occurred in 2018 with the Cybersecurity and Infrastructure Security Agency Act, which "amends the Homeland Security Act of 2002 to redesignate the Department of Homeland Security's National Protection and Programs Directorate as the Cybersecurity and Infrastructure Security Agency." The Act established and enlarged the Cybersecurity and Infrastructure Security Agency (CISA), which is responsible for coordinating cybersecurity programs to protect against malicious cyber activity, including activity related to industrial control systems. It also integrated the United States Computer Emergency Readiness Team (US-CERT), which had been operative since 2003, and the National Cybersecurity and Communications Integration Center, which mitigated cybersecurity between the government and the private sector.[23]

One of the most significant regulations came in late 2022 when the FCC decided to ban Chinese communications equipment based on the 2019 Secure and Trusted Communications Networks Act and the Secure Equipment Act of 2021, which granted the FCC the authority to ban entities from selling communications-related equipment and services on the basis of national security risks, including fear of economic espionage and possible sabotage. Critics have noted that these measures were undertaken not only in response to national security risks but also in response to the trade war between the United States and China. Regardless of the reasons, the FCC banned communications equipment produced by Huawei Technologies, ZTE Corporation, Hytera Communications, Hangzhou Hikvision Digital Technology and Dahua Technology (and their subsidiaries and affiliates).[24] The Secure and Trusted Communications Networks

[21] See Electronic Communications Privacy Act of 1986 (ECPA), 18 U.S.C. §§ 2510–2523. U.S. Department of Justice, Office of Justice Programs. https://bja.ojp.gov/program/it/privacy-civil-liberties/authorities/statutes/1285.

[22] See Children's Online Privacy Protection Rule. 16 CFR Part 312 RIN 3084–AB20. Federal Trade Commission. https://www.ftc.gov/legal-library/browse/rules/childrens-online-privacy-protection-rule-coppa.

[23] See U.S. Department of Homeland Security (n.d.) and Miller et al. (2021).

[24] See H.R.4998—Secure and Trusted Communications Networks Act of 2019, 116th Congress (2019–2020). https://www.congress.gov/bill/116th-congress/house-bill/4998; Federal Communications Commission (n.d.).

Act of 2019 and the Secure Equipment Act of 2021 mark, to my understanding, a significant turning point as the United States began to overtly and fiercely ban unwelcome equipment and services, contrary to its market-driven regulation orientation.

Thus, the United States has several regulatory entities, such as the FCC and the NTIA, and several laws and regulations, like the FISA and CISA acts, as well as agencies, like the *other* CISA that operates the US-CERT, which are all responsible for regulating cyberspace. Alongside these, organizations like the American Registry for Internet Numbers, the international ICANN, and American internet-related companies like AT&T, Lumen Technologies, Google, Meta (Facebook), Apple, Microsoft and many others, all play a role in regulating and managing American cyberspace. Due to Section 230 and the First Amendment, state-level regulation is very limited in the United States, and the above-mentioned federal entities and frameworks largely regulate companies and not users. However, both former President Donald Trump and President Joe Biden have called to change Section 230 as it has allowed companies to avoid regulating themselves and combating hate speech and mis/disinformation. The United States has suffered—is suffering—from widespread hate speech and mis/disinformation. Online racism and anti-Semitism are thriving, dividing American communities and perpetuating hate[25]; online mis/disinformation is also rampant as foreign adversaries use sharp power to harm the United States, as exemplified in Chaps. 4 and 5 (i.e., the 2016 presidential election interference, the Pizzagate and QAnon conspiracy theories, the Capitol riot, which was partly propelled by domestic actors as well, COVID-19-related conspiracies and more). As Table 7.1 concludes, the United States does not regulate cyberspace sufficiently: it has a VCD.

Table 7.1 Restriction of internet layers in the United States

Restriction of network layer	Answer
Does the country regularly restrict or control its physical connections by design? Can it restrict the physical layer on demand?	Partially, the United States does not regularly restrict physical connections; however, it banned certain Chinese equipment in 2022
Does the country regularly restrict or control its network gateways and routes?	No, the logical layer is largely unrestricted and regulated by the market
Does the country regularly restrict or control the content within its borders?	No
Does the country regularly restrict or control the way its citizens and even visitors use the internet?	No, however, it may hold people liable for illegal content like digital piracy or child pornography

[25] See, generally, Topor (2022).

7.2 The British Cyberspace

The United Kingdom was one of the earliest network allies of the United States. The American ARPANET project first transmitted data to the United Kingdom in October 1969 (although data had been transmitted between Norway, the United States and the United Kingdom earlier, in 1968). In 1971, a message was sent from the United Kingdom to the United States, in 1973 University College London transmitted data to California, and full use of ARPANET was gained with the merger of SATNET, ARPANET and PRNET in November 1977. In 1984, another development occurred: the Joint Academic Network (JANET) was established, and it now serves over 18 million users. In 1985, the *.uk* domain was created. The British public gained access to the internet in the 1990s when the company Pipex became the first commercial ISP, offering dial-up access. The pivotal period for internet access in the United Kingdom was around 1994–1997 when the popularity of the World Wide Web surged, and services like email, web browsing, and basic online content like newspapers became more accessible to the general public. This was the time when internet usage started gaining momentum, and more people began to explore and utilize the various possibilities offered by the internet. By 2005, as many as half of the households in the United Kingdom had internet access.[26]

According to the ITU, and true to 2022, there are approximately 67.5 million people in the United Kingdom, of whom 96.7% are connected to the internet. About 95.2% of households in the United Kingdom are connected to the internet.[27] The United Kingdom has several IXPs. Some of the prominent ones include the London Internet Exchange (LINX), which was founded in late 1994, London Access Point (LONAP), IXManchester, IXCardiff, IXScotland, and the Manchester Network Access Point (MaNAP). While the ITU does not explicitly reveal the number of IXPs in the United Kingdom, just as in the American case, alternative databases like the Packet Clearing House organization and the IXP database suggest that there are 30 IXPs in the United Kingdom, with LINX being one of the largest IXPs in the world.[28]

The internet in the United Kingdom is regulated by several related laws, and I present the main ones here rather than an exhaustive list, just as in the other cases. The key laws and regulations relating to the internet in the United Kingdom cover a range of areas, including data protection, online privacy, cybersecurity and digital rights. Laws and regulations governing the internet began to emerge with the growing use of the internet in the 1990s and 2000s, but one of the early laws

---

[26] Belam (2015).

[27] See "United Kingdom" on ITU's DataHub: https://datahub.itu.int/data/?e=USA.

[28] See the IXP Database: https://ixpdb.euro-ix.net/en/; also see "United Kingdom" on Packet Clearing House: https://www.pch.net/ixp/dir#!mt-filters=%7B%22ctry%22%3A%5B%22dropdown%22%2C%22%22%2C%22United%20Kingdom%22%5D%7D.

was the Copyright, Designs and Patents Act 1988, which also addressed, to some extent, the use of copyrighted material online.[29] The Computer Misuse Act was enacted in October 1990, and it was the first main legislation to criminalize unauthorized access to computer systems and data, as well as the act of damaging or destroying such systems and data.[30]

Two other key acts came into being in 1985 and 1994, establishing the Government Communications Headquarters (GCHQ). The Interception of Communications Act 1985 granted the government the right to intercept postal communications and subsequently other types of public telecommunications, and the Intelligence Services Act 1994 de facto established the GCHQ and the Secret Intelligence Service, known as MI6.[31]

In July 2000, the Regulation of Investigatory Powers Act 2000 (RIPA) was introduced to "make provision for and about the interception of communications, the acquisition and disclosure of data relating to communications, the carrying out of surveillance, the use of covert human intelligence sources and the acquisition of the means by which electronic data protected by encryption or passwords may be decrypted or accessed …" RIPA regulates the powers of governmental entities to carry out surveillance and intercept and decrypt communications.[32] Next, the Communications Act 2002 and the Communications Act 2003 were introduced by parliament and came into force on July 25, 2003. Apart from internet, television and radio services regulations, these acts established the Office of Communications (OFCOM) as the regulatory body that oversees electronic communications, including mobile networks, broadband providers and internet service providers. It also regulated the electromagnetic spectrum (including mobile connections and Wi-Fi).[33]

Next, the Electronic Communications (EC Directive) Regulations 2003, also known as the Privacy and Electronic Communications Regulations, were introduced in late 2003. This law implemented the European Union's ePrivacy Directive (Directive 2002/58/EC) and provided specific privacy rights in relation

[29] See the Copyright, Designs and Patents Act 1988, HM Government, United Kingdom. https://www.legislation.gov.uk/ukpga/1988/48/contents.

[30] See the Computer Misuse Act 1990, HM Government, United Kingdom. https://www.legislation.gov.uk/ukpga/1990/18/contents.

[31] See the Interception of Communications Act 1985, HM Government, United Kingdom. https://www.legislation.gov.uk/ukpga/1985/56/contents; the Intelligence Services Act 1994, HM Government, United Kingdom. https://www.legislation.gov.uk/ukpga/1994/13/contents.

[32] See the Regulation of Investigatory Powers Act 2000, HM Government, United Kingdom. https://www.legislation.gov.uk/ukpga/2000/23/contents.

[33] See the Office of Communications Act 2002, HM Government, United Kingdom. https://www.legislation.gov.uk/ukpga/2002/11/introduction; Office of Communications Act 2003, HM Government, United Kingdom. https://www.legislation.gov.uk/ukpga/2003/21/contents.

to electronic communications, including rules on marketing calls, emails, texts, faxes, cookies and keeping communications services secure.[34]

Another law was introduced in 2016, the Investigatory Powers Act 2016, known as the "Snooper's Charter." It provides a new framework to govern the use and oversight of investigatory powers by law enforcement and security and intelligence agencies. It covers the interception of communications, equipment interference, and the acquisition and retention of communications data, particularly the bulk collection of communications data.[35]

Apart from regulating internet surveillance, the United Kingdom also introduced a proposal for handling online hate and mis/disinformation in 2019: the Online Harms White Paper. The paper, published in April 2019, outlines plans to combat online harms like illegal content, terrorist and extreme propaganda, mis/disinformation by foreign actors, crime-related content and more.[36] More laws like the Digital Economy Act of 2017, the Data Protection Act of 2018—which aligns the United Kingdom with the European GDPR—the Consumer Rights Act of 2015, the Audiovisual Media Services Regulations of 2020 and the Telecommunications (Security) Act of 2021 all aimed to make British cyberspace safer and more resilient.[37] These laws and regulations, alongside the establishment of the inter-governmental Digital Regulation Cooperation Forum, are designed to ensure that the internet is used responsibly and safely, protecting the rights and privacy of individuals while also addressing the challenges and risks associated with online activities.[38]

The Online Safety Act (OSA) of 2023, which came into law in October 2023, is another significant piece of legislation aimed at making the internet a safer place for users in the United Kingdom. The main goal of the OSA is to protect individuals, especially children, from harmful content online. This includes illegal content like hate speech, terrorist content and child abuse content, as well as legal but harmful content like cyberbullying, disinformation and content promoting

---

[34] See the Privacy and Electronic Communications (EC Directive) Regulations 2003, HM Government, United Kingdom. https://www.legislation.gov.uk/uksi/2003/2426/regulation/6/made.

[35] See the Investigatory Powers Act 2016, HM Government, United Kingdom. https://www.legislation.gov.uk/ukpga/2016/25/contents/enacted.

[36] See the Online Harms White Paper, Department for Digital, Culture, Media & Sport, United Kingdom. https://www.gov.uk/government/consultations/online-harms-white-paper/online-harms-white-paper.

[37] See the Digital Economy Act 2017, HM Government, United Kingdom. https://www.legislation.gov.uk/ukpga/2017/30/contents/enacted; the Data Protection Act 2018, HM Government, United Kingdom. https://www.legislation.gov.uk/ukpga/2018/12/contents/enacted; the Consumer Rights Act 2015, HM Government, United Kingdom. https://www.legislation.gov.uk/ukpga/2015/15/contents/enacted; the Audiovisual Media Services Regulations 2020, HM Government, United Kingdom. https://www.legislation.gov.uk/uksi/2020/1062/made; the Telecommunications (Security) Act 2021, HM Government, United Kingdom. https://www.legislation.gov.uk/ukpga/2021/31/contents/enacted.

[38] See the Digital Regulation Cooperation Forum, Information Commissioner's Office, United Kingdom. https://ico.org.uk/about-the-ico/what-we-do/digital-regulation-cooperation-forum/; also see Schlesinger (2022).

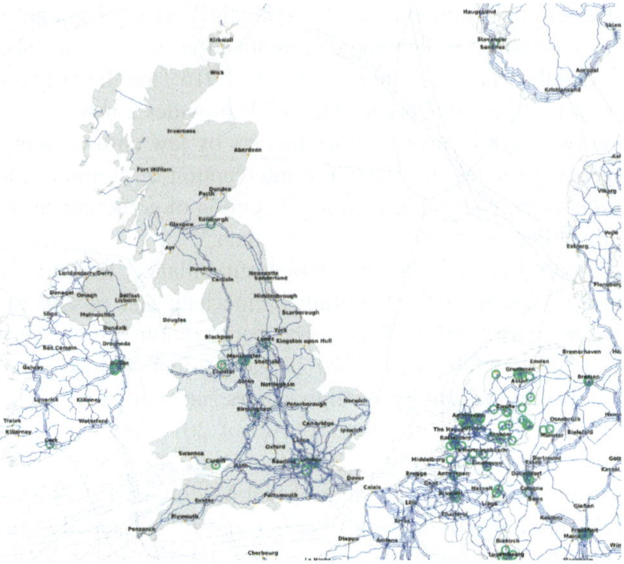

Fig. 7.3 Submarine and terrestrial internet cables and internet exchange points in and around the United Kingdom. *Source* Infrastructure Connectivity Map, International Telecommunication Union. * Blue lines are terrestrial, thin gray lines in seas and oceans are submarine fiber-optic cables, IXPs are in green circles. The United Kingdom is highlighted in gray

self-harm. OSA places new duties on social media companies to protect children and give adults more control over their online experience. It also empowers the regulator, OFCOM, to ensure online safety by tackling illegal content and harmful activity.[39] Interestingly, messaging applications like WhatsApp, Telegram and Signal, and even internet and social media companies like Meta, Google, Twitter and Wikipedia have expressed concerns and put the option of non-compliance on the table before the law was approved, as it makes monitoring obligatory and puts encryption and privacy second to safety. This, of course, has also been done by Russia and China, which have restricted internet and social media companies (see Chap. 6).[40]

The United Kingdom is part of the English-speaking Five Eyes Alliance and is a hub of fiber-optic cables and IXPs that connect the world (see Fig. 7.3). As such, it is committed to Western supremacy, whether in the areas of intelligence, trade or both. Thus, following the United States, it has also announced a ban on Chinese-made cyber-related equipment. While the ban is not absolute, the British government has banned Huawei from supplying equipment for the country's 5G networks

---

[39] See the Online Safety Act 2023, HM Government, United Kingdom. https://www.legislation.gov.uk/ukpga/2023/50/enacted.

[40] Guest (2023) and Spectator (2024).

due to security concerns over potential state influence. The decision was primarily driven by pressure from the United States.[41]

In summary, the United Kingdom has enacted legislation and regulations to restrict cyberspace. Regulations are supported and laws are enforced by several regulatory entities, including OFCOM, the primary regulatory authority for the communications industry. It regulates television, radio, cyberspace and other communication services. Another key governmental entity is the Information Commissioner's Office, an independent authority that upholds information rights and promotes data privacy for individuals. The Department for Digital, Culture, Media & Sport is a government department responsible for digital policy, telecommunications and the creative industries. It plays a role in shaping the regulatory framework surrounding the internet and digital services, as well as in formulating policies related to online safety, data protection and cybersecurity. The Home Office is responsible for issues related to security, immigration and law enforcement. It plays a role in shaping policies and legislation concerning cybersecurity, counterterrorism and the prevention of online harm. It works closely with the National Cyber Security Centre (NCSC), which was established in October 2016 as part of the United Kingdom's national cybersecurity strategy and leads cybersecurity efforts, providing advice and guidance to businesses and government agencies on how to protect against cyber threats. It also runs incident response operations with CERT-UK and collaborates with international partners such as US-CERT.

A particularly powerful entity is the GCHQ, which is the intelligence and security agency responsible for signals intelligence and information assurance. The GCHQ eavesdrops on electronic communications and protects the United Kingdom's own critical infrastructure from cyberattacks, as well as from terrorism. Ultimately, though, the judiciary court systems or bodies like the Independent Reviewer of Terrorism Legislation may decide on internet-related safety issues. Following the 2016–2021 National Cyber Security Strategy, which outlined the main challenges to tackle, the United Kingdom has issued the 2022–2030 National Cyber Security Strategy which aims to strengthen the NCSC and establish more control over cyberspace (mainly to defend it).[42] Indeed, following issues like foreign influence over Brexit, the United Kingdom still has a VCD, but it has been working to gain more control over cyberspace in recent years (see Table 7.2).

---

[41] Perrigo (2020).

[42] See the United Kingdom's National Cyber Security Strategy of 2016–2022 and the following Strategy of 2022–2030: National Cyber Security Strategy 2016 to 2021, HM Government, United Kingdom. https://assets.publishing.service.gov.uk/media/5a81914de5274a2e8ab54ae9/national_cyber_security_strategy_2016.pdf; Government Cyber Security Strategy—Building a Cyber Resilient Public Sector, HM Government, United Kingdom. https://assets.publishing.service.gov.uk/media/61f0169de90e070375c230a8/government-cyber-security-strategy.pdf.

Table 7.2 Restriction of internet layers in the United Kingdom

Restriction of network layer	Answer
Does the country regularly restrict or control its physical connections by design? Can it restrict the physical layer on demand?	Partially, the United Kingdom does not regularly restrict physical connections; however, it banned Chinese-made equipment in 2020
Does the country regularly restrict or control its network gateways and routes?	No, the logical layer is largely unrestricted and regulated by the market
Does the country regularly restrict or control the content within its borders?	Partially, as of 2023 and through the Online Safety Act (OSA) of 2023, it monitors and regulates harmful content
Does the country regularly restrict or control the way its citizens and even visitors use the internet?	Partially, as of 2023 and through the Online Safety Act (OSA) of 2023, it monitors and regulates harmful content and may hold individual users liable for the content they spread

7.3 The Israeli Cyberspace

Israel is considered by many to be a "start-up nation" or a high-tech nation. Indeed, Israel was an early adopter of the interconnected network. In 1984, a limited network was created between universities in Israel, which had opened the Israeli inter-University Computation Center (IUCC), and the European Academic Research Network; this built on an existing single connection between the Hebrew University of Jerusalem and American universities, which had operated since 1982. It is widely believed that the Israel Defense Force (IDF), Israel's military, as well as intelligence agencies, had scouted the idea of such networks—although to a very limited extent. Following the adoption of country code top-level domains (ccTLDs), Israel received the .il ending in 1985, and on November 8, 1988, the IUCC received a legal license to operate a network from the Israeli Ministry of Communications. On June 6, 1991, the Ministries of Industry and Trade, Science and Communications ordered the IUCC to allow private companies to connect. This opened the way for the commercialization of the internet in Israel, and on May 22, 1994, the internet became available to the public via three commercial companies: Elron, Darcom and Netmanage (which later bought out Elron). Soon after, on July 2, 1996, the only IXP in Israel, the Israeli Internet Exchange (IIX), became operational. In the late 1990s, Israeli universities had even joined internet2, a network dedicated to quality of service rather than just availability.[43]

From the moment commercial companies entered the arena, the Israeli internet grew tremendously, and it was quickly adopted by the vast majority of Israelis. On October 26, 2023, Israel even received its own Hebrew ccTLD (.ישראל).[44] According to data from the ITA, and true to 2022, there are approximately 9 million

[43] Hank (2006) and Palter and Nussbacher (1999).

[44] ICANN (2023).

Fig. 7.4 Submarine internet cables and internet exchange points in and around Israel. *Source* Infrastructure Connectivity Map, International Telecommunication Union. * Blue lines are terrestrial, thin gray lines in seas and oceans are submarine fiber-optic cables, IXPs are in green circles. Israel is highlighted in gray

citizens in Israel, of whom 90.3% use the internet; 80% of households have internet access. IIX is still Israel's only IXP, and it is operated by the Israel Internet Association. However, as seen in Fig. 7.4, Israel is only connected to the outside world via fiber-optic cables near Haifa and Tel Aviv (notwithstanding satellite communications and limited land links to Jordan and Egypt), raising the question of civil internet resilience and use in times of possible large wars. According to ISOC, 97% of internet users in Israel use YouTube, 95% use WhatsApp, and 90% use Facebook.[45]

Israeli citizens have thus adopted the internet on a large scale—but who monitors and regulates it to ensure it remains a resilient national asset? In terms of legislation, several laws regulate internet use, considering the fact that Israel has no constitution. First, the Basic Law: Human Dignity and Liberty of 1992 provides a framework recognizing the fact that Israeli citizens are free to do as they wish, as long as they do not harm others. In Israel, freedom of speech is generally protected by the Supreme Court.[46] Some content is censored by the power of the 1945 Defense (Emergency) Regulations, which are a remnant of the British

[45] Wiener and Stegman (2023).

[46] See Basic Laws, Israeli Knesset. https://main.knesset.gov.il/en/activity/pages/basiclaws.aspx; also see, generally, Israel Democracy Institute (n.d.).

Mandate that existed in the land of Israel between 1920 and 1945. These Defense (Emergency) Regulations were adopted as laws, and they are relevant to internet censorship.[47] The court system, alongside the Office of the State Attorney and the Ministry of Justice, has the power to regulate online content. They can censor and block access to websites and can hold people accountable for misuse, according to present Israeli laws and reasonable legal interpretation. For instance, in mid to late 2019, the Tel Aviv District Court ordered Israeli ISPs to block 1700 websites that contained illegal pornographic content.[48] In another example, the Lebanese pro-Iranian Al-Mayadeen website (which was considered hostile) was blocked upon a request from the Ministry of Communications.[49] An additional relevant law is the Basic Law: The Government, which was enacted in 2001 and has since been amended a few times; it can be interpreted as concerning cyberspace in the case of national security relevance.[50]

Until 2017, Israel censored content and users based on the decisions of ministries, which could be overruled by a district or supreme court, and based on the power of the 1945 Defense (Emergency) Regulations. It also censored content and enacted other restrictions by the power of the Counter-Terrorism Law, 5776-2016.[51] Then, on July 26, 2017, Israel introduced the Law on Authorities for the Prevention of Committing Crimes Through Use of an Internet Site, 5777-2017 (Law on Authorities), which came into force on September 26, 2017. The law authorizes a district court judge, selected for this purpose by the president of the district court upon request by a prosecutor, to issue a decree to fully or partially restrict access to a website based on a determination that the restriction is necessary to prevent an offense.[52] As of 2023, this law is the only one to directly address the internet. Before 2017, another relevant law was the 1995 Computers Law, which was adopted on July 25, 1995, and amended in 2012. It prohibits unauthorized access to content, data tempering and other computer-related crimes.[53] An older law that is also relevant is the Protection of Privacy Law, 5741-1981, which prohibits, both online and offline, the infringement of another's

---

47 Tzur (1989).

48 Times of Israel (2019).

49 i24 (2023).

50 Basic Law: The Government, 5761-2001. The Knesset [In Hebrew: חוק-יסוד: הממשלה [התשס"א]]. https://main.knesset.gov.il/Activity/Legislation/Laws/Pages/LawPrimary.aspx?t=lawlaws&st=lawlawsbasic&lawitemid=2000040.

51 Counter-Terrorism Law, 5776-2016. The Knesset [In Hebrew: חוק המאבק בטרור, התשע"ו-2016]. https://main.knesset.gov.il/activity/legislation/laws/pages/lawbill.aspx?t=lawreshumot&lawitemid=568876.

52 Law on Authorities for the Prevention of Committing Crimes Through Use of an Internet Site, 5777-2017 (Law on Authorities). The Knesset [In Hebrew: חוק סמכויות לשם מניעת ביצוע עבירות באמצעות אתר אינטרנט, התשע"ז-2017]. https://main.knesset.gov.il/Activity/Legislation/Laws/Pages/LawPrimary.aspx?t=lawlaws&st=lawlaws&lawitemid=2020878.

53 Computers Law, 5755-1995 (as amended on July 17, 2012). The Knesset [In Hebrew: חוק המחשבים (תיקון), התשע"ב-2012]. https://main.knesset.gov.il/activity/legislation/laws/pages/LawBill.aspx?t=LawReshumot&lawitemid=421693.

privacy without his/her consent. It also sets guidelines for the protection of databases.[54]

In terms of cybersecurity, intelligence and surveillance, the General Security Service Law, 5762-2002 and the Secret Monitoring Law, 5739-1979 authorize the Israel Security Agency (the Shabak) to eavesdrop and monitor content on computers and other devices, as well as online content, including network traffic—the Shabak has operated under the umbrella of the IDF since 1949. The Shabak is also appointed to defend against conspiracies to tamper with critical infrastructures.[55] In December 2023, following the October 7 terrorist attack on Israel and the subsequent war between Israel and the Hamas terror organization, additional amendments to laws concerning cyberspace were added. For instance, the Authorization Law for Penetrating Computer Material Used for Operating a Stationary Camera (Temporary Order—Iron Swords), 5784-2023 grants the Israeli security forces the authority to penetrate computer material and use cameras.[56]

Apart from the IDF and the Shabak—and the Israeli Police, which deals with cybercrime—two additional entities are responsible for the protection and resilience of critical infrastructure. The first is the National Security Council (NSC), the main body that coordinates, integrates, assesses and monitors national security, which was established as part of the Prime Minister's Office in 1999 and later became a partially independent body through legal measures in 2008. Aside from coordinating security and intelligence, is also in charge of strategic planning and crisis management, including cyber-related issues.[57] The other is the Israel National Cyber Directorate (INCD); as stated on its website, "The Israel National Cyber Directorate is the national security and technological agency responsible for defending Israel's national cyberspace and for establishing and advancing Israel's cyber power."[58] It was established as the National Cyber Bureau in 2011. In 2015, the Israeli government decided to operate the Cyber Bureau alongside the National

[54] Protection of Privacy Law, 5741-1981. The Knesset [In Hebrew: חוק הגנת הפרטיות, התשמ"א-1981]. https://main.knesset.gov.il/Activity/Legislation/Laws/Pages/LawBill.aspx?t=LawReshumot&lawitemid=147337.

[55] General Security Service Law, 5762-2002. The Knesset [In Hebrew: חוק שירות הביטחון הכללי, התשס"ב-2002]. https://main.knesset.gov.il/activity/legislation/laws/pages/lawprimary.aspx?t=lawlaws&st=lawlaws&lawitemid=2001389; Secret Monitoring Law, 5739-1979. The Knesset [In Hebrew: חוק האזנת סתר, התשל"ט-1979]. https://main.knesset.gov.il/Activity/Legislation/Laws/Pages/LawPrimary.aspx?t=lawlaws&st=lawlaws&lawitemid=2000169.

[56] Authorization Law for Penetrating Computer Material Used for Operating a Stationary Camera (Temporary Order—Iron Swords), 5784-2023. The Knesset [In Hebrew: חוק הסמכת צבא הגנה לישראל ושירות הביטחון הכללי לביצוע חדירה לחומר מחשב המשמש להפעלת מצלמה נייחת ופעולה בו (הוראת שעה – חרבות ברזל), התשפ"ד-2023]. https://main.knesset.gov.il/Activity/Legislation/Laws/Pages/LawBill.aspx?t=LawReshumot&lawitemid=2211682.

[57] See the National Security Council Law 5768-2008. The Knesset [In Hebrew: חוק המטה לביטחון לאומי, התשס"ח-2008]. https://main.knesset.gov.il/activity/legislation/laws/pages/lawbill.aspx?t=lawreshumot&lawitemid=263865.

[58] See Israel National Cyber Directorate (n.d.).

Cyber Security Authority, and they eventually merged into one entity, the INCD, in December 2017.[59]

All the above-mentioned laws, and a few others that are not covered in this review, contribute to the legal framework with which Israel regulates the internet. The Ministry of Industry and Trade, the Ministry of Science and, mainly, the Ministry of Communications are the regulatory bodies that regulate cyberspace, and communications in general. In terms of cybersecurity, the IDF, the Shabak, the NSC and the INCD all work together to prevent cyber threats. However, as exemplified in Chaps. 4 and 5, Israeli cyberspace is very open and insecure, especially for citizens, who are often attacked by proxy to reach security and intelligence-related targets. Following civil unrest in both 2021 and 2022, even the Israeli police chief, Police Commissioner Kobi Shabtai, called for social media to be shut down as a way to stop the violence. "We are a democratic country, but there are limits," he noted, pointing to the fact that mis/disinformation spread by radical local actors or malicious foreign actors is dangerous. Despite civil society and some Knesset members criticizing his statement, even the Israel Democracy Institute, which is more left-wing, and the Institute for National Security Studies raised concerns about the growing spread of "fake news."[60] Israel has no legal recourse to handle mis/disinformation (see Chap. 5). As summarized in Table 7.3, the Israeli cyber domain can be regarded as a VCD since Israeli civilian internet connections are very fragile (only two main connections exist) and foreign submarines have been spotted near these cables before.[61]

7.4 The European Cyber Bloc

The ITU segments the world into regions: Africa, the Arab States, Asia and the Pacific, CIS, Europe, and the Americas. There are approximately 448 million people in Europe, 89.5% of whom use the internet (true to 2022), and 87.6% of households have access at home. In comparison, Africa has an estimated population of 1.3 billion, but only 39.7% use the internet.[62] According to data from Packet Clearing House, there are 396 IXPs in Europe, more than the 269 IXPs in Asia-Pacific and the 257 IXPs in North America (see Fig. 7.5).[63] Europe is one of the main targets of both American and Russo-Chinese propaganda, including mis/disinformation, as it is a global scientific, economic and political hub that, when united, can compete with the United States, Russia and China.[64]

[59] Unna (2019).

[60] Joffre (2022); also see INSS (2019) and Altshuler Shwartz and Brun (2019).

[61] i24 (2019).

[62] See "Europe" on ITU's DataHub: https://datahub.itu.int/data/?e=5.

[63] See "Internet Exchange Directory" on Packet Clearing House: https://www.pch.net/ixp/dir.

[64] Shuker and Topor (2021) and Zimdars (2022).

Table 7.3 Restriction of internet layers in Israel

Restriction of network layer	Answer
Does the country regularly restrict or control its physical connections by design? Can it restrict the physical layer on demand?	No, it cannot restrict physical connections on demand and needs to enact laws to achieve this
Does the country regularly restrict or control its network gateways and routes?	No, the logical layer is largely unrestricted and regulated by the market. Although it is monitored, this does not affect internet use for the general public
Does the country regularly restrict or control the content within its borders?	Partially, it only monitors and regulates harmful content like terrorist-supported content and illegal pornography
Does the country regularly restrict or control the way its citizens and even visitors use the internet?	No, unless they spread or consume harmful content like illegal pornography or terrorism-related material

Fig. 7.5 Submarine and terrestrial internet cables and internet exchange points in and around Europe. * Blue lines are terrestrial, thin gray lines in seas and oceans are submarine fiber-optic cables, IXPs are in green circles

The European cyberspace is a complex ecosystem that operates across various countries, each contributing to its overall functionality and accessibility. This part delves into some legal and technical aspects of the European internet, focusing on the four layers: infrastructure, the logical layer, information, and users. Additionally, it examines the restrictions imposed on the European internet, mainly due to privacy concerns, and highlights the major laws and regulations governing its use. As in previous cases, this review is non-exhaustive but rather aims to illustrate a crucial point: the gradual emergence of a limited cyber bloc. While the European internet generally allows freedom of expression, certain restrictions are in place. Governments and regulatory bodies have implemented measures to combat cybercrime and terrorism and to protect national security, as well as privacy, trade and copyright. Content deemed illegal or harmful is subject to removal, and efforts to combat fake news and hate speech are ongoing, particularly as Europe is susceptible to American, Russian and Chinese mis/disinformation campaigns. Even American companies are being fined billions of US dollars for violating Europe's cyber regulations.

The European Union has its roots in the aftermath of World War II and had the primary goal of fostering economic cooperation and preventing further conflict in Europe. The precursor to the European Union was the European Coal and Steel Community (ECSC), established in 1951 by the Treaty of Paris. The ECSC aimed to integrate the coal and steel industries of its six founding members: Belgium, France, Italy, Luxembourg, the Netherlands and West Germany. The process of European integration continued with the signing of the Treaty of Rome in 1957, which established the European Economic Community (EEC) and the European Atomic Energy Community. The EEC aimed to create a common market, gradually eliminating trade barriers among member states. Over the years, the European Union expanded both in terms of membership and areas of cooperation. The Maastricht Treaty, signed on February 7, 1992, marked a significant milestone in the evolution of the European Union. It led to the creation of the EU as a political and economic union, introducing the single currency, the euro. The treaty also laid the groundwork for common foreign and security policies. Subsequent treaties, such as the Amsterdam Treaty (1997), the Nice Treaty (2001) and the Lisbon Treaty (2007), further expanded the European Union's competencies and institutional framework. The Lisbon Treaty, in particular, which amended the Maastricht Treaty and the Rome Treaty, aimed to enhance the efficiency and democratic accountability of the European Union.[65]

The European Union operates on a supranational basis, meaning that it has some authority above the national governments of its member states. The European Union's institutions, including the European Commission, the European Parliament, and the European Court of Justice (ECJ), play crucial roles in decision-making and legal interpretation. As stated on the official website of the

[65] See Dedman (2006) and European Union (n.d.).

European Parliament: "The Member States of the European Union have agreed, as a result of their membership of the EU, to transfer some of their powers to the EU institutions in specified policy areas."[66] The European Union thus has several key institutions that have a say in policies, specifically those that concern cyberspace. These include the European Parliament, the European Commission, the Council of the European Union, Europol—the European Union Agency for Law Enforcement Cooperation—the European Union Agency for Cybersecurity (ENISA) and more.

Legally and politically, the European Union has some distributed power. Each member country has its own laws and regulations and national security, including cybersecurity, concerns. On top of these, the European Union divides its power between the European Parliament, the European Commission, the Council of the European Union and more. The legal and political complexity of the European Union deserves its own study; however, there are some key laws, regulations and institutions that together regulate the European cyber bloc. Specifically, these are the European Cybersecurity Act, the GDPR, the DSA and the DMA, the ePrivacy Directive and the Network and Information Systems (NIS) Directive.

The GDPR, the DSA and the DMA were introduced and discussed in Chap. 3; broadly, however, it was in 2016, after the ePrivacy (2002) and Data Protection (2003) Directives, that the European Union adopted the General Data Protection Regulation (GDPR) (2016/679). This regulation governs how the personal data of individuals in the European Union may be processed and transferred. The GDPR applies to organizations that process the personal data of European Union citizens or residents, or that offer goods or services to such people, even if the organizations are not located in the European Union. The regulation imposes strict data protection and security requirements, and non-compliance can result in significant fines. The GDPR aims to harmonize data privacy laws across Europe and strengthen individuals' fundamental rights in the digital age.[67] In addition, the Digital Services Act (DSA) and the Digital Markets Act (DMA), two significant pieces of European Union legislation, came into force in November 2022. The DSA addresses harmful and illegal goods, services and online content, replacing the E-Commerce Directive. It aims to create a safer digital space and protect users' fundamental rights. On the other hand, the DMA is primarily concerned with fostering a fair and competitive digital market, especially for big digital service providers. It sets clear rules for large online platforms and aims to ensure a level playing field for all digital companies, regardless of size.[68]

Another significant law is the European Union's Cybersecurity Act, which was adopted in 2019. It is a cornerstone of the European Union's efforts to bolster its cybersecurity preparedness and resilience, focusing mainly on strengthening

[66] European Parliament (n.d.).

[67] Li et al. (2019).

[68] See Digital Markets Act (DMA), European Commission. https://digital-markets-act.ec.europa.eu/legislation_en; Digital Services Act (DSA), European Commission. https://digital-strategy.ec.europa.eu/en/policies/digital-services-act-package.

ENISA and granting it a permanent mandate, solidifying its role as the central hub for expertise and support on cybersecurity issues in the European Union, and expanding ENISA's powers to tackle threats. Another key development was the establishment of an European Union-wide cybersecurity certification framework for products, services and processes, setting standards for the benefit of the European Union.[69] To strengthen the Cybersecurity Act, the European Union proposed two additional acts. The Cyber Solidarity Act was proposed in April 2023 to improve the response to cyber threats across the European Union and to initiate the European Cybersecurity Shield, and the Cyber Resilience Act was proposed in September 2022 to set requirements for smart or connected devices.[70]

In January 2023, the Network and Information Systems 2 (NIS2) Directive 2022/2555 entered into force, replacing the NIS Directive 2016/1148. The NIS2 Directive constitutes a crucial piece of legislation in the European Union's cybersecurity framework. It aims to enhance the security of essential services across various sectors by establishing minimum cybersecurity requirements for relevant operators. It focuses on essential services like the energy sector, transport, water, healthcare, postal services, public administration and waste management. The main difference between the 2016 and the 2022/3 Directives is an expansion of the scope and the fact that risk management and incident reporting are now mandatory; also, organizations can now be held accountable and receive penalties if they do not comply. NIS2 will likely have a global impact, as the GDPR did, because non-European Union actors will now have to comply with European standards to gain a foothold. It may also intensify the global cyber arms race, as countries and non-state actors are constantly seeking to develop new ways to attack and defend critical infrastructure.[71]

Several of the European Union's institutions that handle cyberspace (the European Parliament, the European Commission, the Council of the European Union and Europol) are not covered in this section due to limitations of scope. Yet there is one particular institution that protects its cyber domain alongside the GDPR, DSA and DMA, and regulations from the European Commission: ENISA focuses on the overall cybersecurity posture of the European Union. It was established in 2004 by Regulation (EC) 460/2004 and strengthened by the Cybersecurity Act mentioned earlier. ENISA contributes to European Union cyber policy, enhances the trustworthiness of ICT products, services and processes with cybersecurity certification schemes, cooperates with member states and European Union bodies, and helps Europe prepare for cybersecurity challenges. In 2011, the Computer Emergency Response Team for the European Union (CERT-EU) was established within ENISA; this permanent team responds to information security incidents and cyber threats affecting the computer systems of all European Union institutions, agencies and bodies, similar to the American and British CERTs.[72]

[69] European Commission (n.d.a).

[70] European Commission (n.d.b).

[71] ENISA (n.d.a).

[72] ENISA (n.d.b).

To conclude, the European internet has a rich history dating back to the early days of ARPANET; some countries, like Germany, had experimented with global networking since the 19080s while others, like Bulgaria, joined later in the early to mid-1990s. Europe played a pivotal role in the development of the World Wide Web, with the first website created by Tim Berners-Lee in 1991 while he was working at CERN in Switzerland (though not a part of the European Union). Since then, Europe has consistently contributed to internet technologies and standards. The expansion of the European Union has influenced the growth and integration of the internet across member states.[73] It is a particularly interesting case as it represents a dynamic and evolving network that balances the principles of openness and security. Due to external threats, it has developed a more dedicated framework in recent years, especially in the 2010s. Legal frameworks such as the GDPR, the DSA and the DMA ensure robust data protection, and ongoing efforts to address cyber threats and online content challenges remain a priority. The European Council tackles mis/disinformation with various legislative proposals and initiatives and harder cyber threats with entities like ENISA and the Cybersecurity Act. However, since each member state is sovereign and can decide on the information it receives, combating mis/disinformation is a significant challenge for the European cyber bloc.

The future of European cyberspace, or the European cyber bloc, might resemble a more secure cyber domain than the American VCD; however, only time will tell where the European wind is blowing as economic inequalities between European countries are prompting some to leave the European Union or to confront it from within (i.e., Brexit and calls for Greece, Spain and even Poland to withdraw). As of 2023, the European Union is also seeking to promote the AI Act, to the consternation of companies like OpenAI (ChatGPT, DALL-E), which has threatened to leave the bloc. The AI Act "aim[s] to ensure that AI systems are overseen by people, are safe, transparent, traceable, non-discriminatory, and environmentally friendly."[74] Finally, this chapter has no concluding table since the cyber bloc is yet premature but also since each member state can have varying requirements and in such a case the bloc should not be compared to sovereign countries, yet.

7.5 Conclusion

This chapter has provided an overview of several prominent global and regional powers and their VCDs, cyber domains that prioritize free information flow and access over national security and sovereignty (compared to the SCDs discussed

[73] See, generally, Shahin (2006).

[74] European Parliament (2023) and Coulter and Mukherjee (2023).

in the previous chapter). The cases reviewed were those of the United States, the United Kingdom, Israel and the evolving European cyber bloc. The ITU's Global Cybersecurity Index (GCI) of 2020 places these VCDs high (or relatively high, compared to SCDs) on a scale of cybersecurity, suggesting that the United States, the United Kingdom, Israel and many European countries have secure cyber domains. How then, can Russia, China, Iran and others so successfully use cyber warfare against Western companies and infrastructure, and sharp power to influence Western societies? Clearly, there is a misalignment. A detailed analysis suggests that the countries inspected here are not as secure as the GCI presents. While it is true that Chap. 6 and this chapter reviewed different aspects of cyberspace than those of the GCI, it is somewhat odd that the most secure cyber domains emerged as the most insecure.

Chapters 4 and 5 and this chapter (the current chapter) have made clear that the United States, the United Kingdom, Israel and many European countries have VCDs and are vulnerable compared to the SCDs of North Korea, Russia, China, Iran and Saudi Arabia. First, the very essence of the internet, a global network of networks, makes countries vulnerable: if a network is open and insufficiently regulated, it is vulnerable. Second, the fact that some countries, like the cases examined in this chapter, prioritize free information flow and financial profit over national security, resilience and sovereignty makes their cyber domains insecure. The approach of this book prioritizes strategic security over human freedom, and indeed, the most free, liberal and democratic countries are also those suffering the most from cyberattacks and mis/disinformation. The United States, the United Kingdom and Israel have all suffered cyberattacks and mis/disinformation campaigns that have had a tremendous impact on national resilience. In the United States, the FCC and CISA did not stop the interference in the 2016 presidential election, nor did they stop the SolarWinds cyberattack. The British OFCOM, NCSC and GCHQ could not prevent the Russian influence on Brexit or the alleged North Korean attack on the NHS. The Israeli Ministry of Communications, IDF, Shabak, NSC and INCD could not stop Iranian or terrorist cyberattacks, nor could they stop mis/disinformation from causing anxiety and chaos in society. The European Union, of course, struggles with Russian influence over its unity and NATO-related issues (see Chap. 4).

One particular case is unique, and it is the case of the European cyber bloc. On the one hand, each European Union member state is sovereign and has independent and sovereign laws and regulations. On the other hand, the European Union operates on a supranational basis: it has some authority over the national governments of member states. For issues regarding cyberspace, the European Commission, European Union Parliament, ECJ and others have the power to implement rules and regulations. For instance, the European Cybersecurity Act, the GDPR, the DSA and the DMA are all mandatory regulations that affect not only European Union members but also non-European countries, companies and individuals. Furthermore, the European cyber bloc has ENISA, and within ENISA, the CERT-EU team. In recent years, this cyber bloc has introduced new rules and regulations that might pave the way for the establishment of a more secure bloc, taking up a central position between the SCDs and the VCDs presented so far.

References

Altshuler Shwartz, Tehilla, and Itai Brun. 2019. Fake news: The next generation. *IDI*, July 14. [In Hebrew: פייק ניוז: הדור הבא]. https://www.idi.org.il/articles/27133.

Ball, James. 2021. Facebook and Google's new plan? Own the Internet. *Wired*, October 7. https://www.wired.co.uk/article/facebook-google-subsea-cables.

Belam, Martin. 2015. Timeline of .uk Internet usage. *Medium*, July 23. https://medium.com/30-stories-of-uk/timeline-of-uk-internet-usage-93b705c78891.

Chen, Kai. 2017. No place to hide: Edward Snowden, the NSA, and the US surveillance state. *Intelligence and National Security* 32 (6): 868–871.

Coulter, Martin, and Supantha Mukherjee. 2023. Focus: OpenAI CEO's threat to quit EU draws lawmaker backlash. *Reuters*, May 26. https://www.reuters.com/technology/openai-ceos-threat-quit-eu-draws-lawmaker-backlash-2023-05-25/.

Dedman, Martin. 2006. *The origins and development of the European Union 1945–1995: A history of European integration*. Routledge.

ENISA. n.d.a. NIS directive. https://www.enisa.europa.eu/topics/cybersecurity-policy/nis-directive-new.

ENISA. n.d.b. ENISA mandate and regulatory framework. https://www.enisa.europa.eu/about-enisa/regulatory-framework.

European Commission. n.d.a. The EU cybersecurity act. https://digital-strategy.ec.europa.eu/en/policies/cybersecurity-act.

European Commission. n.d.b. Cybersecurity policies. https://digital-strategy.ec.europa.eu/en/policies/cybersecurity-policies.

European Parliament. n.d. Supranational decision-making procedures. https://www.europarl.europa.eu/factsheets/en/sheet/8/supranational-decision-making-procedures.

European Parliament. 2023. AI Act: A step closer to the first rules on artificial intelligence. *European Parliament*, May 11. https://www.europarl.europa.eu/news/en/press-room/20230505IPR84904/ai-act-a-step-closer-to-the-first-rules-on-artificial-intelligence.

European Union. n.d. History of the EU. https://european-union.europa.eu/principles-countries-history/history-eu_en.

Federal Communications Commission. n.d. FCC bans authorizations for devices that pose national security threat. https://www.fcc.gov/document/fcc-bans-authorizations-devices-pose-national-security-threat.

Geiger, Abigail. 2018. How Americans have viewed government surveillance and privacy since Snowden leaks. *Pew Research Center*, June 4. https://www.pewresearch.org/short-reads/2018/06/04/how-americans-have-viewed-government-surveillance-and-privacy-since-snowden-leaks/.

Guest, Peter. 2023. The UK's controversial Online Safety Act is now law. *Wired*, October 26. https://www.wired.co.uk/article/the-uks-controversial-online-safety-act-is-now-law.

Hank, Nussbacher. 2006. Internet timeline for Israel—The early years (1984–1998). *Interall*, September 17. https://www.interall.co.il/israel-internet-timeline.html.

Hecht, Jeff. 2021. Biggest tech companies now building the biggest data pipes—Facebook will lay a record-capacity submarine cable across the Atlantic. *IEEE Spectrum*, October 18. https://spectrum.ieee.org/biggest-tech-companies-biggest-data-pipes.

i24. 2019. Russian submarine spotted off Israel's coastline some 3 months ago: Report. *i24*, November 11. https://www.i24news.tv/en/news/israel/diplomacy-defense/1573503505-russian-submarine-spotted-off-israel-s-coastline-some-3-months-ago-report.

i24. 2023. Israel blocks pro-Iran Al-Mayadeen TV website over security concerns. *i24*, November 13. https://www.i24news.tv/en/news/israel-at-war/1699896177-israel-blocks-pro-iran-al-mayadeen-tv-website-over-security-concerns.

ICANN. 2023. The Israel IDN ccTLD manager joins as newest member of the ccNSO. *ICANN*, October 27. https://ccnso.icann.org/en/announcements/announcement-27oct23-en.htm.

INSS. 2019. The campaign over consciousness: Strategic and intelligence insights, May 2019. INSS. [In Hebrew: המערכה על התודעה: היבטים אסטרטגיים ומודיעיניים]. https://www.inss.org.il/he/publication/the-cognitive-campaign/.

Israel Democracy Institute. n.d. Regulation of the media. https://en.idi.org.il/tags-en/1476.

Israel National Cyber Directorate. n.d. About. *Gov IL*. https://www.gov.il/en/departments/about/newabout.

Joffre, Tzvi. 2022. Israel police chief recommends shutting off social media during riots. *Jerusalem Post*, September 21. https://www.jpost.com/israel-news/article-717745.

Kleinrock, Leonard. 2019. The first message transmission. *ICANN*, October 29. https://www.icann.org/en/blogs/details/the-first-message-transmission-29-10-2019-en.

Li, He, Lu Yu, and Wu He. 2019. The impact of GDPR on global technology development. *Journal of Global Information Technology Management* 22 (1): 1–6.

Miller, James N., Robert J. Butler, and Johns Hopkins University-Applied Physics Laboratory. 2021. *National Cyber Defense Center: A key next step toward a whole-of-nation approach to cyber security*. John Hopkins University Applied Physics Laboratory.

National Telecommunications and Information Administration (NTIA). n.d. The Federal Communications Commission (FCC), U.S. Department of Commerce. https://www.ntia.gov/book-page/federal-communications-commission-fcc.

Ortiz-Ospina, Esteban. 2019. The rise of social media. *OurWorldInData*, September 18. https://ourworldindata.org/rise-of-social-media.

Pai, Ajit. 2014. The story of the FCC's net neutrality decision and why it won't stand up in court. *The Federal Communications Law Journal* 67: 147.

Palter, D.C., and Hank Nussbacher. 1999. Internet 2 takes to the air. *Satellite Communications* 23 (11): 36–39.

Perrigo, Billy. 2020. Bowing to U.S. pressure, U.K. bans 5G equipment from China's Huawei over security concerns. *TIME*, July 14. https://time.com/5866643/uk-huawei-5g-ban/.

Pew Research Center. 2021a. Social media fact sheet. *Pew Research Center*, April 7. https://www.pewresearch.org/internet/fact-sheet/social-media/.

Pew Research Center. 2021b. Internet/broadband fact sheet. *Pew Research Center*, April 7. https://www.pewresearch.org/internet/fact-sheet/internet-broadband/.

Schlesinger, Philip. 2022. The neo-regulation of internet platforms in the United Kingdom. *Policy & Internet* 14 (1): 47–62.

Shahin, Jamal. 2006. A European history of the Internet. *Science and Public Policy* 33 (9): 681–693.

Shubber, Kadhim. 2013. A simple guide to the Prism controversy. *WIRED*, June 10. https://www.wired.co.uk/article/simple-guide-to-prism.

Shuker, Pnina, and Lev Topor. 2021. Russian influence campaigns against NATO in the Baltic region: Spread of chaos and divide et impera. In *The Russian Federation in global knowledge warfare*, 295–314. Cham: Springer.

Siripurapu, Anshu. 2020. Trump and Section 230: What to know. *Council on Foreign Relations*, December 2. https://www.cfr.org/in-brief/trump-and-section-230-what-know.

Spectator. 2024. The Online Safety Act is already stifling free speech. *Spectator*, January 13. https://www.spectator.co.uk/article/the-online-safety-act-is-already-stifling-free-speech/.

Times of Israel. 2019. Israel: Court blocks access to 1,700 pedophilia websites. *Times of Israel*, June 17. https://www.timesofisrael.com/israel-blocks-access-to-1700-pedophilia-websites/.

Topor, Lev. 2022. *Phishing for Nazis: Conspiracies, anonymous communications and white supremacy networks on the Dark Web*. Routledge.

Tzur, Michael. 1989. *The (emergency) defense regulations, 1945*. Policy Paper No. 16. Israel Democracy Institute.

U.S. Department of Homeland Security. n.d. US-CERT: United States computer emergency readiness team. https://www.cisa.gov/sites/default/files/publications/infosheet_US-CERT_v2.pdf.

Unna, Yigal. 2019. National cyber security in Israel. *Cyber, Intelligence, and Security* 3 (1): 167–173.

W3. n.d. Tim Berners-Lee. https://www.w3.org/People/Berners-Lee/Overview.html.

Waterfield, Bruno. 2013. Angela Merkel: Spying between friends is unacceptable. *Telegraph*, October 24. https://www.telegraph.co.uk/news/worldnews/europe/germany/10403437/Angela-Merkel-spying-between-friends-is-unacceptable.html.

Weinstein, Dave. 2014. Snowden and US cyber power. *Georgetown Journal of International Affairs* 15: 4.

Wiener, Asaf, and Ofir Stegman. 2023. Social media and digital platforms use in Israel (2023). *ISOC-IL*, August 3. https://en.isoc.org.il/data-and-statistics/social_media_use_il_2023.

Zimdars, Melissa. 2022. Mis/disinformation and social media. In *The social media debate*, 120–136. Routledge.

Chapter 8
The Future of the Internet

We are all living in, sometimes on, the cloud. This imaginary cloud is, of course, cyberspace, which in recent decades has boosted globalization and allowed humanity to disregard the parameters of time and space. In rich countries but also in less fortunate ones, people use cyberspace—the internet—for work, education, leisure and even love. We spend a tremendous amount of our time online, creating and consuming content that in many cases is open to everybody, or not as safeguarded as we think. This "Galactic Network," as Joseph Carl Robnett Licklider of MIT described it in the early 1960s, has indeed succeeded in connecting the whole world by technical means. The problem, however, is that technical means are not enough for humanity, which often needs socio-political means and agreements to get along. The technical aspect of the internet did not fully consider the political reality of the twentieth century—the Cold War—and now, in the twenty-first century, the technical aspect does not address global power shifts, multi-polarity and cultural differences. The internet, it seems, has evolved into a golem, which is now turning on its creator. In Jewish legend, a golem is a man-made creature that is often portrayed as a helper or a protector, but in some cases, it can turn on its creator and endanger him. The internet is humanity's golem; it has been of significant use to people, but it is now turning on its creators.

How has this golem turned on us all? First, this cyber-golem, so to speak, has created cybersecurity threats, which include cyberattacks like infrastructure damage, data breaches, espionage and data manipulation. Second, it has created, or significantly enhanced, the abuse of sharp power and of mis/disinformation and made it easier than ever to spread conspiracy theories. Third, it has enhanced privacy concerns. Our private and personal information is often stored online, but we lack the proper regulatory and security means to protect it. Identity theft and other fraudulent activities are now easier to perpetrate than ever. Since governments control ISPs, and they control our internet, it has also provided governments with excessive amounts of power and the ability to spy on and control their citizens, as Edward Snowden revealed. Moreover, as of the 2020s, emerging technologies like AI, biotechnology,

L. Topor, *Cyber Sovereignty*, Global Power Shift,
https://doi.org/10.1007/978-3-031-58199-1_8

and VR have become more integrated with the internet, and we now face new ethical and political dilemmas. Questions about algorithmic accountability, digital surveillance, technological discrimination and more arise.

One of the most significant problems of the internet is the socio-political and cultural gap between countries. Countries are naturally sovereign, and the concept of sovereignty is a foundational and enduring principle in politics and international relations. True, globalization and industrialization have indeed created great interdependence between countries and subtracted from the Westphalian model of sovereignty, but countries are still the ultimate authority over their domain (land, resources and citizens). As long ago as the sixteenth century, Jean Bodin argued that sovereignty must be absolute, perpetual and undivided. This insight remains valid today—countries constantly strive for absolute control. Yet countries often engage in conflicts over control, resources and outcomes, intervening in others' affairs for their own benefit. The internet, however, undermines the very essence of sovereignty as it is eating away at both the despotic and the infrastructural power of countries. Intervention becomes a matter of just a few skilled mouse clicks. A fully connected and open country cannot properly combat foreign mis/disinformation or even true information that it perceives as dangerous or unwanted. Foreign powers and their proxies can easily intervene in the affairs of their adversaries—digitally rather than kinetically.

During the Cold War, the Soviet Union and the United States did not engage in direct warfare but used proxies to compete for global prominence and dominance and for control of outcomes, actors and resources. As nuclear powers, they wished to avoid a MAD situation. Indirect engagement was also used due to the difficulty of attribution as, by using proxies, war was not legally justifiable—if one considers international norms and laws as an important part of global affairs, that is. International laws indeed play an important role as they tone down coercive desires; such laws compel international actors to maintain a stable global order. There are international laws concerning war, human rights and maritime laws; however, there are no applicable international laws regarding cyberspace. For instance, fake news is not illegal, and espionage or data-wiping attacks that damage infrastructure can be carried out by proxies. Cyber proxy warfare is used to avoid attribution, making it difficult for a country to justify retaliation against a proxy's "boss," not only because there is no direct connection but also because some attacks are below the threshold of armed conflict.

For instance, how can the United States retaliate when Russia and China intervene using proxy hacking groups or by spreading mis/disinformation? On the one hand, interventions such as the 2016 presidential election intervention and the 2021 Capitol riot undermine American sovereignty—undermine the very nature of the democratic idea. On the other hand, these interventions were carried out using proxies and without firing a single bullet. Inappropriate regulatory means can lead to severe state control over citizens, but a complete lack of regulatory means can often harm a country much faster. As there is no applicable international law regarding cyberspace, the United States had the option of retaliating by military, diplomatic or economic means, and it could, of course, retaliate with similar cyberattacks. However, countries like Russia and China have an advantage: they are less free and less open than the

United States, and they can control data and information flows more effectively. They utilize sharp power to threaten the West while preserving or gaining sovereignty and power themselves. The quote by Wu Jichuan, the former Chinese Minister of Posts and Telecommunications and former Minister of Industry and Information Technology during the 1990s, which was presented in the introduction, is very relevant to our understanding of information control:

> By linking with the Internet, we don't mean absolute freedom of information. I think there is a general understanding about this. If you go through customs, you have to show your passport. It's the same with management of information. There is no contradiction at all between the development of telecommunications infrastructure and the exercise of state sovereignty.[1]

China has its GSP, an initiative that protects Chinese sovereignty, mainly through the GFW, which blocks foreign incoming information. Russia has a vast array of laws, technological and social, which also protect its sovereignty, as well as the RuNet project, which can provide networking services solely within Russia or with the parties it deems appropriate. Other countries, like Iran, have projects like the NIN, which aims to create a separate and state-controlled domestic cyberspace. Saudi Arabia also has an extensive legal regime to control data and information flow. North Korea is not connected to the global grid at all, apart from a few limited and private connections with China and Russia and some satellite connectivity; it has created an air gap. Countries like India, Myanmar, Sudan, Cuba, Jordan, Ethiopia and many others utilize whole internet shutdowns to retain national resilience even at the cost of their citizens' access to information. In contrast, there is a constitutional right to free speech in the United States, and Section 230(c)(1) provides immunity from liability to platforms, providers and users of online services who publish information provided by third-party users. Global powers utilize this by becoming the "third-party users" who spread malicious code or mis/disinformation.

In fact, many democratic, liberal, Western countries suffer from the cyber-golem as they are vulnerable to cyberattacks and the spread of mis/disinformation. The United Kingdom, Israel and many European countries continually suffer from foreign interventions and attacks that harm national resilience and create socio-political chaos. In fact, while the United States, United Kingdom, Israel and the European Union have largely open cyber domains, they are the odd ones out. Freedom House lists just over a dozen countries as "Free" in its internet freedom analysis, while the majority of countries are either "Not Free" or "Partly Free." Throughout this book, dozens of examples of the abuse of internet freedom have been described and explained, including examples from the United States, the United Kingdom, Germany and France, Sweden and Finland, Israel and more. An analysis of the cyber domains of global and regional powers led me to define them either as SCDs or VCDs. It seems that more and more countries are suffering from their VCDs, and in recent years they have begun to increase their regulation of the internet, a process that might lead them to become countries with SCDs. For instance, in October 2023, the United Kingdom enacted the Online Safety Act, a law that drew criticism from many

[1] Wu (1996).

Western companies. The Act places new duties on social media companies and it gives the regulator, OFCOM, more power to ensure online safety by tackling illegal content. Companies like Meta, Google, Twitter, WhatsApp, Signal and Telegram, to name just a few, expressed their concerns and put the option of non-compliance on the table before the law was approved. While they claimed it would put encryption and privacy second to safety, they did not address the fact they provide monitoring services in other countries, like Russia.

Another key problem of cyberspace is that it is Western-led and is overwhelmingly controlled by Western companies, organizations and other entities. The entire internet ecosystem, as explained in detail in Chap. 2, is governed by the rules and regulations of ICANN, IANA and PTI, ITU, IETF, IRTF, RIRs like APNIC, W3C, IXPs, CDNs, registries like ccTLDs, IAB, IGF, EIF, WEF, IGOs like the European Union and many other X-letter entities. The internet backbone, as well as platforms, services and smart devices, are dominated by companies like Amazon, Microsoft, Google (Alphabet), Meta (Facebook), IBM, Apple, Lumen Technologies, Cogent Communications, AT&T, Starlink (SpaceX) and many others, which also compete over non-Western markets with their overseas counterparts, including Yandex, Rostelecom, Sberbank and VK (Mail.Ru), in the Russian case, and Tencent, Alibaba, Baidu, JD.com, TikTok (ByteDance), China Telecom and China Unicom, in the Chinese case. All these companies—and many others—lay out submarine fiber-optic cables, launch satellites, manage IXPs and CDNs, and manage cloud platforms, services, internet webpages and social media. In doing so, these organizations chip away at the sovereignty of countries.

Furthermore, in our multi-polar world, China, Russia and even Europe are all competing for dominance in cyberspace, trying to gain more control and influence while undermining the Western (American) grip on the internet. While projects like the Soviet OGAS system have failed (see Chap. 2), others are taking shape. The Russian side has created RuNet, a Russian internet that can also function as an intranet if needed. There are also Russian alternatives to Western companies. VK and Odnoklassniki operate like Facebook, Yandex is Russia's Google, Rutube is just what it sounds like—an alternative to YouTube—and there are more. China's BRI includes the Digital Silk Road project, which aims to improve digital connectivity in Belt and Road countries. It has already exported internet-related services to Vietnam, North Korea, Uganda, Tanzania and more. Even countries like North Korea, Iran and Saudi Arabia have their own internet companies and social media platforms, reflecting their strategic needs as well as their cultural desires.

Some countries, like North Korea and possibly Iran, Russia and China, either have SCDs (or "internet bubbles," as Haber and I named them in 2023) or have the option of creating a closed and restricted network, not fully connected to the outside world. Nevertheless, this process might undermine the desire of countries to collaborate or to project power and influence others. Naturally, we can conclude that some collaboration is necessary to preserve the major benefits of globalization while still maintaining sovereignty. One way to understand this process is to consider Samuel Huntington's Clash of Civilizations theory. This theory posited that the defining fault lines of global conflict in the post-Cold War era would be cultural and civilizational, rather than ideological or economic. Applying this framework to cyberspace presents a complex yet intriguing possibility. This process could be expressed by the emergence of cyber blocs like that of the European Union, which was described in Chap. 7. In this way, all, or some of Huntington's civilizations might develop their own cyber domains, less connected to the outside world, with the gateways very much monitored and regulated. Western, Arab-Islamic, Slavic and Sinic cyber domains will emerge.

In fact, this is already taking shape. Each of these civilizations displays distinct trends when it comes to cyberspace. However, not all countries have the ability to shift the global order in such a manner. Such cyber blocs emerge with the lead of a major international power. Russia is leading the way in the Slavic world, China is leading the way in the Sinosphere, providing services and influencing Thailand, Vietnam, North Korea, Mongolia and others. In the Islamic world, Saudi Arabia and Iran are competing for regional dominance, but they are also providing services and platforms to the Gulf area and most of the Middle East (apart from Israel which is more West-oriented). The most significant cyber bloc that is still striving to remain open is the Anglosphere, with alliances like the Five Eyes Alliance, an intelligence network established between the United States, the United Kingdom, Canada, Australia and New Zealand. One region that can already be considered a partial cyber bloc is the European Union. With its supranational basis, this cyber bloc has legal and operational authority over its member states. The European cyber bloc has developed significant regulatory means with the European Cybersecurity Act, the GDPR, the DSA, the DMA and ENISA. This is true, however, in case the European Union will manage to stay a Union in the following decades.

In more practical terms, although the future of the internet is complex, one fact is clear: it is changing. What are possible options for the future? Generally, there are four main options for the future development of the internet. The first and least probable option is a status quo. That is, cyberspace remains an American and Western-led project. The West will retain control through proxy organizations and companies, and they will lead the global cyber domain. Specifically, the Anglosphere will dominate the internet with the support of allies like European countries, Israel, Japan, Singapore and a few others. The main advantage of this situation will be the option to maintain globalization and draw others toward the West; however, the openness of this type of network is also its main drawback, as other powers will utilize sharp power to harm national resilience and create chaos. Extreme domestic actors within each country might also utilize this to their advantage.

The second option is already being implemented in some countries, but it is a somewhat restrictive option: the emergence of "internet bubbles" or fully independent SCDs. In this case, countries like North Korea keep themselves disconnected from the global grid, effectively operating a closed-circuit intranet. Any information exchange must pass through cyber borders, and information is reviewed for appropriateness by the regime. Other countries are already establishing such SCDs. Russia has the option of disconnecting itself from the global grid, while it also constantly executes DPIs. China, Iran, Saudi Arabia and others also use DPI techniques, and Iran is striving to develop its NIN project. Fully independent SCDs will be more secure and more beneficial to the regimes; however, this will lead to less international cooperation and development, as we can see in the case of the North Korean SCD.

The third option is the emergence of many cyber blocs. These are less interconnected than the global internet as we know it today, but far more connected than sole SCDs or bubbles. In this case, blocs will emerge like economic or military alliances, as described above. Currently, the most prominent example is the European Union's cyber bloc, which operates on a supranational level and, with further development, might emerge to offer robust competition to the American-led internet (even though the European Union and the United States have signed the "Declaration for the Future of the Internet," hinting at possible future cooperation). The one disadvantage of the formation of cyber blocs is to countries with less power and influence. Cyber blocs will be led by global or regional players, and other countries may be compelled to participate or obey the strategic goals of that particular regional player.

The fourth option is the development and establishment of a globally applicable law regarding cyberspace. In this case—which is unlikely to eventuate in the near future but may evolve incrementally over a long period of time—as groups of countries develop specific applicable laws like in the case of the 2001 Budapest Convention on Cybercrime, a legal framework will take shape, similar to maritime law or the laws of physical warfare. Yet, due to the use of cyber proxy warfare, it will have large gaps, and attribution will remain a very difficult issue. Such a global regime of norms and laws will give rise to mutual accountability, something global powers are less likely to desire due to their constant struggle for power and influence. After all, a suitable legal regime will also require a sanction regime.

Interestingly, each of these options reflects a different approach in the field of international relations. Some approaches are more liberal or constructivist in nature, like the establishment of an applicable international law regarding cyberspace and, of course, a sanction regime. Realists will find the options of SCDs and cyber blocs more interesting as, in such cases, countries act in their best selfish interests. Furthermore, the internet is currently led by giant capitalist powers, and Marxists will probably lean toward cooperative options, such as the establishment of cyber blocs. Yet it is important to note, once again, that such cyber blocs will be led by global or regional powers, which may or may not be capitalist in nature. Of course, followers of the English School will likely also side with the establishment of cyber blocs as this option retains the ability to hold both realistic and liberal approaches.

Indeed, it is beyond my ability to predict whether the future of the internet will be more Hobbesian, Grotian or Kantian. It is clear, however, that SCDs in the form of internet bubbles and cyber blocs are emerging as these lines are being written. Referring to Wu Jichuan once more, it makes perfect sense that data and information will need to be approved when crossing "cyber borders" as they can influence another country's target audience. Similarly, countries shut down their physical borders and denied foreign people from entering during the COVID-19 pandemic due to concerns over public health and safety. As all the cases described in this book prove, information may also harm national resilience and public safety.

The internet is constantly evolving, and the future holds some exciting—or certainly interesting—possibilities for future interactions. As humanity dives into the next technological developments, more problems might emerge. The rise of the metaverse, a virtual world, will blur the lines between the physical and digital worlds even further, especially with the use of VR and AR. Will the metaverse be borderless, or will it have regional spaces? Will the call by liberal actors to decentralize the internet make the spread of conspiracy theories and hate speech more prominent and dangerous? AI is already a difficult issue as many countries worry that it may harm their economy. Of course, the question of accountability also arises—who is responsible for an unacceptable action by an AI? Its creator? AI tools may be used in the exertion of sharp power and cyber proxy warfare, making the process of attribution in cyberspace even more complicated.

Another issue is the attempt to shift the industry from submarine fiber-optic cables to satellites with projects like Starlink. Is it ethical to pollute space when satellites break down? Moreover, can a country block or shoot down satellites that bypass its communication regulations? If an American satellite or related debris crashes on Russian soil, how should Russia respond? Also, as our lives become even more connected with smart devices with the IoT, issues of cybersecurity may become a political demand as people require their smart homes and smart cars to be safe and secure. One thing is certain, as technology evolves and our internet changes, new cybersecurity challenges—but also socio-political and legal challenges—will emerge and it will likely be the responsibility of sovereign countries to tackle them.

Reference

Wu, Timothy S. 1996. Cyberspace sovereignty—The internet and the international system. *Harvard Journal & Technology* 10: 647.

Uncited References

Center for Strategic and International Studies. n.d. Significant cyber incidents. https://www.csis.org/programs/technology-policy-program/significant-cyber-incidents.

Chen, Kai. 2017. No place to hide: Edward Snowden, the NSA, and the US surveillance state. *Intelligence and National Security* 32 (6): 868–871.

Comerford, Ruth. 2023. Violent protests after Quran burning in Sweden. *BBC*, September 4. https://www.bbc.com/news/world-europe-66706937.

European Parliament. n.d. Supranational decision-making procedures. https://www.europarl.europa.eu/factsheets/en/sheet/8/supranational-decision-making-procedures.

Financial Tribune. 2017. Iran launches 6th internet hub in Khuzestan province. *Financial Tribune*, May 28. https://financialtribune.com/articles/economy-sci-tech/65386/iran-launches-6th-internet-hub-in-khuzestan-province#:~:text=Company%20of%20Iran.-,Internet%20Exchange%20Point,%2C%20Tabriz%2C%20Shiraz%20and%20Qom.

Jeppesen, Sandra, Henry Giroux, Michael Hoechsmann, Chenjerai Kumanyika, David VanDyke, and Miranda McKee. 2022. *The capitol riots: Digital media, disinformation, and democracy under attack*. Routledge.

Radio Free Europe Radio Liberty. 2021. Apple reportedly agrees to preinstall Russian software on gadgets. *Radio Free Europe Radio Liberty*, March 16. https://www.rferl.org/a/apple-russia-iphone-software/31153385.html.

Shultz, Richard H., and Roy Godson. 1984. *Dezinformatsia: Active measures in Soviet strategy*. Pergamon-Brassey's International Defense Publishers.

L. Topor, *Cyber Sovereignty*, Global Power Shift,
https://doi.org/10.1007/978-3-031-58199-1

Index

L. Topor, *Cyber Sovereignty*, Global Power Shift,
https://doi.org/10.1007/978-3-031-58199-1

The manufacturer's authorised representative in the EU is Springer Nature Customer Service Centre GmbH, Europaplatz 3, 69115 Heidelberg, Germany. If you have any concerns regarding our products, please contact ProductSafety@springernature.com

Printed and bound by CPI Group (UK) Ltd, Croydon, CR0 4YY

30/09/2026

02225239-0004